THE TREATMENT

The
Treatment

"First do no Harm"

SALLY J ROBERTS

Matador
9 Priory Business Park,
Wistow Road, Kibworth Beauchamp,
Leicestershire LE8 0RX
Tel: 0116 279 2299
Email: books@troubador.co.uk
Web: www.troubador.co.uk/matador
Twitter: @matadorbooks

ISBN 978 1838591 328

British Library Cataloguing in Publication Data.
A catalogue record for this book is available from the British Library.

Printed and bound in the UK by TJ International, Padstow, Cornwall
Typeset in 11pt Sabon by Troubador Publishing Ltd, Leicester, UK

Matador is an imprint of Troubador Publishing Ltd

To my darling Neon and Elektra,
with all my love.

This book is the result of my search for a new paradigm
where *the treatment* is justified and beneficial.

Where there are lovers there will always be haters.

Where there are believers there will always be non-believers.

The principle of duality is Universal Law…
and so it should in our healthcare system.

Balanced by natural and unnatural.
Conventional and complementary.

Throughout history, it has been possible to observe the accusations of, or people's reactions to, certain individuals shaping our futures. Like Sally Roberts, we feel that something good will come out of the harrowing case of her son, Neon. Neon and his mother have been in the media spotlight, both within the UK and further afield, but rarely has Sally had an opportunity to make her case.

Rob Verkerk, PhD.

Contents

Foreword

A testament to a mother's natural instincts, intuition, protection, strength, determination and the uncompromising fearlessness of pure love. *The Treatment* is a primal scream echoing from the depths of Sally's womb – to create conscious awareness and awaken the nation to the dangers we will all face, if 'inalienable' sovereign (parental) rights are not respected or 'lawfully' enforced.

The Treatment is an exposé about the untold truths and powerful control of our medical establishment – safeguarded by their own 'laws' – borne out of Sally's personal experience and brave attempts to protect her son (Neon) from the documented harm caused by aggressive 'cancer treatments' available on the National Health Service (NHS). Sally expresses her story with raw emotion; she clung on to hope, desperate to shield Neon from long-term harm, whilst the medical authorities callously used emotional blackmail and clever manipulation to convince her ex-husband and the public that she was an irresponsible, cruel mother, hell-bent on denying her son life-saving cancer treatments. Moreover, (as seen in Sally's case), a parent can also be prosecuted, heavily fined, imprisoned or their children put into the care of social services.

The truth will simply blow your mind.

Being a mother myself and natural health advocate, I can attest that *The Treatment* reveals 'the truth, the whole truth and nothing but the truth'.

The medical establishment cannot deny that chemotherapy and radiotherapy not only cause cancer, but also more deaths than the disease itself. But these proven facts are openly ignored because we have been manipulated and misled into trusting that scientists and doctors know 'best'; have the 'best' treatments available and our 'best' interests at heart. When in truth the medical establishment is a corporation and the 'cancer business' is their most lucrative, financially driven and heartlessly exploited... to our detriment. Sally is just one of thousands (if not millions) of parents, whose rights have been violated without lawful redress, and left with the aftermath of caring for a seriously damaged or disabled loved one for the rest of their lives – or even worse, they may have died because of 'medical' abuse, ego, arrogance, ignorance and an outdated/unbalanced healthcare system... reliantly safeguarded by the 1939 Cancer Act, unethical regulations and 'gold standard' methodologies. The medical establishment's reputation clearly proceeds itself; therefore, one needs to ask who are the true 'Charlatans'?

Sally's case clearly demonstrated that although she was Neon's mother, the National Health Service's 'rights' superseded her parental rights. No words can express the depth of fear and sheer horror of having to helplessly watch your child being used as a deterrent, to ensure other parents do not oppose the medical establishment.

Hence, Sally's fight was certainly not in vain, and although she was vilified by the media, just two years later her case alerted the King family to proton beam therapy for their five-year-old son Ashya, suffering from brain cancer. And even though Mr and Mrs King were jailed for a few days for defying the NHS and also lost temporary custody of Ashya, the authorities' atrocious mishandling of their case (which showed an absolute lack of compassion and empathy), caused a huge national outcry which reverberated around the world. It also drew attention to the abuse of parental rights, as well as highlighting proton beam therapy as a less invasive 'orthodox' treatment for brain cancer. The entire fiasco brought shame and embarrassment to all involved and thankfully, Ashya was successfully treated in Prague. Plus that same year, another mother (Ms Barnes) also elected proton beam therapy for her son 'Alex', who was successfully treated in America.

Seven years later, after being treated like a criminal; hounded like a fugitive by the police; losing custody of Neon – who against her express wishes was forcibly treated with aggressive radiotherapy – proton beam therapy was finally introduced to the UK on 23 January 2019.

It therefore gives me great pleasure to endorse *The Treatment*, and I commend Sally for bravely and unashamedly pouring out her heart for the love of her son. *The Treatment* shines a bright light, exposing the darker side of the medical establishment and is a poignant reminder to those in the profession to 'first do no harm'. Hopefully with proton beam therapy now available in the UK and with the integration of natural treatments, no one else will have to endure Neon's torturous 'treatment' or Sally's heart-wrenching experience. Only through reading this book will people truly understand what Sally had to suffer – for the benefit of others.

This book is a 'Neon' torch and shining beacon of hope for all cancer sufferers. Lighting and guiding the way for safer treatments and raising awareness for the protection of 'inalienable' sovereign (parental) rights.

With love, light, peace, gratitude and abundant blessings.
Dounne Alexander

Prologue

December 21, 2012 was a cold and gloomy winter's day. Helicopters were hovering overhead in the sombre sky, people with notepads and cameras were pressing in and surrounding me as I stepped out of the taxi outside the Royal Courts of Justice on the Strand in Westminster, London. The sound of cameras clicking echoed through the air despite the chopping noise of the helicopter blades circling above.

I walked towards the flashbulbs that created a wall of bright light. Photographers scrambled all over each other, eager to get the best pictures and journalists were doing whatever they could for their sought-after soundbites.

'Sally.'

'Over here, Sally. Look this way.'

I was front-page news and being painted as a monster who was denying her son life-saving cancer treatment. In reality, I was seeking the best post-surgical treatment for a medulloblastoma brain tumour. The conventional treatment was an umbrella approach: life-threatening, overprescribed and outdated. There were better ways to treat Neon, but these other techniques were not yet available in England.

My son's brain tumour had been successfully removed. However, the post-surgery protocol prescribed a course of whole brain and spine radiation and a year's course of chemotherapy as a precautionary measure to destroy *the possibility* of a floating rogue cancer cell.

The physicians caring for Neon warned me about the devastating side effects of the treatment. With the medical team unable to show me any credible statistics or studies proving radiation was necessary, all while making it difficult for me to obtain a second opinion, knowing there were more advanced treatments elsewhere I could not agree to allow the radiation to proceed. With the strict time restrictions, the medical industry (backed by the legal establishment) had used their full force against me.

Up against the time constraints of the protocol and needing more time to decide on the safest and most effective treatment, I disappeared with Neon. The NHS informed the High Court that my son was "gravely ill" and would die if brain and spine radiation treatment did not start immediately, triggering a huge police hunt and media frenzy. We were tracked down like criminals and Neon was taken away from me by social services.

Neon's words, "Mummy, am I ever going to see you again?" will haunt me forever.

My little boy was traumatised by a system set up to *protect* the nation's health and I was severely criticised for not accepting the bog-standard treatment. I was obliged to attend court whilst Neon was in the hospital when I should have been with him. Instead, I was the centre of controversy and at my most vulnerable, crucified by the press.

CHAPTER ONE

Mysteria

My mother and father were rather traditional. They met in Butlins, Bognor Regis. Mum had been born in the UK and Dad was from New Zealand. His father had been taken out to New Zealand from England as a baby. In 1959 dad came to the UK. Not long afterwards he met my mum. Dad was Mum's first serious boyfriend and after they married in 1962, they wanted children. My two eldest brothers Michael and Tony were born in the UK. In 1965 my parents decided to go back to New Zealand by boat, a journey that took five weeks. They settled in the North Island, where Dad's family were from, years later buying a house in the lovely suburb of St Heliers, Auckland. That is where my third brother Russell was born in 1966 and I was born nine years later on May 1, 1975.

Dad had got a job with Air New Zealand. By the time he was made Chief Purser he was flying all over the world and it was one of the perks of the job that Mum and I could fly with him. We went to all the places Air NZ went: Singapore, Tahiti, Fiji, Hawaii, LA, Tokyo and Canada. I always loved to travel. We came to England frequently to see Mum's side of the family, eventually buying a flat in Southfields near Wimbledon Common.

It was while I was in England that I got my first job working for my brother Michael, who at the time was living in the UK. I had always respected Michael, who was a qualified engineer. He was also a courageous, adventurous man and had set up his own bungee-jumping company, Natural High Bungee. It was a wonderful introduction to English musical festivals with Michael, overseeing and organising jumps from a 200ft crane. I did several jumps while I was working for my brother. Michael was a bungee-master having done over 400 jumps, including out of helicopters. I much preferred the safety of the cage and watching other people take the leap of faith; I found going up and down in the cage thrilling enough.

My early twenties were spent continuing to travel the world. Having an ear for music, I had invested in some professional equipment while in Tokyo. With my parents' home in Southfields and my brother Michael living in High Barnett, London, I enrolled on a sound engineering course at the Liberty School of Music. My move to England wasn't going to be permanent, my friend Amanda lived in South Africa and had a recording studio on her property. I had given her a little money to invest in some land and was sure that after completing my course, that was where I was going to be spending the fast-approaching millennium.

I had only been in London for a few weeks when I met Ben Roberts, my future husband. Ben's time at school had been very different from mine. He had been sent to a prestigious boarding school when he was seven but he had not enjoyed it and spoke about it bitterly.

'My children both loved boarding school,' Ben's mother Christine said on one occasion.

'No, I did not, Mum, I hated every minute of it,' Ben had scoffed back. 'Dad loved Cranleigh, not me. I will never understand why you sent me there. We only lived around the corner. Why did you not send me to Bedales with Lucy? She had a great time.'

Ben's high school days had come to an abrupt end, expelled when a random drug test came back positive after a weekend at home. Since then, he had been living in his parents' basement flat in Knightsbridge. Christian, Ben's father, owned a five-star beach-side restaurant in the West Coast on the Caribbean island of Barbados where they spent much of their time, leaving Ben the London flat to himself. When Christian and Christine found themselves wanting to spend more time in the United Kingdom they encouraged Ben to start looking for his own place to live.

Ben and I met through a mutual friend on the doorstep of the record label where Ben was working as an assistant sound engineer. Ben was fun; he had a big smile, blond hair and wore glasses and over dinner that night we talked about music, studios and technology. We got on well, we both loved a certain style of music, were interested in production and loved to dance. After spending time together in the studio, days turned into weeks and then months. I was hardly going home to my parents' place and made the decision not to go to South Africa as planned, choosing to help Ben look for a house where we could set up a studio of our own. London was impracticable and too expensive and we wanted to be somewhere we didn't have to worry about our music offending the neighbours. A place in the countryside seemed like the obvious solution. We took a week out to drive around the West Country to look at houses. We were ready for a long search but as luck would have it we fell in love with the first place that we saw and moved in March 2000.

———

Weeke Barton was an 800-year-old farmhouse in the small West Devonshire town of North Tawton, near Dartmoor National

Park. Both Weeke and Barton are names often associated with farms that have significant features proclaiming them as important dwellings in the past. The ancient market town, property and house itself oozed character. There were no straight walls; it had sloping floors, exposed beams, a well, inglenooks and fireplaces in almost every room. The spiral staircase tucked in the corner of the main living room was so narrow and low you had to duck your head to enter and practically crawl on your hands and knees up and down the stairs. It was written in the deeds of the house that if ever there was a water shortage, our well, which backed onto our dining room, would supply the town with water. Close by, there was Weeke Farm and Weeke Cottage. I wanted to give our house more of a sense of identity, so I registered it with the local council calling it Mysteria.

Mysteria was positioned down a winding country lane. It had a courtyard with old stables and various outbuildings. I was told the previous owners had sold off all the adjacent land that surrounded the property all the way down to the river, which was just as well – we had enough to look after. It felt like our own bit of paradise. In a sense, it was idyllic.

With the River Taw running right alongside the front of the house and surrounded by fields and woods, it was picturesque. Occasionally, I would see a fox hunt go by with all the finely dressed riders on horseback following the foxhounds raring to catch a scent. It was impossible not to feel the adrenalin pumping with at least fifty hounds who all looked exactly the same, bred for the hunt. I always had my fingers crossed for the little fox.

As much as I loved England, I always thought I would eventually end up back in New Zealand; I loved the sub-tropical climate and the outdoorsy lifestyle. I had even loved my all-girls Catholic school, Baradene, where I had studied religion taught by nuns and had made some great friends. Although I missed my friends and family and having passion fruit vines, citrus trees, feijoas and guavas growing in my backyard I liked being nestled away deep in the English countryside, enjoying being surrounded by farms and nature. I adored the feeling of the old land, the narrow country lanes and the rolling pastures.

I walked our Staffordshire Bull Terriers Jasmine and Venus every day and never tired of the legendary Tarka Trail that was right on our doorstep. In one of our outbuildings on our property, we had a huge old cider-press. Mysteria had been around a long time with diversified uses from farming crops and animals to being an old school house. There was also village gossip that it had once been a brothel.

My father said that he compared the age of our house to when the Maoris had first landed in New Zealand. It really put it into perspective how long the old house had been standing. Although Mysteria was no longer thatched, the rendered walls that had stood the test of time were primarily made from mud and horsehair. Our garden was bursting with apple trees, berries and herb and vegetable patches. In the warmer months, I was kept busy planting and harvesting. Meanwhile, Ben with the help of his father Christian embarked on turning one of our old stone barns into a state-of-the-art recording studio.

We spent two long years renovating the studio, alongside developing our skills as sound engineers and music producers. We appreciated that having a studio of our own was an incredible luxury and Ben and I would spend most of our waking hours there. Together with a friend, Adrian Shortman, we formed a group called Starmagix and worked solidly on our albums. Adrian, who had been a sound engineer for singers such as Nenah Cherry and the Sugababes, was known as Professor Stretch. We had another project called Dev'n'Dub, which was devoted to a more diverse style of music, and Ben was working with me to compose my album, which I took great pride in producing. Ben and I existed in a flow of fulfilment and our partnership went from strength to strength.

When I wasn't in the studio, I was carefully and lovingly bringing Mysteria back to her former glory. Working on the old property was satisfying. It was uplifting restoring the house with more of her beauty revealing itself. I cut down the conifers in the back garden to let more light in and made a fence from them. The majority of the oak beams, including the floors, had been painted with sticky black paint that had been fashionable in the sixties and seventies; this had to go and so I hired a sander to strip them back.

Never a dull moment. My neighbour, who specialised in old buildings, showed me how to repoint brickwork in order to repair the leaky exterior walls of the studio. My parents would lend a hand when they were over from New Zealand and sometimes friends helped out but most of it fell on my shoulders. Mysteria was literally a money pit. It was a large house to upkeep and the previous owners had really let it go. It needed serious updating. I could not help sometimes feeling a little weighed down by the workload but once Ben and I were in our studio it was like nothing else mattered.

———

'So, Sally, what's going on with you and Ben?' my friend Rachel asked, sitting down outside at her garden table in the heart of Devon while enjoying the midsummer sunshine and sipping tea.

'What do you mean?' I asked putting down my cup.

'Well, you know, you've been together for ages... five years isn't it? If you had a baby what would you call it?'

'If I had twins,' I laughed, 'I'd call them Tyla and Tylo.'

Although twenty-nine, I had not thought about having children with Ben. We were quite content being caught up in the house and studio and happy just enjoying life as it was. I had grown up with the Disney-imprinted dream that someday

I would meet my prince and we would live happily ever after. However, Rachel's question had got me thinking.

———

It was only weeks after speaking to Rachel, one late afternoon while I was stripping off the stubborn, icky black paint above the open fireplace in the living room, that I began to feel lightheaded. It was one of those awkward jobs; I had been stuck up a ladder for days, having to do most of it by hand because the electric sander would not work on the curved wooden beams. At first, I thought it was the toxic fumes from the thick black paint that were making me queasy. However, I was over a week late with my cycle and thought I should probably do a pregnancy test so I drove into town to buy one. It came back positive.

I ran to the studio to share my discovery with Ben.

'I think I'm pregnant,' I gushed, unable to contain my momentous news.

Ben swivelled his blue orthopaedic chair around and peered over his glasses. 'I'll support you whatever you decide to do.'

I did not question what Ben meant in his matter-of-fact manner. I was thrilled to be having a baby; it felt right. 'I'm so happy. I feel ready.' I beamed.

'We're ready.' Ben paused. 'It is amazing, Sally, but how can you be sure that you are pregnant?'

'It makes sense. Remember our little weekend trip to Paris last month?' I recalled. 'That might have something to do with it… and with the way I have been feeling, it explains everything… and the pregnancy test… look… that confirms it.'

———

My pregnancy went smoothly. I did not put on much weight, I just grew a belly and boobs and my only craving was for pancakes. At twenty-one weeks Ben and I went to the hospital for our first scan. The nurse squidged the cold gel over my belly and we both looked eagerly at the screen.

'Oh crikey,' the nurse said, rolling the handset around on my tummy.

'What is it?' I asked, praying everything was okay. The nurse did not say anything but continued to look at the screen and move her handset over my bump. 'Is there a problem?' I asked.

'Well, dear,' the nurse hesitated. 'Have you got twins in your family? It looks like there are two in there.'

'You are kidding?' I giggled. 'Really?'

'Don't move, dear, or I'll have to stop,' the nurse frowned. 'You're last on my list today and I want to go home. If you don't keep still you'll have to come back tomorrow.'

I had been happy before but now the joy had doubled. On our way home Ben called his parents to tell them the news – they were thrilled, as were mine. Mum and Dad were out on my brother's boat in Auckland harbour when I told them. My mother squealed with glee. Twins did not run on either side of our families, I felt blessed.

CHAPTER TWO

Trouble in Paradise

During one of the routine scans I had been told that Twin One (Neon) was breech and because of this I was being monitored extra closely. At thirty-four weeks I still had a little while left to go. Having read all about giving birth to twins, I was aware it would be highly unlikely for me to do a full-term pregnancy of forty weeks but I presumed that I had at least a few weeks to go before the big day.

It was the evening before my scan was scheduled. I knew something was not right when I was having trouble focusing. To be able to see things properly I had to look at them sideways. In my peripheral vision, I was seeing white sparkly spots, my body felt heavy and I became lightheaded. I had some pamphlets and pregnancy information and compared my symptoms, double-checking on the Internet. I knew the symptoms I was experiencing were something I had previously read about and it wasn't long before I self-diagnosed myself with pre-eclampsia. When I relayed my self-diagnosis to the nurse at the hospital early the following morning she was quite cutting.

'I'll tell you what you've got,' she told me.

After they checked me over and did a series of tests, the nurse confirmed I was right. Because of my sky-high blood pressure and diagnosis of pre-eclampsia, I was admitted to hospital.

Later that night, I was wide awake when the gates opened at one o'clock in the morning. I buzzed for the on-duty nurse to tell her my waters had broken. I was monitored carefully and given steroids and various other prescribed drugs as part of the process of giving birth to premature twins being born at thirty-four weeks. The nurse told me the steroids would help the babies' lungs to mature, which were likely to be a little underdeveloped because they were preterm. This was all a standard procedure. I was glad to be in the hospital and trusted the medics implicitly.

It was the middle of the night when Ben arrived and even though he curled up on the single sofa in the corner of the room and went straight to sleep, it was good to have him there while I lay awake observing my contractions getting closer together. I had to wait until the morning for the surgeons to arrive.

The on-duty nurse had become concerned about the twin babies' heartbeats.

'We would like to give you a spinal, Sally,' the nurse said, 'we don't have time for an epidural. We have to do an emergency caesarean.'

As Twin One was breech I had been advised to opt for a caesarean anyway, so it came as no surprise. It was just happening much quicker than I had anticipated. I agreed to whatever the experts suggested. All I wanted was my babies to be born in good health with no complications.

At 10:04am our little boy was born, followed at 10:06am by our little girl. There was no crying, just pouting and indescribable sounds of pleasure as they were welcomed into the world. They were wrapped up and whisked away so fast I barely got to see them. When the spinal wore off after the surgery and

I was allowed to leave the recovery room, Ben wheeled me down to see our babies, which were each in their own incubator.

I was struck by their beauty. Even though they were so tiny, the first thing I noticed when I saw Neon were his big feet. I was in awe of how exquisite our little boy and our little girl were, they were absolute newborn perfection. Love poured out of me, I felt like the luckiest mother in the world to have given birth to the most gorgeous babies I had ever seen. Considering how tiny they were, Neon weighing only three pounds ten and Elektra three pounds thirteen, I thanked my lucky stars they were both okay. Being premature it took one month before both babies latched on to my bosoms and were feeding properly. That milestone achieved, we were allowed to take them home.

With such perfect babies, we had to find perfect names. Ben and I agreed that if we had a boy we would call him Neon. We asked Ben's sister Lucy what she thought. She let out an excited laugh, clapped her hands with joy, jumped into the air and shrieked, 'Yes!'

My parents weren't as impressed. 'You can't call your child that, Sally.'

Laying eyes upon him no other name would do – we just had to call him Neon. Elektra was the same, we simply had to call her Elektra – she suited it beautifully; after all, you need electricity for Neon to light up.

'Are you sure?' Ben's mother Christine asked us.

'Yes, absolutely,' we replied, thrilled at our choice, choosing to ignore the dislike written across her face and festering in her voice. Having given our twin babies double-barrelled names, Neon-Luca and Elektra-Lily, Christine chose to call them Lily and Luca.

Anyone who has had the good fortune of having a multiple birth can appreciate how much twins kept me busy. One baby must be such a breeze. Sure it was double trouble, but it was twice as nice. Soon after the twins' birth, my parents announced that they were selling their flat in Wimbledon and would buy a house in Devon to be near us. Although they only ever stayed the summer before returning to NZ, having them around when they were in the UK made all the difference.

Ben and I had talked about getting married, but I couldn't help but be surprised when one evening in the studio he proposed to me. We had an eighteen-month engagement and got married in 2009 in Barbados on the coral sand beach beside Ben's parents' restaurant, The Lone Star. We invited our nearest and dearest to come and join us in the tropical sunshine. Neon and Elektra looked like angels in their white outfits. It should have been a perfect day, but there was trouble in paradise. It was a series of mini-disasters and I could not help noticing that Ben's sister Lucy, my maid of honour Claudia and my brother's girlfriend Antonia, had all chosen to wear black dresses.

'I'm going for the ying yang thing,' Clauds commented.

Lucy, who had been doing a detox, was crying as Ben and I said our vows. As the sun went down a friend told me why. 'She says it's because she feels like she is losing her only brother.'

'She could see it as gaining a sister. It's just what I have always wanted,' I said in all seriousness.

Lucy left the next morning back to London. I could not help wondering if it was all an omen. At least the rings were not dropped in the sand.

Back home in the UK the recession had begun to bite. The strain of our long engagement and the wedding had taken its toll and our relationship began to deteriorate. Ben was constantly in the studio and it was bothering me that when he was coming back to the house it was very late, he was making himself tired and often grumpy the next day, especially in the mornings.

Although Ben was always around, it was burdensome to ask him for any help. It was far easier to do whatever needed doing myself rather than disrupt his time in the studio. I questioned our relationship and wondered if we had made a mistake. If we were both not happy and it was not working, how were our children ever going to be truly happy? As I was doing pretty much everything on my own with the children, I considered perhaps being a single mother wouldn't be so bad.

I gave Ben an ultimatum: either he could make more of an effort, be a bit more pleasant, play more of an active role in the lives of our children and we could work it out or we would have to think about going our separate ways.

I hoped that a short period apart might help and, taking Neon and Elektra with me, I left for New Zealand. It had been eight years since I had been back to Auckland, and I wanted to see my friends and family and introduce them to my delightful children. Putting space between us, I thought that on our return he would appreciate us and want to do more together. Although not married for more than a year, we had been together ten years... maybe we were just growing apart.

When we arrived home from New Zealand, Ben was there to greet us at the airport, but the initial signs weren't good. Whatever we once had was not there anymore. Back at Mysteria there was another issue. Our friend Michele had been accepting our hospitality for quite some time and liked living out in the self-contained flat attached to the studio. We were well accustomed to friends coming and staying with us and Michele, who was a singer for a band called Shpongle, liked to be part of our recording studio. I did not usually mind. Michele had a great art of telling joke after joke, and she was easy-going. However, with our marriage on the rocks, the timing couldn't have been worse. It was a strain, but Ben reminded me she had no fixed abode and I agreed it would be unkind to ask her to leave.

When my parents arrived back to England, they were forthcoming offering their advice. 'Sally, why don't you ask her to go?' Mum voiced over breakfast at their home, number 9, Strawberry Fields, conveniently one mile up the road from Mysteria. 'If something is going on they are being brazen about it. Why doesn't she give you any space? There must be somewhere else she can go?'

Michele was one of Ben's oldest friends. They had known each other long before Ben and I met. They had met out in Barbados. Michele used to date Ben's best friend's brother. She frequently called to chat to Ben and often came to stay. When we first got together, I asked Ben if there was anything going on between them. He reassured me their relationship was purely platonic.

With my friend Fiorella confirming that Ben had confessed to her about his feelings for Michele earlier on in our relationship, it turned out I had been right all along. I felt the fool and wished Fiorella had told me sooner. Ten years is a long time to keep a dirty secret. Then again, life would have been very different. My children are my world and for that, I would not change a thing.

Michele eventually did give us some space, flying out to Australia to spend a few months with her mother who was living there. Nonetheless, as soon as Ben came clean in April 2012 that he had developed "more than friends" feelings for Michele, she soon returned to our studio to stay as his live-in lover.

'The government will help you out,' one friend suggested a few days after Michele's arrival. 'Why don't you apply for housing benefit and move somewhere else with the children so you can just let Ben and Michele get on with it?'

As I stood with a towel wrapped around me, still dripping wet from the shower, it was difficult to know what to say to both Grantly and Ben who had come into my bedroom and were waiting for me to reply.

'But what about the children's school?' I eventually responded. 'It's just up the road. It wouldn't be fair on them.'

Our friend Grantly did not have children. I did not expect him to understand. Regardless, it was difficult for me to comprehend how he found it acceptable for Ben to flush our marriage so conveniently down the toilet and freely parade his mistress so flamboyantly around our home and expect me to "simply" move out, taking the children with me.

That Grantly supported Ben and Michele made no difference, there was no way I was budging. It also made me realise that having no morality was more common than I initially thought. Moreover, if they wanted to be together, I was of the mindset that they were the ones who should be moving out. In fact, I would have loved nothing more than to kick them both out into the gutter where they belonged. Sadly, that was not an option. Ben had purchased Mysteria with money inherited from his grandfather that was controlled by their family trust and until the house sold, neither of us were financially in a position to go anywhere. When I asked Ben what the hell did he think he was doing moving in a mistress and where were his morals, he told me "my house, my rules".

It was an impossible dilemma and I was in a real quandary while paying my £20,000 business loan back to the bank that I had taken out to set up my production company, and until now, I had been helping keep us afloat with my various bank loans and three credit cards. Also, ever since our children had been born, Ben had a £2,000 per month allowance from his parents which helped pay the bills but in a nutshell, we both needed to sell the house to be able to move on. There was no spare cash and I refused to go to social services to seek alternative accommodation. It would have been far too disruptive for Neon and Elektra and the only ones benefiting from us moving out would have been Ben and Michele. Of course, it did not stop me ringing a removal company to order some packing boxes.

Since having Ben admit his feelings and Michele becoming a permanent resident in our studio from mid-May 2012, it all snowballed very quickly from Auntie Sandie commenting, 'Why is Michele always staying at your place? Are you sure nothing is going on there?' to several weeks later my mother commenting, 'Gosh, Sally, they are very skimpy, colourful knickers. Not your usual style.'

'They are not my knickers, Mum, they are Michele's. They look uncomfortable. You should know they are not to my taste.'

'She is coming into your house and doing her washing and hanging her smalls in your kitchen? The audacity.' Mum's jaw dropped.

'No, Mum. Ben is doing her washing and hanging her smalls in my kitchen.'

'That man is unbelievable. Most men would have the common decency to wait until their wife had at least packed her bags before moving another woman in,' Mum proclaimed opening a drawer and taking out my kitchen scissors, 'let alone hanging out his girlfriend's fluorescent knickers to dry neatly across the radiator in his wife's kitchen. This will make him think twice about doing it again.' Mum was livid.

'That's better!' Mum exclaimed cutting through another crotch of bright flamingo pink lace panties. 'I will put them in the rubbish where they belong. I would like to put her there too.

'Sally, I have not told you half of what the neighbours are telling me. Those two are the talk of the town. They have no shame parading themselves around. I've got Wendy, my neighbour, telling me how they have been sitting outside the local café drinking their coffee openly smooching and canoodling. Apparently, even the children at their primary school are asking questions. It's Neon and Elektra people are most concerned about.'

———

When I returned from a working trip to Switzerland to be informed by my daughter that while I was away Michele and Daddy had been sleeping in my bed, I told him enough was enough and that his behaviour was inappropriate and unacceptable.

'Where else could we sleep?' he replied. 'The children could not sleep out in the annex with us, there is only one bedroom. We had to sleep in the house. If you're not happy you can always take the children and go and stay at your mother's place.'

Apart from my sheer disbelief at such outrageous conduct, I wished with all my heart they would be more discreet in front of our children. It was the children I was worried about and who I made every effort to protect. With Ben and Michele being so open about their feelings for each other it created confusion and Elektra liked to ask questions.

'Mummy, why is Daddy living out in the studio with Michele? Is he going to marry her now?'

'Daddy has feelings for Michele now, darling, but I don't think they will be getting married just yet.'

The children were somewhat troubled by the situation, particularly Neon. He was much more subdued than normal and often appeared to be lost in thought, but Michele had been our friend and part of our lives since they were born, she had been a guest at our wedding. Having her move in across the courtyard as Ben's mistress was unsettling for us all.

'You are handling this all very well,' Ben's father Christian commented on a visit down to celebrate Ben's thirty-fourth birthday.

'Thank you, Christian,' I replied. 'It's an impossible situation that would be made much worse if we did not have a united front.'

Mum and Dad were not of the same view, having declined Christian's invitation out to lunch. 'It is morally wrong,' Mum expressed. 'We will not be seen to condone such behaviour. We all know Christian has a mistress out in Barbados. Both your father and I were shocked at the way he rubbed up and down that Bajan woman at your wedding. It's like they think it's normal to have a floozy on the side. Well, it's not.'

As bizarre as the whole awkward situation was and the extreme emotions I was experiencing, I had no pangs of jealousy looking at Ben and Michele walking ahead together hand in hand. I knew I did not want to be with him anymore. He was not my usual type and if I am to be honest, I wondered what I ever saw in him. Indeed, it was still a shock to see how quickly he had moved on, allowing her to literally slip into my slippers and to be so comfortable.

Ben and I did not argue in front of the children and if we had anything to discuss regarding the separation we would do so in private, away from them. However, with Ben moving out to stay with Michele in the studio annex and no longer sleeping in our house, I worried about the effect it would have on our children now and in the future. With their father so openly sharing his affection for another woman, it was not helping them master concepts such as "right and wrong".

No matter how seamlessly it was all unfolding for Ben and Michele, it did not change the fact that their father was not with their mother anymore and openly involved in an intimate relationship with somebody else. For the children's sake as well as my own, we had to resolve the situation and fast. In preparation for moving, I started giving whatever I could away to friends. I ordered a large skip for all of our bulky waste and packed anything I could into boxes. In serious need of a quick sale, the house had been put up for auction: I shed tears of relief when it sold. It felt like I had gone through hell; I truly thought things could not get any worse.

CHAPTER THREE

Comes in Threes

In 2007 when Neon was two, he had developed flu-like symptoms that would not go away. For ten days I persisted in taking him backwards and forwards to the doctor's surgery and A&E. The doctor prescribed antibiotics and assured me that he would get better soon, but I was not convinced. I had a gut feeling it was more serious than the doctor's diagnosis and the antibiotics prescribed were not the answer, they were not helping.

With Neon unable to eat and experiencing so much pain he could not stand up, I had driven him back to A&E. One doctor eventually guessed that Neon had appendicitis and needed an emergency appendectomy. The doctor admitted that she could be wrong and I had to acknowledge the risks by signing a waiver giving permission for the surgery to remove his appendix. The diagnosis was fortunately correct. Neon had a really "mucky appendix", it had been a really close call.

The appendectomy had been difficult but five years on in 2012, having Neon diagnosed with a medulloblastoma gave new meaning to the word "difficult".

It was the beginning of the August school holidays when I first noticed a rash beginning to break out over Neon's whole body. His neck was stiff and off-centre and Neon, who was normally not one to complain, said that his head hurt. Alarm sweeping over me, I took him to our general practitioner.

The doctor's initial concern was that Neon could have meningitis but after some routine tests at the Exeter A&E it was suggested that he had scarlet fever, a contagious disease. However, after more tests, a nasty bout of tonsillitis was diagnosed. We were sent home and told the course of antibiotics administered would clear it up. Over the next few days, I periodically got Neon to open his mouth wide and check his throat, but I could not see any sign of ulcers. The symptoms lessened over the next few weeks but his neck remained rigid and the headaches continued. I was worried.

I kept taking him backwards and forwards to our GP but we were prescribed paracetamol and sent home or back to A&E. Neon became withdrawn and terribly lethargic; most evenings as early as 5pm he could not wait to get into bed. The doctor prescribed physiotherapy, anticipating that would help his headaches to subside and reposition his neck but it did no good. Then one morning Neon said that he could see two of me. I took him back to our GP and he agreed to refer Neon to a specialist. After a long wait, almost three months after first taking him to the GP for his wry neck, we got the letter for the initial consultation scheduled on 23 October 2012.

———

In the middle of various doctor, hospital and physiotherapy appointments, our family home sold on 10 September 2012. We did not have long to vacate. I took comfort from the thought that the children and I were going to be able to move away from the Southwest and get on with our lives. With the house selling pre-auction, we had a forty-two-day countdown upon us.

'Where shall we move to, Neon and Elektra?' I asked, wondering where we would go. I could not help but laugh a little when the children suggested in chorus – 'New Zealand'. They had only been once last year and loved it.

'I think that is a great idea but it would be too far away from your father.'

Devonshire was beautiful, and our home Mysteria with its recording studio was perfect when Ben and I had been passionate about developing our music careers, but now I felt cut off living in such an isolated and rural environment. I didn't want to live in the sticks anymore. I wanted to live somewhere with more of a pulse, somewhere with more of a community feel. Friends were keen to offer suggestions: East Grinstead, Oxfordshire, Hampshire, Bristol, London, Wiltshire and Gloucestershire.

Brighton was mentioned several times, and so I decided to drive there and take a look around. I had not been to Brighton in my adult years. It was nothing like I remembered as a child. It seemed a great place to settle. There was everything we could wish for: lovely sea air, open countryside and close to London.

Under pressure to find somewhere to live, just two weeks after the sale of Mysteria, I found a perfect home in the suburbs. We would be living on top of a beautiful hillside. There were rolling pastures behind us with views of the downs, yet we were able to glimpse the seaside. It was heavenly, overlooking the beautiful city of Brighton. It was a far cry from living surrounded by huge hills at Mysteria. Our new home was south facing with all-day sun. Because Mysteria had been positioned in a valley, we had missed out on the luxury of sunrises and sunsets.

After living in a dip several years, I had become acutely aware of how dark and damp our old home had become. Neon suffered from asthma every winter and was prescribed the brown preventive inhaler, which the doctor suggested he needed to take daily for the rest of his life. The doctor had tried hard to persuade me to administer the brown inhaler to Neon insisting that he needed it to overcome his asthma. However, having noted Neon's symptoms eased when we took him away on holiday and in the summer months, I knew the issue was environmental and declined the offer. The dampness issue was one of the many influencing factors adding to the mountain of reasons why I could not wait to move.

———

Living in the heart of the English countryside came with its advantages, but there were downsides and none more than now. The affair situation was uncomfortable for anyone looking in with a peep-hole perspective but actually living through it, of course, as a devoted mother of two, I was most concerned for my children, and my mother, well, she was worried sick about us all and I was constantly having to reassure her everything would be okay. Truth be known, it was anything but okay. Having come to the conclusion heaven and hell was on earth, I wondered how far into the depths of hell I had fallen.

Trapped in a region of Dante's Inferno, the extreme situation was taking its toll. I counted the days until we moved. At times, it was difficult to comprehend how I had landed in such unfortunate circumstances. It felt the only thing I was learning from the situation was how bad things could actually get. It was hard to understand how two people could behave so outrageously and get away with it. Ben's family appeared to think it was acceptable. Most people with principles would agree that cultivating a new relationship on the marital property is wrong.

'I'm sorry you're moving,' Tony said. 'This is such a lovely old property. I'm going to miss coming here to Devon.' My big brother was always there to help. We had filled three skips in ten days.

'It is sad, Tony, but bring on Brighton I say.'

'Pretty shocking stuff that Ben is not here to help you though, but then again it's probably best he's not. I'm so angry with him at what he has done. I probably wouldn't be able to control myself. How dare he treat my little sister with such disrespect. His behaviour is off the scales. I've never seen anything like it in my life, and believe me I've seen some things. I thought I'd seen it all until he moved Michele into your annex under your nose like that. I would liken their behaviour to that of a couple of alley cats.'

'As Sasha said the other day, Tone, no morals. He's more focused on cultivating his new relationship than anything else.'

'Mum told me how last week Ben asked you to sign all sorts of forms before he left. A waiver of occupational rights? Asking you to sign your rights away?'

'I know it looks bad, Tone, but I'm sure it's Ben being dictated to by his legal team. Don't forget his strings are being pulled by his parents and his over-controlling sister.'

'Yes, but at the end of the day he's his own person, and you should stop making excuses for him. He's behaved well out of line. I admire you though for keeping your side of the street clean. Keep doing that and it will all work out in the end. It's hard to see what you saw in him anyway.'

My mother, most of all, had found the breakdown of my marriage overwhelming. Even so, upset as Mum was by what was happening with my recently estranged husband, she was always there to support me. Living in the middle of nowhere had been made more complicated with Ben taking our family car to London. Without my parents, I would have been left stranded.

'Have you noticed that Neon can't walk in a straight line?' I asked Mum, walking down the long, windowless corridor towards the consultant's reception at the Royal Exeter Hospital. Neon was walking a few paces ahead and was struggling to balance himself properly; every step he took he slightly swerved side-to-side. Part of the problem was he appeared to be having difficulty focusing. Quickening my pace, I held his hand to steady him and sighed with relief that we were walking towards our referral.

Mum nodded in agreement. 'At least we're finally being seen by a specialist who can help.'

We were called into a room by an attractive lady with long, wavy blonde hair pulled back in a half ponytail. She wore a fitted knee-length red skirt and matching jacket over a satin-like white shirt and introduced herself as Dr Shelley. I had never met such a cheerful doctor. She had the biggest smile framed with rose-pink lipstick and a definite bounce in every step she took in her black patent high-heels that matched her over-sized black belt. While she ran some observational tests on Neon, I sat in the corner. I had a lot on my mind. My head was buzzing with not only my concerns about Neon but everything that was going on and what I had to do. When the doctor finished her observations, she informed us she would get back to us shortly.

Early the next morning I received a call from Dr Shelley. She told me I needed to bring Neon back to the hospital to have an emergency MRI scan. We rushed to the hospital and were seen straight away. I was initially told the scan would take about forty-five minutes, during which time Neon was to remain completely still.

Throughout the procedure, I stood at his feet and tickled his toes. My gorgeous son was totally engulfed by the huge, white machine. Despite the pneumatic-drill noise and the claustrophobia he must have been feeling, he lay still and did not complain once. A thick panel of glass separated us from the radiologist. Several others joined him and huddled around the screen.

'We're taking pictures of your spine – now lay nice and still. You're being so good. Well done, Neon, almost over,' the voice said over the speaker.

It was coming up to two hours when we were told the scan was finished. We were asked to wait back by the bed Neon had been allocated. I was growing more anxious with every passing moment. Neon had found himself a playmate on the ward. It had gone four o'clock when a doctor came for us. A nurse was sent to keep an eye on Neon. There was a heavy sense of dread in the air. Mum and I knew something was seriously wrong as we were led down the long hallway towards her office. Dr Shelley was there. Unlike the poker-faces of the radiographers, she was frowning and looked upset.

'I'm sorry, I'm so sorry.'

'Oh no, what is it?' I asked.

'We have found a tumour in Neon's cerebellum. I'm so sorry.'

'A brain tumour?'

'Yes, we think it's a medulloblastoma.'

'No, why not me? Why not me?' Mum cried out.

My legs turned to jelly and gave way. Two of the doctors caught me as I heard a voice echo in my ears that I needed to sit down. Mum was wailing in anguish.

'It's going to be okay, you have to believe everything is going to be okay,' I sobbed looking into my mother's tear-filled eyes.

'Could you show me the scan?'

They pulled the image up on the computer and indicated a tumour. 'It's huge,' I said.

'Yes, it is big, about as big as a golf ball,' the doctor confirmed.

'How long has it been there?'

'Sorry, we can't say, Mrs Roberts.'

'But over the past few months I have taken Neon to our GP and A&E department so many times. That's countless times I was told to take Neon home and he was prescribed antibiotics and painkillers. My requests for a scan were always dismissed. How much has the tumour grown as a result?'

'We cannot say. It is a rare malignant tumour and we cannot do anything here,' Dr Shelley said. 'Neon will have to go to Bristol. We have ordered him an ambulance to take you there right away. The team in Bristol know that you are coming. Mrs Roberts, rest assured where you are going they have some of the best neurosurgeons in the world. I mean it when I say he will be in the very best of hands.'

The door to the small office we were all crowded into had opened and closed several times but the entire world had melted away, including everyone in it. Words were coming in fast and furious. All I could see was what I saw on the screen; an image of my worst nightmare. Sensing my distress and total disbelief, one sympathetic doctor put their hand on my shoulder. 'What is your situation at home?' she asked.

'I have recently split up with Neon's father. I've got a removal truck booked to move out of our house on Friday,' I told her. 'The house is bare and the heating has already been turned off.'

'You're meant to be moving house in two days?' the doctor asked.

'Yes.' I nodded.

'Nobody would expect you to move under these circumstances,' she said. 'There is no way you could do it.'

When Ben arrived at the hospital, he disagreed.

'They've told us the operation will happen straight away, and that Neon will be able to come home in ten days,' Ben said. 'Do not postpone the removal truck. You cannot take him back to a cold, empty house once he is out of the hospital. I cannot and will not let that happen. If you do not do the move as arranged, he will have to come to London with me until you sort it out. You will only be making it worse if you don't move this Friday. You know how busy the removal men are. It will take another month to get another slot, and that's if you're lucky. This time of year if you don't do it Friday you will probably have to wait until after Christmas.

'Think about it very carefully, Sally. Neon is going to be under a general anaesthetic all day. The doctors say at least eight to nine hours. Clear everything off the property and get to Bristol as fast as you can. The new owners are moving into Mysteria on Monday whether you like it or not. You best be gone. If you want your house in Brighton, there can be no delays. All you have to do is get everything loaded onto the truck, come to the hospital, then drive to Brighton on Monday and get your keys. Let's face it, otherwise you will be sitting around in the waiting room, which isn't good for anybody, I will be there with Michele. We will need to get back to London as soon as you arrive. You will be there for Neon when he needs you the most… when he wakes up.'

———

Leading up to the diagnosis I could not wait to leave North Tawton, I had been counting down the days. I dreamt of driving away and never looking back. The breakdown of my marriage; my husband openly conducting an affair with our friend, moving and now my only son being raced into emergency brain surgery. I wondered how much more I could take.

Our marital home where I remained with our twins had been sold pre-auction five weeks ago. The initial asking price was £750,000. Desperately wanting out we accepted £515,000. I had been kept busy packing up our belongings driven by the thought of a bright new start. One week previously Ben's removal men had taken all his belongings to storage and Ben, together with his girlfriend, had driven to London to his parents' flat in Knightsbridge. They were staying there while the sale of Mysteria went through and they found somewhere suitable to live.

'Why is Ben not here helping you?' Mum asked. 'It's the final countdown. You cannot possibly be expected to move everything by yourself.'

'But I have got you,' I answered, 'and there's Tony. Sasha is coming over later. Please don't worry, Mum. Everything will be fine.'

'It is anything but fine. It's a disgrace. You have more than a marriage worth of stuff here, and there's still so much to do. Everywhere I look there is something to do. It's a big house, and as for the studio, how could Ben and Michele have left it like that? It should not fall on your shoulders to clean up their mess. Who does he think he is? As for that tramp… it just makes me so angry. Typical Ben though, making excuses and shirking his responsibilities when he should be here helping. Where is he anyway?' Mum fumed.

'He has been asked by Lucy to network computers together for a friend of hers, Sarah Burkeman. She owns a small production company,' I explained. 'He is doing what he does best, working on computers. He has never been much of a helper around the house. Your expectations of him seem awfully high when you know what he's like. Besides, it's good he is actually working don't you think?'

'The first job he's had in years conveniently falling when you are moving out of your marital home… no, it's not good. Nothing is as important as this. All he's doing is something he enjoys. Ben loves nothing more than sitting around twiddling his thumbs and playing on computers. All with the added bonus of doing his sister Lucy a favour. I'd be surprised if he's even being paid. He has tactfully avoided helping you. Whatever he is up to, it could have waited.'

I shook my head in disagreement. 'Ben is not exactly my favourite person anymore. To be honest, Mum, I'm glad to see the back of him.'

'I wonder how he feels sitting in his parents' warm flat in London leaving you and the children stranded in the middle of nowhere with no heating, no electricity, no fridge and no car, all while he lives the high life.'

'I guess he feels warm with a full tummy,' I half-joked. 'Beer and fags for brunch every day, wandering around Harrods, he probably hasn't given us much thought.'

Mum was frustrated, as was I; Mum just showed it more. The past few months had been hard on her having to bear witness to Ben and Michele's relationship blossoming so openly before our eyes.

———

To see my gorgeous boy, usually so full of life, laying so still, hooked up to various machines, made me ache with grief. He was scheduled to remain in the high dependency unit (HDU) for the weekend. His head was wrapped in a bloodstained bandage. There were cables and wires connecting him to various machines, which were beeping rhythmically as they performed their tasks.

Every four hours the nurses would come and have to turn him because of the risk of blood clotting. The painkillers could not subside the agony he was in. Having to turn him to lay on his right side could be done with ease but it caused immense suffering to move him to lay on his left side, because of the way his neck had been misaligned over the previous months and it took two nurses with my help to be able to do so.

Neon was groggy from the morphine he was being administered amongst a concoction of other drugs, some for the inflammation, some to avoid infection and some for the pain. I was told by one of the nurses that he was suffering from "posterior fossa syndrome", which is quite common from operations on the cerebellum where the tumour had been removed. The cerebellum is the part of the brain that controls speech, balance and coordination and was why since the operation he was unable to swallow and could not yet form words.

My parents (who were looking after Elektra) came to the hospital. The tears welled up in my mother's eyes as she looked down at Neon, who appeared to be in a deep sleep. Elektra, sensing the seriousness of the situation, tip-toed towards her twin; cautiously approaching the bed, her blonde curls fell around her face as she leant over her motionless brother.

'Neon, this is what everyone made you at school,' Elektra whispered, presenting a very thoughtful, impeccably made card. Neon's eyes flickered and he stirred at the sound of Elektra's voice. 'I'll put it right here,' she said placing it on the bedside table and tip-toed back. Elektra looked sad and confused. She did not know what to do when Neon did not respond.

Picking up the card I put my arms around her. The card had Scooby Doo on the front, and it opened out intricately. A real work of art. I was having difficulty reading what Neon's classmates and teachers had written; thoughtful individual messages strategically glued in place. It was impossible to focus through the tears. I had never seen such a beautifully made card. Elektra looked more angelic than ever and to see her look so stunned at the sight of her brother tore at my heartstrings even more.

'Mummy, is Neon okay?' Elektra asked, her piercing blue eyes looking deep into mine for answers.

'Neon has had to have a big operation to remove something that should not have been there. It's all gone now and he is feeling very tired. Neon needs to rest so his body can heal while he sleeps.'

Seeing tears streaming down my face, my mother reached for Elektra's hand. 'Come on, Elektra-Lily, let's go home now. We have to make your dinner. We'll come back tomorrow morning to see Mummy and Neon.'

Alone once more I looked down at the post-surgery notes. The words "full resection" beamed from the page. Eternally grateful the tumour had been removed I counted our blessings, telling myself, 'It's all going to be okay, Neon will be okay. Everything is going to be okay.'

———

'Am I going to die?' Neon asked when he regained the ability to speak and was able to form slow, stuttering sentences.

It had only been a few months since he had asked, 'Mummy, what does it feel like the day you grow up?'

'Don't you worry about a thing, Neon. Every day you are going to get stronger. You are going to live a long life and grow to be a fine young man.'

CHAPTER FOUR

Broken Promises

Neon's operation was four days previously. He was extremely weak and still in the high dependency unit (HDU). It was hard to imagine him being discharged in one week, but I remained hopeful.

Ben had returned to Frenchay, the Bristol hospital, on Sunday night after spending the weekend in London. He was adamant that my move into the new house could not be delayed, and so I agreed to drive to Brighton to do what was asked of me. Ben wished me well on my way and in the early hours of Monday morning I left Bristol with my jam-packed car and set off for Brighton. I would complete the mission and drive back to Bristol as quick as I could... I was almost there.

It was 11:11am and I was only twenty-three miles away from Brighton when the driver of the removal company called me. 'Mrs Roberts, we've arrived. We've made really good time. We're an hour early, but I don't think you're going to be very happy.' He paused. 'The vendor is still in the house.'

Pulling over at a designated rest area on the side of the motorway, I started making calls. Only to learn that there had been a problem with the paperwork. Ben's legal team had made demands I could not meet and, because of this, the sale had not been finalised. When I called my conveyance solicitor, he informed me I was no longer his client and that he was now acting for my husband. He asked me to drive to his office to sign some paperwork in order to complete the sale. When I had left the Bristol hospital early Monday morning the plan had been to drive to Brighton to get the keys, get the boxes and furniture sorted and drive straight back to Bristol. The arrangement had been to meet the removal men and my older brother Tony at the new property on Monday at midday. With Ben not forewarning me of any complications, I did not anticipate standing on the pavement outside my new property unable to get in.

I called Ben. 'Well, you should have signed the piece of paper when I first asked you to, shouldn't you?' Ben seethed. 'Drive to the lawyer's office, sign and the house is yours.'

When I spoke to the removal men the news was not good. 'We're pressed for time, Mrs Roberts. You need to decide what you want to do. We've got to be back on the road by two o'clock at the latest. We're only allowed to be on the road for a limited time. We've got to get back to Devon.'

I saw no choice but to do what was asked and drove to the solicitors. With the paperwork signed, the vendor agreed to be out of the house by the next day. I now needed to figure out what I was going to do with the fully loaded truck. Tony told me to leave it with him. After making some phone calls he found a solution. He booked a self-storage unit and would help me unload.

A short drive later we were outside the unit and in a rush to get my belongings safely stored.

'Out of all the messy breakups I've seen this is by far the worst.' Tony spoke his mind while loading up another trolley. 'I know you wanted to remain friends with Ben but it was never going to happen, Sis, not with another woman on the scene.'

'I know, Tony, but he's the father of my children. We need to remain amicable.'

'We all want to remain on good terms with our exes in a perfect world but look at what he's done to you. You don't deserve this. You need to be at the hospital with Neon, not in a warehouse loading boxes into a unit. I'd never dream of doing something like this to my worst enemy. You've been nothing but good to that guy. He never deserved you in the first place. You can't trust him. The way he has behaved these past few months, please do us a favour and do not believe a word that comes out of his mouth.'

Half of my furniture and boxes were outside and it had started to rain. We were working at top speed, but somehow we managed to move even faster. There was no hiding from the wintry chill. I could see every breath I took with condensation forming a smoky haze and clouding the air in front of my face. Acutely aware a bad situation could always be worse, I thanked my lucky stars I had Tony with me. He was big and strong and helped me transfer everything into the unit. Every time the industrial trolley was fully loaded, Tony would disappear into the old-fashioned cage lift to return and do it all again. It was a laborious task: sofas, tables, beds and big boxes and so much of it.

It was 4:30pm on the verge of getting dark when my mother and father pulled up with my very lively daughter and vocal cat. Elektra brightened the warehouse finding fun in everything, her eyes ablaze with excitement. Boxes galore, it closely resembled a play-park with so much to climb on.

'Mummy, look at me,' Elektra giggled, scrambling on top of a pile of furniture.

'Oh, Mummy, can I ride on the trolley?'

My Oriental Siamese cat was not as amused having just done the 230-mile journey from Devon to Brighton. She peered out of her cage watching our every move with pure dissatisfaction.

Listening to her loud, drawn-out, wailing meow resonating through the warehouse added to my torment and the already tense atmosphere. My mother was even more upset than my cat and took me to one side to have a few words.

'So now he's made you homeless?'

'It's only temporary, Mum. I'll get the keys tomorrow. It's because I'd not signed their piece of paper relinquishing all my rights,' I explained.

'You didn't sign it did you, Sally?'

'What choice did I have? They had me over a barrel.'

'More like tied up in a room and blindfolded with a gun held to your head. As if you haven't been through enough.' Mum was furious. 'So much for securing your new home.'

'I'm sure Ben will do the honourable thing, Mum… he did promise.'

'There is more honour amongst thieves than that family. They don't have an ounce of honour between them. The sooner you see that the better off you'll be.'

'I'm sure this is all formalities to do with the lawyers. You know what they're like.'

'Yes, Sally, I do, but they have control over their lawyers. You are deluded to think Ben and his family are ever going to do right by you. Can you not see they are trying to screw you over? You are far too trusting.'

'But Ben promised,' I sighed. 'I want to believe he will do the right thing.'

Tony had overheard our conversation. 'Ben looked me in the eye and promised me the house in Brighton was Sally's. To be fair, at the time I believed him too, Mum.'

'Well, why has he tossed Sally and Elektra onto the streets then?' Mum said through gritted teeth.

'Hopefully, it's just for the night. Please do us a favour and go and find us a nice hotel to stay in. Elektra must be starving, and you too – and Dad looks like he could do with a beer. After that drive, he deserves one. Everything is going to be fine,' Tony said in my defence. 'We will have to stay in a hotel tonight and with the paperwork signed we'll get the keys for the house tomorrow. This will all have to stay in the storage unit until next week.'

We both heaved a huge sigh of relief when they pulled away.

Tony and I were left with Pebbles, who remained crouched in her wicker basket. Her piercing green eyes watched our every move, voicing her long, disapproving, yowling cry sometimes quietly, but mostly it was so loud it echoed throughout the warehouse. We finished in haste as the self-storage warehouse closed at 8pm. We then drove to the Mercure, a hotel on the seafront close to Brighton Pier. The delay was dealt with the next day. At last, I was able to collect the keys and drive back to the hospital.

———

Back at Frenchay, I was confronted with the devastating bombshell that Neon was booked in for second-look surgery later on in the week.

'We will know more in the next day or two,' the doctor said, 'we have had great difficulty interpreting the postoperative imaging.'

'But the notes say he had a complete macroscopic resection,' I cried.

'I'm sorry, I know how hard this must be for you. We can only go by the images. We have to do another scan. We will let you know closer to the time,' the doctor apologised.

Neon had regained a little strength and had been released from the HDU the previous afternoon. He could not yet sit up by himself but was starting to be able to swallow, and with a little help, he could take sips of water through a straw. Hearing they may need to operate because they were unsure if they had got all the tumour out scared me. Brain surgery for an adult is inconceivable, let alone for a seven-year-old boy who had not yet recovered from the first surgery.

Having been out of the HDU for less than twenty-four hours, Neon was very shaky and remained attached to various machines. He was still having to be tube-fed and remained hooked up to a shunt, which continued to drain any surplus fluid. The pain when he was awake was written all over his face. Any movement we encouraged, he cried out in pain. The thought of adding to that torment was unimaginable. Surgery was pencilled in for Thursday. If there was any tumour left, needless to say... they had to get it out.

––––––

Late Wednesday afternoon, the day before Neon's second-look surgery was due, one of the paediatricians came in to talk to me.

'Mrs Roberts, you will be pleased to hear that Neon's operation tomorrow has been cancelled. We are satisfied by analysing the images that it is unnecessary. What we thought may be a tumour remnant, we are now confident is inflamed scar tissue and enlarged ventricles.'

I let out a shriek of pure delight and hugged the doctor.

'The images from the most recent MRI show there is extensive high signal change around the surgical cavity as on the immediate post-op scan. Diffusion weighted imaging [DWI] was added to the examination and suggests most of these changes represent post-surgical change rather than there being any significant residual tumour volume. It has been difficult for us to analyse the images. It is sometimes very hard to tell.'

The heavy weight that had been pressing down on my shoulders lifted. With the tumour confirmed all gone, we could focus on his recovery. It was more good news when they disconnected Neon from the external ventricle drain (EVD), which had been keeping his ventricles decompressed by draining the excess fluid from his brain. Having it removed gave Neon a sense of feeling freer and indicated that his intracranial pressure was normalising.

The hospital personnel were all very helpful and good at explaining everything that was happening. Rebecca, the neuro-oncology specialist, had introduced herself and gave me her direct line in case I had any questions. The lead paediatric oncologist was away on holiday. Rebecca informed me he would be back the following week and if I had any concerns, I could discuss them with the consultant on his return.

CHAPTER FIVE

First Do No Harm

Although the lead consultant was yet to return from holiday, I caught wind of what the specialists planned to do next. They were satisfied the operation had been a success, but they considered radiation and chemotherapy necessary in case there were any remaining runaway cancer cells. With all the numerous tests indicating he was in the clear: that the tumour had been fully removed (full resection) and that the tumour had not metastasised (spread), I questioned if there was a need for radiation.

My research indicated this was to be the next step but I was not convinced; it was far too risky. "The primary focus in radiotherapy is to increase DNA damage in tumour cells, as double-strand breaks are important in cell death."

This same damage applies to healthy cells causing irreparable damage to living tissue. As the ionising radiation causes chemical changes by breaking chemical bonds, it threatens the integrity (and survival) of normal cells and Neon would undoubtedly face the unavoidable side effects of the radiation treatment.

Playing a game of chance with my son was unacceptable. It was too big a gamble and would unravel a whole load of irreversible devastation. How could this be common practice, to subject a seven-year-old to such dangerous toxic extremity while blindly attacking a phantom culprit cell?

The short-term effects from radiotherapy include: burnt scalp and spine, inflammation of the lining of the mouth which can cause difficulties in chewing, speaking and swallowing, personality changes, seizures, chronic fatigue, hearing and memory loss, hair and weight loss, nausea and not only aches and pains but total immune system annihilation. In the long term I was warned his growth, fertility and IQ would almost definitely be affected as well as bone and nerve damage. The information I was given at the hospital clearly stated that as a result of being treated with radiation my son may be at risk of strokes, secondary cancers and even death. All of these side effects intensified if chemotherapy was added to the radiotherapy. Long-term side effects for children were reported to be more common because the nervous system was still developing.

If you look up "poison" in the dictionary: "a substance with an inherent property that tends to destroy life or impair health. Something harmful or pernicious, as to happiness or well-being." That pretty much sums up our modern-day cancer treatment. Polluting the body with toxins and contaminating our way back to health.

Everything about the radiation/chemical treatment flew in the face of the Hippocratic oath once held sacred by physicians:

"First do no harm" and "I will never do harm to anyone. To please no one will I prescribe a deadly drug, nor give advice which may cause his death."

A physician by definition is a person who is skilled in the art of healing. Where is the brilliance when it comes to modern medicines approach to cancer: bringing the immune system to its knees before (hopefully) reviving it?

As my search went on I discovered the conventional protocol of surgery, radiotherapy and chemotherapy had not changed much, if at all, since World War Two. Different variations, doses and combinations of drugs had been tried and tested, forever chasing the "magic bullet" theory but with very little progression with the treatment since the discovery of *medicinal* radiation and its cousin chemo.

So why had the treatment for cancer become so stuck and not moved forward at all?

It could not be described as "breakthrough" or "cutting edge", indeed the complete opposite. Where were the life-saving pioneering therapies in our current system?

An elaborate charade had unfolded where all the emphasis from Neon's clinical team was fixated on the removed tumour and its follow-up treatment. Such arrogance overshadowed my pursuit to nurse Neon back to strength. The hospital was all for a drastic treatment programme that would completely compromise Neon's well-being, but this was my son they were talking about and I needed to know absolutely everything there was to know about what they had scheduled in next.

Growing more curious about the background of the treatment, I asked various staff about the prescribed protocol they proposed for my seven-year-old child. It was unsettling that none of the clinicians seemed to know anything about the history of the treatment that they swore by.

How had radiation and chemotherapy after surgery become the only accepted treatment for cancer in hospitals? How had it become known as the "gold-standard"?

Why were the doctors and nurses prescribing and administering these highly toxic drugs unaware of their background or how they had come to be?

There was only what is referred to by many alternative advocates as the "cut, burn and poison" options: surgery, radiation and chemical therapy. This ruthless regime requires every child to have the same treatment irrespective of the severity. An adult, although strongly advised to accept the conventional, still has the right to say no. A child (or his parents) does not have that privilege.

Given my past experiences with having to push to get the right diagnosis and treatments, I was mindful that the doctors' interpretations can sometimes be incorrect. It seemed logical to search internationally for statistics on survival rates of children diagnosed with medulloblastoma, who like Neon had a full resection and clear cerebral spinal fluid (CSF): classified as standard risk. On the bright side, everything was in Neon's favour, with one doctor referring to the type of tumour that had been removed as "the best of the worst".

———

Neon was beginning to show interest in solid food and had begun to eat a little. There were a variety of grocery stores close to the hospital, which supplied organic produce and while my mum and dad were with Neon, I could go out and shop for his favourite foods.

Although disconnected from the various machines, Neon still had the nasogastric tube, which he found very uncomfortable. It wasn't helping to encourage him to swallow and it kept popping out of his nose. Neon and I were happy when the specialists agreed he was taking in the calories through eating and removed it. That he was able to eat again, say a few words and give the thumbs up sign was all amazing progress. With his bodily functions also starting to work, I hoped to soon be able to take him to our new home.

As part of Neon's ongoing journey back to well-being, I intended to play safe and be cautious about foods, drinks and cooking methods that are said to promote cancer. Wherever possible, I knew it would be best to avoid well-known toxins. We were already good about not consuming processed foods, cow's milk products or using microwaves but I thought it to be wise to introduce an abundance of foods, supplements and drinks that are known to hinder and kill cancer cells. With a healthy mind and body being key for Neon's full recovery, my approach was if there was a rogue cancer cell it would certainly struggle to survive in such a healthy environment.

Having become aware that sugar feeds cancer cells, it was a mystery to me why the doctors with all their expertise did not acknowledge this. If cancer cells have been shown to break down significantly higher amounts of sugar than healthy cells, this strongly suggests glucose fuels cancer. With evidence indicating the link between sugar and cancer, I could not brush it off like the doctors I spoke to did.

Sugar has an acidifying nature, which together with an overburdened immune system can lead to acidosis; a condition in which cancer can thrive. To wreck the environment that would be supporting any cancer cells (should there be any) I acknowledged as a fundamental part of the armoury, it would be sensible to limit Neon's sugar intake. I was not going to take any risks. If sugar can have a disastrous toll on health, then, for now, I wanted to (wherever possible) avoid it.

With sugar everywhere and the average person eating their body weight in sugar every year, it can be difficult to escape and takes commitment. I preferred natural substitutes; organic maple syrup was my family's personal favourite. The challenge was preparing healthier choices and making it work while staying in the hospital. It was all do-able. Anything was possible. It was getting friends and family on board... that was the hard part.

'You cannot *not* give a child sweets, Sally, that's mean,' Lucy commented.

There was no way I could argue with Ben's sister. She loved her sweet stuff. However, Neon did not eat much junk food, he didn't like sugar-laden drinks and had never tasted cordial, so it wasn't going to be much of a change.

Neon was drawn to healthier options, his favourite food was cucumber but with his father's side of the family all offering him pizza, crisps, ice-cream and biscuits, he would not say no. Family generally like to show their love with food. I asked my family to bring grapes not chocolates.

Staying in the hospital, Neon was offered food and drink by brands we choose not to consume at home. It was part of my armoury to avoid processed food that has no nutritional value. We never bought any of the brightly coloured snacks that would pull up in our ward on a trolley at least twice daily but were encouraged to eat them by both staff and even other parents.

'Don't you live?' one parent asked when both Neon and I turned down the offer of Coca-Cola at his son's birthday party across the ward. This was demonstrated on a bigger scale in the *Helping Your Child to Eat* booklet provided by the Children's Cancer and Leukaemia Group (CCLG):

"Sipping fizzy drinks such as ginger ale and cola can be helpful."

"Use extra sugar with cereal and desserts."

"Avoid filling your child up with low energy, bulky foods such as vegetables and fruit."

"There is no need to stick to traditional breakfast foods, why not try custard or cakes and biscuits instead."

If it were not so tragic it would be comical.

Whoever wrote this pink booklet or had a part to play in it should be ashamed of themselves. To be frank, they either suffer from a severe case of idiocy or are immoral. All else aside, one of the biggest issues is that they count calories not nutrients. Despite what the mainstream advisors say, you can keep your weight up without having to eat processed convenience (denatured, sugary and saturated fatty) foods.

It also shows the health system up. The nutritionist we saw in the hospital who gave me the "how to feed cancer" booklet also provided us with complimentary Build-Up Nestlé Nutrition sachets. The hospital worker could not answer me when I asked, "How can a product that provides zero valuable nutrients be called nutritious?" Nestlé's "nutritious shake" ingredients are unnatural. The chemically laden ingredients including GMOs, synthetic vitamins plus minerals and contaminated whey protein are not helpful and should not be given to any child, especially children recovering from a critical situation.

At every opportunity, I was pouring my spare moments into searching for ways to help Neon to ensure I was doing the best for him to help his body heal from the surgery while continuing to boost his immune system. Most importantly, I needed to find the right place to take him.

Germany was reported to have the best centres, and when I looked, I was overwhelmed by choice. Alongside the conventional, there were many natural solutions for cancer. Some were based on nutrition, and there were other treatments that imitated the body's natural healing reactions.

I started to contact the places that stood out, hoping that by reaching out I would find the best clinic. Contacting no less than thirty highly regarded treatment centres and sending out Neon's medical records, I trusted I would find the right one. Body support therapies made sense: safe removal of toxins, boosting immune response, increasing the blood flow and killing cancer cells without harmful side effects.

There was a book I had bought about the Gerson therapy, which recommended a strict and wholesome organic, vegetarian diet for cancer patients. Days after Neon's surgery the Gerson Clinic in Budapest was the first place I contacted. Hungary was only a short two-hour thirty-minute flight away. I wanted to take Neon there straight after getting out of the hospital to help achieve a healthy body terrain and implement an anticancer regime while deciding what to do next. Shortly after making the enquiry, I heard back from them informing me that I could not take him there as they did not take on children. This was the case for many clinics. Centres in the United Kingdom that specialised in complementary therapies proven to speed up healing were mostly unable to treat children due to current restrictions, including legislation that was in place.

Serving up good meals for Neon while he was in the hospital wasn't easy. Not only did Neon not like the food he was being offered by the hospital, but it also seemed to lack any nutritional value. Providing our body with nutrients made sense to me; the human body is a self-healing organism that is capable of so much more than modern medicine gives it credit for. We accidentally cut ourselves; we heal. We accidentally break a bone; we eventually heal. We get sick; we get better. For all that, if you succumb to cancer, we are told that "to heal" it is necessary to destroy our immune systems. It's quite a paradox, like going to war to achieve peace. "Step aside immunity. We're going to blast this cancer out of there. Hopefully, you'll survive."

Perhaps, if our bodies are capable of creating cancer, given the right tools our bodies are capable of overcoming it too. Relying entirely on toxic measures is unbalanced and is why the treatment on offer continues to fall short of expectations.

It is a crying shame our healthcare practitioners are not trained in nutrition at all and overlooking the one thing that can boost our health. It was difficult for me to have full faith in the conventional methods when cancer treatment hospitals did not come close to resembling healing centres. In comparison to torture chambers, radiation would be right up there. To make a bad situation worse, the standard of food that the average cancer patient gets given while in hospital leads to additional undernourishment. Is this not another crime? To say the least, it made me further question the "experts" expertise.

They say "we are what we eat". Surely not providing food with any nutritional value in hospitals is an oversight that only further burdens the healthcare system?

Food is our energy source. It is our fuel. It is the one thing we spend money on that literally becomes a part of us. As much as food can be our medicine, it can also deteriorate our health. There are foods that can heal us and foods that can harm us.

Why isn't there more focus on training, promoting and encouraging healthy eating?

Is it because our doctors study disease and not health in medical school? If the curriculum included teaching our practitioners vital information about nutrition and boosting our immune systems rather than strictly promoting pharmaceutically funded procedures and drugs, surely we would be better off and degenerative diseases would be less common.

When I spoke to the lead consultant about nutrition, he said he "appreciated good nutrition may be of some importance", and then dismissed it by saying "there was no evidence to back it up". This baffled me as there are scientific studies proving nutrition to be valuable for good health. I had friends who were qualified professionals varying from ex-GPs turned naturopaths to nutrition experts who gave me their advice and recommendations.

I was grateful to have sound advice when it wasn't available in the hospital. How did it come to be that we are governed by a medical institution that holds itself above nature and all it has to offer, including food? A boosted immune system has the capability of restoring health, yet the current conventional approach only favours manufactured drugs and therapies that will never cure cancer. If they could, they would have already.

Knowing it was crucial to provide Neon's body with good nutrition, I developed a daily plan for him. This began first thing in the morning when I would offer Neon some juicy organic grapes, particularly red and black grapes that contain compounds in the skin and seeds that can destroy cancer cells. I found reading about "Johanna Brandt's grape cure" very interesting; hearing such positive results from resveratrol alone, I thought it valuable to implement it into Neon's routine. I would then offer Neon a teaspoon of bee pollen, which is known to be one of nature's most nutritious and complete food sources. I trusted it would be beneficial to help him recover on a cellular level from the surgery. I was keeping E3 algae in the freezer. Aware that it was good for the brain I would give Neon some with a tablespoon of omega-rich flaxseed or hempseed oil that I was keeping in the staff fridge. Essential fatty acids work synergistically with chlorophyll-rich super greens like E3, chlorella and spirulina, working like a postbox service and delivering the healthful nutrients directly to our cells.

Next, it was upstairs to the parents' kitchen to make a freshly squeezed juice from a variety of organic celery, carrot, broccoli, kale, spinach, herbs and cucumber. Having learnt about the benefits of turmeric being both anti-inflammatory and anticancer, I would occasionally add some and make the juice more palatable for Neon using a few apples as the base. It would take Neon a while to drink his juice but as long as he had a straw he was happy enough to drink as much as he could.

Luckily I had the use of a Champion juicer a friend had lent me having recently given my Oscar 900 juicer to my brother. My love for juicing ran deep since discovering the benefits of slow masticating juicers. Given our current crisis, I ordered what the Gerson therapy suggested for overcoming cancer: the Norwalk juicer… it was already on its way from America.

For Neon to have developed a medulloblastoma, I guessed his pH balance must have slipped. I presumed his body was likely to be too acidic and a good way to alkalise and maximise the bioavailability of vital elements (vitamins and minerals) was to regularly juice. With the stress I was under my body thanked me for it too. It seemed a highly effective way to rebuild, support and rebalance Neon's immune system and gave me the energy to do so.

Having explored the cooking facilities, I had recently discovered a steamer deep in the back of the cupboards of the parents' kitchen and was cutting up some broccoli when a hospital cleaner came in and stopped and stared. 'In all my days and I've been here a while, I've never seen anyone use that before, I didn't even know it was there.'

I'd guessed by the build-up of dust I had to clean off that it did not get much use. Other parents were forever using the microwave. The fridge was packed full of their ready meals, and there was no oven.

'Health and safety won't allow us to have an oven because of the fire risk,' the cleaner explained.

Healthy eating at the hospital took careful planning and I was being watched.

One fellow parent had seen me get a small bottle out of the fridge and add a couple of drops to Neon's passion fruit. On this occasion, I had added a few drops of marine phytoplankton, which is known to be good for the brain and promotes healing. The sweet and sour tanginess of the passion fruit hid the salty taste beautifully. There is much to be said about the healing powers of nature and dynamic living medicines to assist in correcting imbalances. I was encouraging Neon to consume anything packed full of antioxidants that had anticancer and anti-tumour properties whenever possible.

'Mrs Roberts,' the nurse said, 'we have reason to believe that you are adding unknown substances to Neon's food, could you please explain to me what you are giving him?'

'I'm giving him things like marine phytoplankton and this is chaga.' I showed the nurse my tincture.

'And what is chaga, Mrs Roberts?'

'Chaga is an adaptogen that has very powerful anticancer properties including beta-glucans.'

The nurse looked puzzled. 'But what is it?'

'It's a medicinal mushroom.'

'It requires approval by the doctor,' the nurse frowned. 'I need to have it and anything else you're giving your son.'

The superfoods and supplements were bagged up and taken away to be inspected. They were given back to me later on that day. Once approved by the doctor and returned to me I continued giving them to Neon at every opportunity.

Both Neon and Elektra love pineapple, which has a mixture of enzymes in both the stem and flesh called bromelain. As well as boosting immunity, bromelain has been shown to exhibit tumour-fighting properties. Pineapple also has anti-inflammatory effects and is reported to be helpful post-surgery to promote faster healing. On learning about apricot kernels, which have B17 in them that work synergistically with bromelain to target and destroy cancer cells, I encouraged Neon to eat them.

The hospital medics knew next to nothing about living medicines as they only dealt with synthetic drugs. Pharmaceuticals are most certainly good and have their well-deserved place, but natural remedies should not be entirely ruled out and categorised as useless.

It did not cross my mind to discuss the apricot kernels with the doctor. He was not trained in what is known as "nature's chemotherapy". They are controversial because they are packed full of cyanide, which gives them their distinct flavour. For most of us our natural reaction is cyanide, why would you want to take cyanide? It is poisonous but need I remind you that so are radiation and chemotherapy, and far more so than a little dose of cyanide.

Nature is very smart. Our bodies use different enzymes to perform different tasks. An enzyme called rhodanese is found throughout our body but is not present in cancer cells. Rhodanese quickly breaks down the B17 when it is introduced to the body. When the B17 comes in contact with the cancer cells, there is no rhodanese to neutralise it and break it down. Beta-glucosidase is an enzyme only present in cancer cells. If somebody has cancer and consumes foods such as apple seeds, cherries, blackberries, millet, buckwheat and particularly high concentrations in the humble apricot kernels, then the beta-glucosidase enzyme unlocks and releases the cyanide. Consequently, this releases benzaldehyde directly into the cancer cells, destroying them. Ultimately, this stops the fast-dividing cancer cells in their tracks and in no way whatsoever harms any healthy cells. No beta-glucosidase (cancer cells) means no hydrogen cyanide will be formed from the B17. Unlike the reckless conventional method, this is a process known as "selective toxicity" where only the cancer cells are targeted and destroyed.

You have to really dig around to find any recorded cases of cyanide poisoning from apricot kernels or any other B17 foods and even these stories don't add up and are open to debate. Compared to radiation and chemotherapy where countless millions have paid the price with their lives.

———

I was beginning to grasp how common childhood cancer was when I attended my first meeting in the paediatric oncology wing in the Bristol Hospital for Children.

Neon's lead consultant had returned from holiday and set up an appointment. The first piece of paper I was presented with and asked to sign at this initial meeting was to give my consent for signing the tumour over to the Children's Cancer and Leukaemia Group (CCLG) Tissue Bank. I understand research needs to be done but it gave me the impression Neon was simply another statistic. In view of the rarity of medulloblastoma (one in a million), every bit of evidence needed to be captured and gathered to boost statistics.

Dr Lucock confirmed they were confident there was no evidence of disease but to make sure they had Neon scheduled in for another lumbar puncture the following week, where he would have to be anaesthetised again. Although radiation and chemotherapy had been previously mentioned, in this meeting it became evident that it was to start much sooner than I thought… whether I agreed to it or not.

Dr Lucock explained their plans. 'The optimal window for treatment is that radiotherapy must begin within forty-two days of surgery.'

'If it fell out of the forty-two days does that mean he cannot be part of your trial?' I asked warily, dubious about the radical medical interventions timescale. I had just come out of another forty-two-day countdown with the sale of Mysteria and pondered on the significance… why forty-two days?

'We recommend the current UK guidance for treating medulloblastoma which for both standard and high risk recommends for a child of Neon's age the use of a combination of craniospinal radiotherapy and chemotherapy based on cumulative evidence from multiple clinical trials. We need to facilitate this on a timely basis and this, of course, requires attendance for recommended investigations and planning.'

'Why is there no mention about boosting Neon's health to build up his natural resistance and giving his body a chance to find its own defence?' I asked. 'If there is a rogue cancer cell surely this would work better than radiation?'

'Whilst you make of it what you will, Ms Roberts, at the very least, treatment for Neon would involve radiotherapy, and that has to happen soon.'

'Is Neon to be used in a trial treatment programme?' I asked again.

'Neon will be receiving treatment that is based on a trial. He will be part of the PNET 3 treatment protocol. It is too soon for him to be part of the PNET 4 trial, that starts to the best of my knowledge early next year,' Dr Lucock replied.

A chill ran up my spine. 'With all due respect, without being shown that it's necessary, I must decline your offer to irradiate my son. All tests so far confirm there is no evidence of disease. I would like to take Neon to a clinic in Germany or possibly America, where we can work on detoxifying his body while incorporating proven anticancer therapies and boosting his immune system, something your protocol does not appear to acknowledge.'

'There is nothing to say that boosting immunity is at all beneficial,' he answered. 'Your son has a chance of cure with our treatment, and it must begin imminently.'

'Dr Lucock, it appears we are at loggerheads. I consider your treatment to be too risky and what concerns me is you pay no attention to the numerous other ways to go about killing a fugitive cancer cell, which various tests you have performed have confirmed is not even there. Otherwise what is the point of all the tests poor Neon is having to have?

'What else concerns me is rather than supporting his immune system you not only want to wipe it out, you are going to completely obliterate it. All while not giving me any clear indication of why you are doing such a thing other than because it's protocol. I'm afraid I fear more the treatment you are offering than the cancer itself. Would it not be more sensible to wait until we have had sight of the results from the latest lumbar puncture before deciding what to do next? If his cerebral spinal fluid remains clear, this shows us the tumour has not metastasised. What is the point of putting Neon through more pain and the trauma of being anaesthetised for another lumbar puncture if it's not going to make a difference in treatment?'

'You are right, Ms Roberts. It will not make a difference but what you need to understand is that Neon must have radiotherapy. All that changes in medical terms would be the category of risk and consequently the radiation dosage, that is what we need to ascertain.'

'If you could please help me get Neon's full medical files, there appear to be missing chunks from what I've been provided. The clinics I'm in contact with are requesting more information, and I need a tissue sample of the tumour, a second opinion is paramount.'

'I appreciate your need for a second opinion,' the doctor replied. 'Can I suggest the name of a paediatric oncologist in London?'

'That is very kind of you, but is it not true that all doctors within the United Kingdom must abide by the same guidelines and follow the same protocol? If you could please provide me with Neon's notes and medical records, I can send them to the various international centres I have been in contact with.'

CHAPTER SIX

The Forty-Two Day Countdown

With the operation deemed a huge success, I cried down the phone to my mother.

'We've been given a second chance, they've got the whole thing out.'

I could not have been more grateful for the skilful surgeons and their expertise in such a complex operation and thanked them with all my heart.

'Mummy, when can we go home?'

'I'll be able to take you to our new home soon Neon.'

'Are Candy and Venus there?'

'No, they're not there yet – they are staying with Sasha. As soon as we are ready we'll pick them up.'

'What about Pebbles, where is Pebbles?' Neon asked. 'Is she in Brighton?'

It was impossible to tell him that our precious Pebbles had disappeared out of the cat flap and could not be found.

Our stay on the ward was dragging along. It was clinical and monotonous. With Neon having been in the hospital far longer than the recommended ten days, I wanted to take him to our new home and was told he could soon be discharged. Neon wanted nothing more than to go "home". However, home as he knew it no longer existed. Mysteria now belonged to another family and everything we owned was packed away in boxes.

We were kept busy with constant monitoring and various tests, activities, meals and visitors but the hospital's sterile atmosphere with all its smells and noises was bleak. Neon had always loved to be active and to be in familiar surroundings with all his own things. It concerned me that being in the hospital environment for so long might be slowing down his recovery.

My spirits were lifted by the replies I was getting from the emails I had sent out to the various international cancer centres. They offered solutions, hope and general advice for Neon to make a full recovery. With the medical notes saying full resection, my focus was directed towards looking at other countries' protocols and the many ways to boost immunity. Above all else, I needed to find an acceptable treatment that would not compromise Neon's health. To educate myself, I became immersed in acquiring knowledge about radiation and chemotherapy from well-known published medical journals and other reliable sources.

A survey from the National Cancer Institute of the USA estimated that more than half of the children after the standard treatment for a brain tumour would have some sort of physical problem, for example limb weakness, poor balance or shakes (tremors). Studies indicated radiotherapy to the pituitary gland or nearby area meant the brain may not ever be able to make enough growth hormone and would most probably affect puberty and fertility.

The Internet was littered with information. Looking on the Internet, it helps to know where to search and you need to have your wits about you in order to filter through the masses of misinformation. The more I learnt about radiation and its serious side effects, the more I feared it. My instincts and research told me the relentless regime the NHS was offering us was not the only treatment available and certainly not the best. My suspicions were confirmed when I met Dr Lucock for a second appointment where I spoke openly about my reasons for hesitating to consent.

'Radiation should only be used as a last resort. If he still had a tumour I could try and understand. Neon, however, does not; the tumour has been removed in full, and he has been confirmed cancer free from the numerous tests you have done. What concerns me the most is that radiation would cause irreparable damage. It is classed as a carcinogenic. It is an unnecessary immunosuppressive assault and a violation of my son's body.'

'I am not completely dismissing what you are saying, Ms Leese. There are most certainly consequences from the treatment. Medical and radiotherapy oncologists have been trying for many years to reduce these consequences of treatment whilst still maintaining a good chance of cure and to a considerable degree have been successful.

'The problems which were severe for children ten and twenty years ago are now substantially less so, as a result of better surgery, better technology to deliver radiation and the use of chemotherapy so that less radiation is needed. It is important you understand if there are any floating cancer cells which we have to presume there are, we have no choice but to fry the whole brain and spine.'

The discussion was getting heated. Did I really hear that right? I was glad to be recording the conversation.

'Excuse me?' I exclaimed. 'Fry his brain? Doctor, this is my son we are talking about, and I most certainly will not allow you to fry his brain. You mention problems not being so severe as a result of better surgery. Presumably, in days gone by, the majority of children died during or shortly after the surgery? Surgical practices have come a long way. Besides, all his tests say he is clear. The treatment you are suggesting to *cure* my already cured son will cause a huge onslaught of other problems and is a massive insult to injury. Your radiation would cause devastation to his whole body with the possibility of causing cancer while you go about curing something that all tests confirm is no longer there. Do you not realise how crazy that sounds?

'I can't let you irradiate him just because you presume there is a slight possibility of one or two cancer cells lurking around. You have not shown me any studies to prove that your protocol is beneficial. Where is the evidence that it works? You're giving people false hope calling radiation a cure and it is anything but safe.'

'Without treatment, there would be a forty per cent chance of him dying. With treatment, he only has a twenty per cent chance of dying,' Dr Lucock persisted.

I was silent for a moment as I let Dr Lucock's words sink in.

'Where are the studies? Could you please show me the studies? Where are you getting your statistics from?' I asked. 'Is it taken into consideration, if children are fed food with very little nutritional value and adding to the problem with junk food and sugar-laden drinks? The difference is going to be huge if children are being fed a diet high in nutrition including freshly squeezed juices, compared to fast food and artificial soft drinks. Even more so if they are following an integrated anticancer approach, embracing immune boosting methods like metabolic therapy.'

'We recommend a balanced diet including sugary foods. We encourage eating chocolate, cakes and sweets. They are good sources of energy,' Dr Lucock declared.

'But it's common knowledge that sugar feeds cancer. Evidence indicates glucose fuels the growth of tumours,' I replied. 'Research suggests there are clear benefits of a low GI diet for many chronic diseases. Surely at least limiting high-sugar processed foods must be seen as an attractive tool in combating cancer?'

'There is no evidence to prove following a sugar-free diet boosts the chances of survival and following restricted diets can hamper recovery and be life-threatening. We do not suggest avoiding sugar in any way.' Dr Lucock maintained his stance.

The doctor had his toolbox and nutrition was not part of it. I knew their views, it was becoming all too familiar, having been told by hospital staff that people who want to use natural cures to potentially improve the outcome were "wasting their time".

'Surely in my son's position, an anticancer strategy used alongside various complementary therapies would be sufficient to manage one or two floating cancer cells if by some chance they are there?'

'Ms Leese, we have a protocol to follow and we must follow it; a six-week course of radiation is to be followed by one year's chemotherapy.'

'But you have said yourself, the tumour is gone and the tests indicate there is no trace of cancer. Therefore, is it not true that he is more likely to survive the treatment and will be recorded in your statistics as a cancer cure, with no mention that he was already cured?' I continued. 'It concerns me that you are relying on biased, passé statistical data. It's far too premature to prescribe such a minefield with all tests indicating he is already in the clear. He would be far more likely to develop the disease in the future should he be subjected to your treatment… it is insanity which I cannot allow.'

'We have to presume there is a floating cell,' Dr Lucock said.

'But what if there is *not* a floating cell? That's an awful amount of unnecessary suffering you are inflicting upon my son *just in case* there is the *possibility* of one or two phantom cells. Don't we all have the odd floating cancer cell anyway? Isn't it our immune systems that keep it under control and cancer at bay? It's like burning down a whole forest to get rid of one diseased tree that is *possibly* infected.

'All Neon's blood tests, all his CAT scans, all of his MRIs, everything indicates that he is cancer free. I cannot agree to let you *fry his brain*. You have not shown me anything that proves the radiation is necessary apart from telling me there *might* be a floating cell and that doing a "mop-up" is protocol. I'm sorry, but it's not good enough. This is the most important decision I will ever have to make. It's the most important decision in Neon's whole life and his twin sister's. If I would not accept this archaic treatment for myself, how can I accept it for him?' I looked into the professor's eyes. 'The tumour is gone. Would you want this treatment for your child? Would you consider it acceptable?'

The professor crossed his legs and leant back in his chair. 'When you are talking about doing radiation to the whole brain, there are many incidences where you do think it is not the therapy you want to do, but it is our job to try to cure him and ensure his best chance of survival.'

'I understand you are doing the best to your knowledge,' I protested, 'but is it possible there are other approaches you may not be aware of which could be more effective? For whatever reason, your treatment provided here courtesy of the National Health Service is restricted to chemotherapy and radiation alone, and as a consequence, you do not seem to have knowledge of or specialise in any other treatments. Using radiation will negate the benefits of having a successful surgery. Therefore, I'm determined to find a more acceptable way forward.

'What matters to me is Neon being treated as an individual and that he gets the right treatment for him. Where are the studies showing it will come back without radiation? Hearsay is not enough. Without seeing any studies giving weight to your words, I will not be giving my consent. If there are studies indicating that radiation works or that he will die without radiotherapy, I need to see them. I will agree to radiation if proven necessary.'

'Are you okay?' the taxi driver asked on the journey back to Frenchay hospital. 'You look like you have the weight of the world on your shoulders.'

'I kind of do,' I replied, managing a hint of a smile as I caught his eye in the rear vision mirror. 'I'm deep down a rabbit hole doing my best to understand radiation treatment and no matter how hard I try I cannot comprehend why it is unavoidable as a treatment for children, especially my son who no longer has a tumour. It's like they're all completely mad, yet I'm the one they're questioning.'

'Oh, that's heavy, Alice.' The taxi driver turned and gave me a little wink. 'Is it your son with cancer?'

'He had a brain tumour, and it's been removed. He is thankfully in the clear, but they want to irradiate him anyway to do what they describe as a mop-up,' I replied. 'Out of the frying pan and into the fire.'

'Why would they do that? That don't make sense,' the taxi driver remarked.

'Well that is what I'm faced with... overexcited oncologists telling me I have no option in the treatment choice for my son as it's only radiation and chemotherapy served up after surgery on their very limited three-course menu.'

'But that ain't right, it should be your choice,' the taxi driver frowned. 'He's your son.'

'Can you imagine?' I sighed. 'Not only are they wanting to treat my son with radiation when there's no sign of cancer in his body, but most people also don't realise it's the same radiation from radioactive sources used in a massive industry which generates energy production that is used in health care. How did radiation from the nuclear industry become the same radiation that is used for medical purposes in our hospitals?'

'No, it ca… can't be. The same kind of radiation?' the taxi driver stuttered. 'I… I thought it was a different type of radiation. Like, you know… medicine radiation?'

'If only,' I replied. 'Radiation is radiation. Any hospital where radiation is being used has to take serious protective measures to minimise the risks to staff. Why? Because of the potential problems of being exposed to radiation. Radiation's dangers are fierce and life-threatening. We all know the terrible consequences of the Chernobyl nuclear tragedy and the more recent Fukushima disaster, many of the first responders died from radiation poisoning. The radioactive material claimed countless lives where the particles dispersed and travelled far in the wind. It is said that many who survived the radiation suffered from cancer. Yet we allow radiation to be used in hospitals on terribly sick people… to heal them. How backwards is that?'

'But how can radiation cure cancer when it causes it?' he asked.

'Exactly. It's false hope,' I replied. 'It can't.'

———

Mum and Dad were with Neon and waiting patiently for my return.

'How did it go?' my father asked as I walked through the door. Neon did not stir. He looked fast asleep. Dad was sitting in the chair next to him.

'I'm having doubts,' I replied. 'The treatment demanded by the MDT [multidisciplinary team] is outdated. I cannot let them irradiate him when there are other non-toxic treatments available, which would suit Neon better. I'm just waiting for the reports I have requested.'

Dad sided with the medics. He believed the conventional big three (surgery, radio and chemo) were the answer to cancer; after all, it is what the medical profession recommended and is what we had been brought up to know and trust. The hospital team preached, "if we do not do radiotherapy soon he will die". We were all scared, the forty-two-day countdown weighing heavily down on us.

'We want our grandson to live.' My father pushed that an urgent decision must be made. 'They know what they're doing. You have no choice but to let them get on with it.'

'If it were a safe treatment and was going to benefit him in any way I would agree to it without question,' I argued. 'There is no tumour, and the tests all say there is no remaining cancer. There are other anticancer therapies that can be used, just not by the NHS. How can I allow them to proceed with the radiation knowing how dangerous it is? Radiation is a cause of cancer, not a cure. Dad, can we talk later?' I said, gesturing towards Neon who was starting to wake.

A group of consultants arrived soon after my parents left to discuss the regime and conversed candidly about how Neon needed to begin radiotherapy in a matter of weeks. A well-rounded lady with wiry white hair stood at the end of Neon's bed and spoke on behalf of the team. She spoke slowly with her eyes closed. 'We need to make arrangements for Neon to be transferred to London soon, Ms Roberts. Your husband informed us you will be moving there. The team in London are expecting him. Planning needs to begin as soon as possible.'

'Much time has passed since I have requested Neon's full medical notes, I do hope to get them later on today or at the latest tomorrow. It has come as a surprise to hear Ben told you we would be moving to London, it's the first I have heard of it. Dr Lucock has been unable to provide me with a tissue sample or histology report of the tumour. This was requested quite some time ago. It is preventing me from getting a second opinion without the sample, scans, detailed notes and reports. If you could help speed up the process and provide me with what I need to obtain a second opinion, I would very much appreciate it. In terms of your protocol I'm pressed for time and am quite aware a decision needs to be made quickly.'

'I'm not sure a second opinion is what you need, Ms Roberts. Radiotherapy and chemotherapy are both standard practice, and if your son does not receive the treatment he needs very soon, then he will die.'

The doctor's callous tone bothered me. I squeezed Neon's hand and looked into his sorrowful eyes. 'It is not true, don't worry, Neon.'

Looking at the doctor, I saw red. Apart from finding it very off-putting having her talk to me with her eyes clenched shut, she seemed to be drained of any colour everywhere except her face, which resembled an overripe cherry. 'Excuse me, Doctor, if you would like to talk to me and state your opinion in such a way would you be so kind as to do so in private.' Standing at six feet tall, I towered over the stout doctor who was no more than four foot ten.

'I'm sorry about this, Neon,' I whispered in his ear. 'I've just got to go and talk to this doctor. She's got some strange ideas. I'll be back in a minute.'

Outside the ward, I expressed how I felt about the doctor involving the Grim Reaper and speaking about Neon as if he was not there, but the doctor had her own ideas.

'Ms Roberts, I am not sure if you understand, but there is no choice of treatment. Your son has to begin radiotherapy very soon. We are quite sure that he would not survive without it.'

'Yes, you are making your view most clear, and I will resort to bludgeoning any cancer to death with your chosen methods if there is any cancer found in his body and you can confirm with studies that your radiation treatment is shown to work. It would be good to know that it is safe too, but given the list of side effects, we both know radiotherapy is incredibly unsafe. Your tests confirm he is already cancer free. We will get much better results from a non-toxic approach that has a good track record. All I need are Neon's medical notes so I can find the right one.'

'Ms Roberts, there is no other treatment available that can cure your son. If there was, I would be sure to know about it.'

'Respectfully, I appreciate your opinion, but perhaps it is because you are not taught patent-free therapies in medical school?'

The doctor's eyes flickered, her chin tilted even more towards the ceiling than it already was. 'We do not have the luxury of time to examine your strategy. All my colleagues would agree with me that the only treatment options are radiotherapy and chemotherapy.'

CHAPTER SEVEN

Tidcombe Hall

'I'm impressed with the way you're coping and dealing with all of this. You're doing admirably well,' Ben said.

'Thanks, Ben, you too.'

'You know, Sally, after we get him out of here, any follow-up care we will be going private. It will be good to get him out of the clutches of the NHS. We all want to access the best possible care for Neon.'

'It has become complicated though,' I responded. 'They're pushing to begin the planning phase. While I'm busy concentrating on building up Neon's strength and immune system, the doctors are fixated on something that all tests have confirmed is not there anymore and because of their outdated protocol, want to irradiate him.'

'I know,' Ben replied. 'Just keep doing what you are doing. If there is another way to treat Neon you will find it, but whatever happens, Neon is going to be fine.'

There had to be another way. I had to find a solution. Neon was too frail to be subjected to such a torturous treatment.

In my search for answers, I found a much-needed source of support: Kevin Wright, the founder of an online health store based in Tiverton in Devon.

Over the past few years, I had regularly bought supplies from Bobby's Health Shop and knew of the story about Kevin's son, Bobby. I had read about their family's experience with childhood cancer. I found Kevin to not only understand and be supportive of my reluctance to treat Neon with radiation, but he knew all about an integrated approach to treating cancer. Bobby had been diagnosed with neuroblastoma when he was three years old and given only a fifteen per cent chance of survival. Kevin and his partner Jacquie had refused radiation treatment and developed a personalised plan based on an organic diet, supplements and complementary therapies. They accepted chemotherapy on the basis that the body can recover, unlike radiation where it causes irreparable damage. More than a decade on after the dismal diagnosis, Bobby remains in remission.

Speaking to Kevin on the phone was helpful. I was extremely grateful for the time he spent talking to me about Neon and our situation. After visiting Kevin, Jacquie and Bobby at their home in Tiverton, conveniently close to the Bristol hospital, with my life still in boxes, I accepted his invitation to take Neon there once he was discharged from the hospital so we could use the hyperbaric chamber they owned.

'You never think it will happen to you, but when it does you need all the help you can get,' Kevin said when we first arrived.

Hyperbaric oxygen therapy (HBOT) involves breathing pure oxygen in increased atmospheric pressure. Being in conditions where the air pressure is increased, our lungs can gather more oxygen than is possible if we are breathing air at normal pressure. Our blood carries this oxygen throughout our body and promotes healing by increasing the levels of oxygen in the blood plasma, with another advantage that it helps create an internal environment that hinders cancer cells. It is well documented that HBOT helps to remove the toxic effects of chemotherapy and radiation. Hyperbaric tanks are commonly used in clinics using an integrated approach to overcome cancer.

'Oxygen therapy seems like such an obvious solution. Why are hyperbaric chambers not used by the NHS alongside radiation and chemotherapy?' I asked. 'Shouldn't it be part of the protocol?'

'That's a good question,' Kevin answered. 'They know hyperbaric improves quality of life; they've been using it for years. It certainly would increase the overall outcome of all their patients, especially important when treating children who are not fully grown and most vulnerable to the debilitating side effects. The medical tormentors should be hung for dosing young children with the level of deadly drugs and radiation they subject them to. If the survival and quality of life of cancer patients were paramount, the use of oxygen therapy would not be overlooked. Who is your consultant at Bristol?'

'Dr Lucock.'

'Are you serious?' Kevin said with audible disdain. 'Professor Lucock… I know him well. Send him my regards. That's the consultant who wanted to irradiate Bobby ten years ago.'

'But Bobby didn't have radiation. How did you manage to avoid it?' I asked eager to learn.

'It was mandatory back then.' A soft cheeky chuckle escaped Kevin's lips. 'All kids diagnosed with neuroblastoma had to have it as they do now with medulloblastoma, but there was no way they were going to fry my Bob. Alone in his office, I got Professor Lucock pinned up against the wall with one hand around his neck, and my other hand I got him tightly by his balls and told him what I would do to him and his family if he irradiated Bobby. I told him if I was inside I would still get to him. There was no way I was going to let them irradiate Bob. It would have killed him. Radiotherapy is no longer standard treatment here in the UK for a child diagnosed with neuroblastoma.'

'Wow. That goes to show. Bobby had cancer all through his body and survived without radiation. Neon has no trace of cancer yet they say he has no choice but to have radiation telling me he has less chance to survive without it.'

'The allopaths make out as if they drink from the fountain of knowledge and that radiation is some arcane branch of physics with magical powers when it's not. When your child develops cancer, it is like being dealt a hand in the highest stakes poker game imaginable. You can only play the hand you have been dealt with the best of your ability. The trouble is we have an epidemic of misinformed doctors misinforming their patients. It's because of this ignorance in cancer care we have a complete healthcare system failure and people end up looking into alternative treatments after the doctor says there is nothing else they can do and organs have been removed and their bodies have been ravaged by chemotherapy and radiation.'

'Can't you go and grab Dr Lucock by his balls again and tell him to leave Neon alone?' I asked.

'I wish I could, Sal, I wish I could,' he replied.

Neon and I were with Kevin and his family for nearly three weeks. We were able to eat delicious, nutritious, consciously cooked food and I juiced daily. Neon had access to complementary treatments including a resonant light machine that Kevin had bought for Bobby.

The technology was based on the research of Dr Royal Raymond Rife. It was about the same size as a printer. The resonant light machine worked by using different frequencies of light and sound waves mimicking microorganisms. Rife built the world's first virus microscope and developed a means of killing viruses by resonance. Rife's breakthrough enabled him to demonstrate that bacteria could change their form and cancer cells could potentially be transformed into healthy cells again. Rife's theory also suggested that because everything is energy vibrating at different frequencies, you can destroy pathogens by making them over resonate at their own vibrational frequency until they burst, all without affecting human tissue.

Rife paved the way for this remarkable discovery but his life's work was tabooed by the medical profession. By 1939, anyone who supported Rife had their silence brought about by the pharmaceuticals. Any practitioner who made use of his discoveries was stripped of any privileges and unable to continue working as a member of the medical profession. Rife's theory of how to cure cancer used electricity (cheap and unpatentable) and only became known to the public again in 1986 through the author Barry Lynes, who published a book called *The Cancer Cure that Worked*.

I was in awe, admiring the frequency machine that was clearly the result of many years of patient labour. It certainly looked the part with its big dials and large glass bulb. Kevin presented me with the manual and showed me how it worked. The unit was easy to use, mesmerising to look at and pleasant to listen to. Both Neon and I liked having it in our bedroom. It was placed on a table at the end of the bed, and we both enjoyed its nightly cycle, never ceasing to transfix us as we watched the static luminous light glow, listening to its gentle humming taking about an hour to complete.

Neon had needed the use of a wheelchair the few weeks while in the hospital, but within a few days of staying at the Wrights', he was walking again without my help. The improvement was noticed by everyone. The difference was incredible.

'In all my days I've never met a child like Neon before,' Kevin remarked, not letting anything go unnoticed, always giving Neon constant praise and encouragement. 'It's something else to drink those vegetable juices, eat those apricot kernels and get into the hyperbaric chamber. To have a boy that good is a credit to you… he just gets on with it. To think Neon is only seven, I've not heard him complain once. His father must be alright to have a kid like that, does he know how lucky he is?'

'He does. He's perfect isn't he? I couldn't be more proud.'

One morning while staying at Kevin's, I turned my phone off airplane mode to make a call.

'Would you mind going outside?' Kevin asked. 'I'd appreciate you not using your smartphone in our house. Nobody is allowed to use one in our home. I wouldn't own one. I don't like to expose Bob to the microwave radiation.'

'Sure, no problem,' I replied. 'I appreciate where you are coming from. Who wants to be bombarded with all that extra electromagnetic stress? It's great to meet someone who knows about it and puts it into practice.'

Kevin and Jacquie were inspiring. They walked the walk and talked the talk. Together, Kevin and Jacquie had written a helpful booklet packed full of advice and recipes for people like myself who had a child going through the unthinkable. They wanted to do everything they could to ensure parents were informed and children were being provided with the best to help them heal and stay well. Having studied herbalism, nutrition and practised healthy living for many years, most of it was not too foreign. I found their little green booklet to not only be a valid source of information, but it also highlighted Kevin and Jacquie's commitment and dedication to "support and maintain optimum, vibrant health", illustrating the lifestyle and food choices they adopted to save their son. *Stage 4 Cancer Defeated: How to make the foods kids love in a healthy way* gave a good insight into the Wrights' passion and overall mission. This branched out even further into Bobby's Health Shop, which supplied many of the products that they knew were well researched to help combat cancer, having had a child go through it all and come out the other side. Bobby was thriving.

The reason Bobby was doing so well was because of all his devoted parents had done and continued to do for him. The medical *experts* had only given Bobby a fifteen per cent chance of survival. Bobby was a *miracle* by medical standards. The Wrights had not accepted the diagnosed fate and embraced an anticancer lifestyle and integrated approach to treating Bobby. With all their years of experience, they knew what they were doing.

Bobby had been diagnosed with neuroblastoma, which had metastasised throughout his adrenal glands but Kevin with his tenacious diligence and added support from his partner Jacquie, with the extra help from the team he put together, researched and applied a cancer-fighting health-embracing strategy to their day-to-day life. They were well informed and recognised that radiation was not going to help Bobby.

'I wasn't having it. There was no way I was going to subject Bobby to that radiation and the damage it would undoubtedly do to him. It would have caused him intense suffering or, at worst, killed him,' he said. 'I stuck to my guns. It was hard, but I got my way.'

Although the Wrights agreed to the conventional chemotherapy (the hospital would have done it with or without consent), they focused mainly on rebuilding and supporting Bobby's immune system.

'The other kids were losing lots of weight and going from one infection to the next. Other parents were feeding their kids McDonald's and Fruit Shoots and wondering why they could not eradicate their untold pain and suffering and why they were not getting any better. Bob had loads of energy, kept his hair and took it all in his stride. We took his portable air filter everywhere, fed him blueberries, raspberries, black grapes and home-cooked food,' Kevin told me. 'Bob needed all of his energy to fight the cancer, not the toxic effects of radiation which would have made him deteriorate and caused serious immediate and lifelong problems *if* he had of survived, which I know he wouldn't have.'

Kevin and Jacquie implemented some dramatic changes in their lifestyle choices, reflected mainly in the foods they chose to eat and the way they cooked. Refusing to be railroaded into harsh treatment choices that he did not agree with, Kevin took Bobby overseas to some of the most well-renowned cancer treatment centres in the world.

Bobby was gravely ill when Kevin flew to the United States with him. The care in America was more advanced than what was being offered in the UK. At Memorial Sloan Kettering, the integrative medicine service offered a wide range of wellness therapies and ready to spend all the money in the world on saving their son, Kevin sought out the most effective therapies to support his immune system and overcome the neuroblastoma.

To boost his immune system and do a full body detox after Bobby had chemotherapy, Kevin and Jacquie took Bobby for four weeks to Hufeland in Germany, which specialises in holistic immunobiological therapy.

I contacted the Hufeland Klinik to inquire about taking Neon. One well-respected therapy the clinic offered was ozone therapy, which improves the oxygen transfer from our blood to tissue and is said to destroy (mop-up) cancer cells (if there were any) and was not at all damaging. It is included as standard practice in Germany and used by at least seventy per cent of physicians alongside the conventional.

As ozone has an extra atom of oxygen, it is electrophilic, wanting to balance itself with another unbalanced charge. Cancer cells are also imbalanced. When ozone is administered regularly as part of a protocol, the cancer cells are attracted to the ozone (a perfect attraction) and forced into apoptosis and die off.

With the tumour removed would this not be the perfect treatment for Neon? Unlike chemotherapy and radiotherapy, ozone cannot react with healthy cells and selectively kills cancer cells *if* they are there. Additionally, ozone therapy benefits our immune system and strengthens the body's defences.

Ozone provides our Planet Earth with a protective layer from the sun's UV rays and for almost one century has been used medicinally to treat a wide spectrum of diseases including cancer. Oxidative therapies are one of the many holistic "immune therapies" which embrace a crucial component (that conventional therapies are missing) – the inherent healing power of the human body. Given the right tools, it can do its job. Using therapies like ozone as common practice explains why Germany is at the forefront of treating cancer: a balanced approach to healthcare.

Conventional medicine does not investigate the mechanisms of the healing powers of our immune systems, instead only focusing on treating the disease with heavily financed pharmaceutical products. Imagine the improvements to our healthcare system and our health if it were part of the NHS protocol to help nudge the immune system back to doing its proper job, supporting the whole organism (cleansing, nutrition, supplementation and immune therapies) to reverse the cancer-friendly environment that has contributed to the disease.

Hufeland Klinic explains logically, "When introduced into the bloodstream, ozone triggers an avalanche of beneficial changes: it boosts circulation, activates the immune system and improves the exchange of oxygen in the blood," as well as strengthening our body's defences. "Ozone therapy also activates the body's own antioxidants and radical scavengers that help to detoxify the body."

This surely was a more humane way to treat a child who no longer had a tumour. Why did the NHS neglect these advanced/proven therapies? Ozone therapy would not cause irreparable harm and sounded far more promising to me than the conventional treatment. However, despite the dismal data, I remained open to radiation to be used as a last resort if proven necessary.

I was thrilled to hear back from the Hufeland Klinik and be told they would accept Neon. They recommended their very intensive immunobiological treatment to detoxify his body and to strengthen his immune system. It made me feel better knowing that his long-term chances of success would significantly increase. It was great to hear a clinic's first aim was to get rid of the body's toxins and to strengthen the defence mechanisms and work on supporting his overall general condition. It all made perfect sense to me, much more so than the bog-standard offer here in the UK which only wanted to bombard a cancer patient's body with harmful toxins with no mention of detoxing as it was not part of their protocol.

For a condition like cancer to take hold, there was obviously an underlying issue. The medics gave no consideration to how or why a tumour came about in the first instance and only wanted to steamroller into treating a toxic condition with toxic treatment. Integrated practitioners treat the whole body system and don't just focus on a disease, which in Neon's case had been removed.

Although I was finding it hard to understand why our doctors were so restricted and not using the most effective and least toxic treatments for cancer, it was not my biggest issue. What I was discovering in the bigger picture of cancer and its treatments was the total separation between the conventional and non-conventional therapies. Because of the trouble we have with our mainstream health providers not being trained in integrative treatments, they know very little about them, contributing to disbelief among medical professionals that they work.

Generally, physicians are under the impression that if they worked, they would know about them. Patients feel the same; if complementary therapies worked, their doctor would know about them. With the disbelief factor so prevalent, putting all of our trust in our doctors can lead to tragedy. It really requires the patient, or in my case, me, the mother of the patient, to do their own homework so I could make a fully informed decision about any future treatments Neon should receive. The only way to make an informed choice is by being informed. Until we have a fair and balanced healthcare service, any integrated advice is not coming from our mainstream medical establishment.

Holistic clinics such as Hufeland (like so many other complementary therapy clinics), commonly deal with patients who have progressed to advanced stages of cancer. All too often desperate people go to them when the "trusted" treatments have been unsuccessful. When the conventional fails, cancer patients are cast out by the clinicians whom they have entrusted their lives to and often told there is nothing more they can do. Some are left with no hope and told to go home and say their goodbyes.

These patients are often knocking on death's door with their bodies not only riddled with cancer but drained of life and totally annihilated by the ill effects of the radiation and chemotherapy. Many people believe what they are told by their doctors and, thinking nothing else can be done, they give up and die. Then there are those who refuse to give up, instead choosing to implement serious changes to their daily routines/eating habits and given the right approach/therapies, fight for their lives.

Many patients once in the hands of clinics such as Hufeland improve not only the quality of their lives, but many regain full health and overcome cancer. These success stories are usually labelled "miracles" by the mainstream medical establishment.

Recovering from surgery is one thing but doing all you can to ensure your child stays in the clear and survives is another. It was helpful to have first-hand information from people who had experience. I had been modifying my diet for years, often cutting down on the usual culprits that trigger intolerance reactions: gluten, dairy and sugar. Due to having hypersensitivities as a result of having amalgam (mercury) fillings since teenagehood (puberty), I was familiar with candida and other immune response issues that I had experienced. Once

I had the fillings removed when Neon and Elektra were three, the difference in my body (for the better) both mentally and physically was undeniable. This had all helped me accumulate vital background information, which was coming into good use while nursing Neon back to full health.

There were various reasons I had been avoiding cow's milk for many years, choosing to drink hempseed milk, oat milk and nut milk. I am also very partial to goat's milk, especially unpasteurised as it maintains the goodness. It was a delight to see at the Wrights' house they sourced their goat's milk locally by bulk and according to their booklet, not only was goat's milk acceptable for a child with/recovering from cancer but for a growing child it was advisable as it was nutritious and has health benefits.

In Kevin and Jacquie's booklet, it explained that goat's milk has a mildly alkaline effect and takes about twenty minutes to digest, as opposed to the three to four hours that it takes to digest acid-forming cow's milk. It also explained how goat's milk is not mucous forming, and unlike cows, goats are not routinely given antibiotics and growth hormones. Many people avoid cow's milk because it's hard on digestion, which is no surprise when you think about it. Putting aside the way it's inhumanely produced, it is really for baby calves, which grow rapidly. Kevin explained where cancer is concerned, "drinking cow's milk if you have cancer is like throwing petrol on a fire".

With so many substitutes on the market, it wasn't hard to avoid.

I'm a big fan of apple cider vinegar (ACV). The hyperbaric chamber we were using daily was close to the cellar where the vinegar was being made. It was lovely seeing a whole room of it in its various stages, brewing in its massive containers. The shelves were full of bottles and my eyes lit up every time I saw it.

'Look at that web-effect bacteria,' Kevin said as he stopped and picked up a bottle. 'That's what is known as "the mother", pure living enzymes with life-giving nutrients. We give Bob some every day.'

I had been using the unpasteurised murky tonic for years. Some said it was a miracle medicine used for many an ailment from the common cold to cancer.

'It's how I first discovered Bobby's Health Shop,' I explained to Kevin. 'I'd been searching online for apple cider vinegar specifically with "the mother". My mum got me into it years ago, and rather than using the American Bragg's brand, I wanted to source some locally and came across your Bobby's Health Shop. That's how I first learnt about Bobby. Who would have thought I would end up here under these circumstances – that is how I knew about you and thought to call you about Neon.'

'Nobody could possibly imagine how it feels or what it's like... what a wake-up call. You should have seen us before. Unlike you, we weren't very healthy. We have made some real changes. I didn't have a clue about any of this stuff until Bob was fighting for his life. We've all heard an apple a day keeps the doctor away but who'd have thought that apple cider vinegar is the ultimate form of the apple, packed full of beneficial nutrients that are unlocked during the fermentation process and that it is a great way to alkalise the body. Most people don't know anything about alkalising, let alone that some decent vinegar could help towards good health.'

'I've tried to get Neon to take it mixed with water, but he does not like the smell or taste. Elektra and I love it.'

'Bobby doesn't mind it at all.' Kevin paused. 'What do you think caused Neon's tumour?'

'I wish I knew,' I replied. 'I've racked my brain for answers. We were living in a highly acidic situation... talk about toxic. I've heard that cancer can sometimes be a result of tragic events. With the heightened chronic stress situation in Devon, it definitely impacted on Neon hugely. Before the diagnosis, I thought it was Neon who was being affected the most. It seems like too big a coincidence that Neon's diagnosis happened the same week as us moving house, not long after his father moved his mistress into our home. I'm certainly not blaming anyone, but the emotional trauma was off the scales. It was without a doubt the worst time of my life... and then for Neon to get diagnosed with a medulloblastoma... just when I thought things could not get any worse. Have you got any idea what caused Bobby's?'

'I can't say for certain. You're right though, emotions and post-traumatic stress do have a part to play with cancer, the body can only cope with so much. If the sympathetic nervous system is on overdrive nonstop, and the adrenals are taking a beating, it will eventually alter the genetic code, which can result in various pro-cancer processes. With Bob, I thought it was largely our lifestyle, we used to eat a lot of shit, but that's not the case with you, sounds like you ate really well and apart from choosing a dickhead for a husband, you were doing everything right.'

'We did eat well. Neon had his first shop-bought chocolate when he went to nursery at three. It wasn't because of any crap we were eating. He's never tasted Haribo and doesn't like fizzy drinks.'

'Makes you wonder, doesn't it? I know you've just moved but where was your home positioned?'

'A small town called North Tawton in Devon.'

'Your property wasn't surrounded by commercial farms by any chance was it?' Kevin asked.

'Yes, it was,' I replied.

'Did it ever cross your mind or did you remain blissfully oblivious to the extent of the constant spraying of industrial pesticides, which would have happened from early spring until harvest time?'

The penny dropped like a lead balloon.

'It's up to the discretion of the farmers to inform neighbours of any planned spraying, but I can't imagine anyone knocking on your door or the farmers talking about it down at your local pub.'

Kevin was right. Even though we ate organic, I did not put much thought into contamination through our environment and groundwater, ingesting pesticides through rain or irrigation runoff and that pesticides were probably one of the worst offenders when it comes to cancer-causing factors. Until now, we had lived in North Tawton for Neon and Elektra's entire lives. I appreciate that small exposures may be considered harmless but daily exposure over time could have certainly added to our problem.

'Another influencing factor could have been the pulsing microwave electromagnetic radiation beamed at him constantly from the WiFi. Ben was all over the wireless technology like a rash and had our whole property networked. The main hub was in the room right below where Neon slept. As soon as I learnt about it, I asked Ben to turn off the WiFi at night and hardwire the whole property, but that was not until a few years later when Neon was about three or four. Who knows what damage happened in that time. It certainly can't have helped.'

'At least you're aware of it being a problem, Sal. Most people love their wireless communication systems too much to consider that it's experimental technology. In 2011, the World Health Organization classified microwave frequency – WiFi – as a class 2B, possible human carcinogen.'

'A friend of mine came over with her Acoustimeter and showed me our EMF reading, she was the one who made me aware of the damage it could do to our DNA. It's like a continual tapping. It's not too bad if it just happens for a little bit, but over the years if it keeps tapping away at the same place, our DNA eventually breaks. The reading in our house was ridiculously high as not only did we have WiFi but we had cordless phones too, which are also a hazard. Ben's mother sleeps with one beside her bed, and she's got early signs of dementia. Apparently, it's like having a mini-mast.'

'Exactly why I don't have one of those stupid smartphones, and we have everything hardwired. All those poor people walking around with them constantly held up to their heads, especially kids. You know me, Sal, if I see it, I tell them how it is. Children's brain tissue is more conductive, the skull is thinner, and their smaller brains and softer brain tissue allows more radiation to penetrate than adult skulls. The kids are bound to have no idea, but their parents should know better. They are supposed to be protecting their children, not helping along with genetic damage and defects.' Kevin paused. 'As for Ben's mother, did you tell her it could be part of the reason she's losing her memory?'

'Yes, but she didn't want to know,' I replied. 'How could a cordless phone next to my head all night every night (for twenty-something years) have any effect on my mind? Don't be ridiculous.'

With the wonderful web at our fingertips, Kevin made me think about something else I had remained blissfully unaware of: the phone masts. I knew phone masts were going up all over the place for better reception, 4G for mobile phone networks were the latest hype. Obviously, capable of heating our tissue with low levels of microwave radiation, it was dangerous to live right next to, or particularly under a gigantic mast... or a smaller one. A burgeoning body of research reported various health effects people had been suffering from as a result of exposure to mast radiation including sleep disturbance, headaches, memory loss, mood changes and cancer but little did I know that around our old property we had three masts that formed a triangle and were in a close range, too.

———

I will remain forever grateful for the friendship and extra support that was offered at Tidcombe Hall. Tough times were made bearable by playing games (Frustration was a favourite that Neon wanted to play again and again) and reading books in a relaxed home environment. Compared to the physiotherapy that I was still taking him for at the hospital, it was like heaven and hell. "Home" was improving his strength and coordination. Neon strongly disliked our trips back to the hospital, he dreaded going, and could never wait to leave.

One of the hardest parts was Neon and Elektra being separated. They had never been apart before. It was difficult for Elektra to understand why her twin was not himself and did not have the energy to play. Ben and Elektra came to stay at Tidcombe Hall but only for a short time. Elektra is such a bright and bubbly child, having her around was amazing for us both, finding joy in all we did. When we went into the hyperbaric chamber, Elektra wanted to join us.

'Can I come in, Mummy? It looks fun.'

'Maybe next time, Elektra.'

Patiently waiting outside for the one-and-a-half hours we were in there, she circled the chamber and blew us kisses.

Unfortunately, the logistics didn't work. Elektra had started a new school in Knightsbridge and Ben wanted to get back to London.

––––

With the limited time schedule, another meeting was organised by Professor Lucock. On one hand, I was told that all tests indicated Neon was cancer free and on the other hand that the NHS's protocol was inflexible, and radiation and chemotherapy had to be used as a preventive in case of the possibility of a phantom cancer cell.

I was certain that radiation was a severe case of overtreatment, confirmed when Dr Lucock produced a study done in 1942. We like to believe our National Health Service is modern and offers treatments based on groundbreaking research. The reality is the cancer treatment offered to us by our mainstream medical centres was primitive.

The study was based on an investigation done over seventy years ago involving seventeen children. Not thousands, not hundreds, only seventeen children. Moreover, the study was done at a time of limited diagnostic and medical equipment, far less advanced surgical procedures and allopathy had lacked the *skilfulness* we now have in the modern era. I asked Dr Lucock if I could see the full study and not just a snippet. It was impossible to establish whether the children in the study died because they did not have radiotherapy.

A much more recent study I had been shown by Kevin on the outcome prediction in paediatric medulloblastoma was far more interesting and made more sense. Array-based karyotyping was a new technique for assessing chromosomal copy number changes that provided information previously unobtainable.

The Pfister Setal study stated that, "supplementing conventional diagnostics with molecular information should help to identify patients with aggressive tumours for whom maximal therapy is appropriate and others who might survive with less toxic adjuvant therapy of reduced intensity".

'Could you please tell me, Dr Lucock, about array-based karyotyping testing? One of the four subgroups has a good chance of not recurring. It is my understanding that Neon would be in the low-risk group if there was one?'

'The Myc and MycN results are being processed in London, but it is new to us, and this more complex testing is not currently the normal practice for treatment in the UK.'

'But it is being used as standard practice in other countries? Would this not affect the type of treatment used and doses given? Shouldn't we wait to see the results before planning which treatment Neon needs?'

'Ms Leese, treatment decisions are not yet affected by cytogenetic aberrations. Cytogenetic analysis is not a standard clinical test for medulloblastoma, and it is therefore not helpful to wait for the results of these before planning.'

'But integrated genomic studies abroad have revealed that medulloblastoma is composed of four subgroups, surely this makes a difference to treatment?' I asked.

'I am sorry, Ms Leese, even though there are differing prognoses, there is no current stratification of treatment in the UK.'

'America varies treatment depending on 6q and 17q amplification, the cytogenetic aberrations, the basis of resection and cerebral spinal fluid results. The four subgroups: WNT, SHH, group three and group four will help identify patients in the future for whom treatment may be reduced in intensity but that doesn't help Neon does it?'

'I'm afraid not,' the consultant replied.

'I would like to seek other opinions in the United States and Germany. They seem to have made advances that the National Health Service in the United Kingdom has not.'

'We have asked for these tests to be done, Ms Leese. As you know, we arranged for staining with β-Catenin, which does have prognostic significance, and I will forward the report of this, which confirms what I have said to you. Myc and MycN analysis have been performed by the pathologist in London, but the result of this will not be available until next week at the earliest. The result of this would not ever justify withholding radiotherapy. It would help to know whether the specific knowledge of 6q and 17q would affect the proposed therapy, which might be offered by hospitals in the USA. I have not sought these results because my understanding was that Neon-Luca's care was to be in London.'

'I have made preliminary contact with overseas specialists who are waiting for copies of all Neon's scans to date, the tissue sample, the lumbar puncture report and histology report. Dr Lucock, I understand your protocol has time restrictions and not being given what I need is only causing further delays. I'm afraid I cannot proceed with the treatment you are offering until I have at least one other overseas expert opinion.'

'There is a process, and he has a better chance of survival if we treat him. It would be best if Neon remains with you throughout treatment, Ms Leese, I do hope you understand.'

Dr Lucock opened the door to his office. I knew exactly what he meant. He was threatening to take Neon away from me. His words of warning terrified me. 'I have given some thought to your requests,' he continued. 'Releasing tissue sample is not a standard practice of *the Trust,* and we cannot see how it would help you in any way.'

'I understand perfectly well what you are saying, but I too hope that you appreciate I cannot move forward without a second opinion. I'm hoping for no more delays in getting what I have been asking for. Of course, Dr Lucock, should all opinions be that the radiotherapy and chemotherapy must be carried out, I will agree and give my consent for the treatment to start straight away. I realise how busy you are. Thank you for taking the time to talk to me.'

'This is the most important meeting of my day, Ms Leese. I'm sure we will speak again soon.'

For the avoidance of doubt, I requested to communicate with Dr Lucock and his colleagues in writing. The resultant email trail made my position clear and illustrated the delays that were caused by Dr Lucock (and his team) in not providing what I had been asking for in order to be able to obtain a second opinion.

To my dismay, Neon's care had been transferred over to the MDT in London, and despite our discrepancies, I was urged to engage with them so the planning process could begin. The pressure was building up, heightened by the tone of Dr Lucock's intense emails. With the NHS needing at least a week to plan the radiation fields correctly, I was racing against the clock to find a more favourable treatment plan for Neon. Dr Lucock promised a disc would be available for me in London. This would contain all up-to-date scans and the histology report that would be given to me at the hospital meeting by one of the team.

CHAPTER EIGHT

The Planning Phase

It had become much colder, it was icy, and the weather was affecting the trains. To make the journey more comfortable, I drove Neon up to London for his first hospital appointment to meet the London team. Neon and I left straight after breakfast and drove the four-hour journey from Tiverton to Knightsbridge, where Ben was expecting us at his parents' flat. We had arranged to taxi into central London together, but our journey had taken longer than expected. With the timing so tight the taxi was waiting for us, and we hurried to the hospital. Cutting it fine, we made it just in time to be greeted by an intimidating panel of paediatric oncologists and co-workers, who all formed a half-circle directly facing us. We stood frozen in the doorway of the children's ward, where our meeting was being held.

'Please, come in, we won't bite.'

Neon stepped into the overcrowded room sandwiched between Ben and me as we were introduced to the welcoming clinical team. 'Thank you for coming, please sit down.'

Neon's eyes hardly left the floor as he answered "good" to all Professor Gadd's (chief radiologist) questions about how he was now and had been since the surgery. Professor Gadd's intent gaze was firmly fixed on Neon. The confined, stuffy surroundings we were crammed into magnified the awkward atmosphere. Feeling the heavy weight of his steady stare on Neon, I sat cross-armed holding my elbows and noticed Neon doing the same as if hugging himself. There was no escaping the feeling of dread creeping over me like poison ivy. I sensed Neon's discomfort, and then huge relief when introductions had been made and Professor Gadd suggested he went next door with Gemma, a trained *play* specialist.

'We like the children to do play therapy for at least a week so that they get used to the idea of wearing the mask,' he explained. 'They must not move while they're having the radiation, and if they do, we have to anaesthetise them every time. Most children keep still though. I'm sure Neon will be fine.'

I sat fixed to my chair wide-eyed and speechless. Play therapist? Anaesthetised daily if he couldn't keep still? It all sounded like something out of a horror movie. How could a seven-year-old child be expected to tolerate a procedure of being bolted down to a table by a heavy-duty made-to-measure mask, which would cover his entire face and neck so he could not move a muscle and then engulf him in a huge machine that would spin around him on all angles to irradiate him? Being abducted by aliens maybe? Dr Frankenstein's monster? Nazi concentration camps, perhaps?

Two of the walls were painted orange and reflected the harsh fluorescent tube lighting, which added to the overall brightness of the room. An effort had been made to add some artwork to the walls giving the children's ward more of a personality, but it was far from cheery. The heavily bleached sterile surroundings and listening to such lunacy were making me feel faint.

'Ms Roberts, I can understand your concern. My name is Dr Sarah Stone. Any questions you have, please just ask.'

As I faced Dr Stone, it came to my attention how unhealthy everybody looked in the room. Dr Stone had a severe case of adult acne, and Dr Gadd had droopy dark circles underneath his eyes and the worst teeth I had ever seen. The pale winter pallor enhanced the spidery red veins that stood out on the exposed skin of another ghostly-looking clinician sitting opposite me. Although I gave a courteous acknowledgement to Dr Stone, I could not wait to leave.

The chief paediatric oncologist was a tubby man and had a noticeably sweaty brow. He wore a dated brown tweed suit jacket and was unusually upbeat, probably the most enthusiastic person I have ever encountered, which I found disconcerting considering the subject content. Dr Harper got himself all worked up, and was way too overexcited when he spoke and the slight one-sided smirk never left his face as he talked about the current UK guidance for post-surgery treatment for medulloblastoma. The stocky professor reiterated in his highly skilled manner what I had learnt in Bristol; the treatment was based on cumulative evidence from multiple clinical trials. Trials that never involved any other treatment other than surgery, chemotherapy and radiotherapy.

As Neon's healthcare providers I respected their opinions, but I rejected their assumption that there was no other choice. I could not ignore why the scope for treatment had remained the same for over seventy years despite the poor prognosis and injurious effect the conventional therapies had on the body. Surely the inhumane radiation trials conducted in war camps could not have possibly continued by subjecting the weakest and most vulnerable to extreme doses of toxicity? It made me wonder who manipulated the strong hand of the medical establishment, or was it that conventional care had been hijacked by drug companies? With doctors agreeing to a Faustian deal with the Blair government in 2004, allowing NHS doctors to be *paid for performance* there was a mismatch of priorities.

The pursuit of targets had redefined doctors' relationships with their patients. I wanted to think that it was only Neon's welfare the doctors had at heart but having financial incentives in order to maximise their income, I was dubious of the framework that would lead to a lifetime of drugs, including repeated blood tests and a multitude of endless investigations.

After the meeting, I was given the disc with the images but no reports. I couldn't wait to get back to Tiverton and send out the scans to the overseas practitioners I had been in touch with.

'We can't be doing that again. Nine hours travel time, Neon is shattered,' I complained to Kevin as we stood in his kitchen later that night. 'What an ordeal.'

'What did the assessment involve?' Kevin asked.

'They say they have Neon's welfare at heart, but they just wanted to meet him. All he did was say hello, and then he got taken to another room to draw a picture with a torture therapist that they had the audacity to call a play therapist. It was traumatising. I can only imagine how Neon felt. There has got to be another way, Kevin, and I have to find it fast.'

I was seeking views and treatment options from specialists all over the world, set on finding a more favourable way to do a "mop-up", but it was impossible to fully engage with any experts abroad. I had hit a brick wall since composing another email and sending it out to the centres of excellence. They all said they needed more information. Time was disappearing and by the end of the next week, the forty-two days within which Neon was said to have to start treatment would be up.

Acutely aware of the restrictive timescale and desperate to find Neon the best care possible, I continued pressing for the various reports. However, with Ben telling the MDT we would be having treatment in London, matters had become drastically confused and it had become a big problem. Ben had not thought it through properly. Where would we live? Neon was to be a day patient with his medical care performed on an ambulatory basis, but we had nowhere appropriate to stay in London, and neither of us wanted to reside in the "home from home" outpatient hospital quarters. Ben was living in the heart of Westminster; to suggest treatment in London was for his convenience, not ours.

Dr Lucock, who stated in an email, "I am at a loss to know how best to act", was undoubtedly pleased to see the back of us, and then there was the London clinical team who were waiting to welcome us with open arms. However, London had proved to be a nightmare, and that was just a day trip. The only viable option was to stay where we were. Kevin had invited us to remain at his place for as long as we needed. Having asked for the transfer back to Bristol, I thought it could all be worked out.

Dr Lucock wrote:

Dr Gadd has not referred Neon back to me. I think it would not be in Neon's interests to do this. The preparation for treatment will have begun already, and if you remain under the care of the London team, he will – I hope – still receive his treatment at the appropriate time. If you were to come back to Bristol, I am afraid we would not be able to begin the planning process until next week at the earliest, and we would certainly miss the forty-two-day time-point since surgery. I am afraid our paediatrics radiotherapist is on leave this week.

My 4x4 was temporarily unsafe to drive, and it didn't help that the weather conditions were atrocious. We were housebound. I could not drive my car to the garage. Due to such bad weather, the trains were sporadic, if working at all.

News reports said to "avoid all travel". The whole country stood still. Tiverton had roads closed due to snow, ice and flooding, causing us to miss two appointments in London. Aware this would exacerbate the problem but unwilling to expose ourselves to treacherous weather conditions, it was a paradoxical catch-22 situation; we were damned either way. The timing could not have been worse, and there were consequences.

In a follow-up email, Dr Lucock said:

> *I will talk with the Trust solicitor today, to see whether it would be considered appropriate to transfer Neon's care back to Bristol. It is my opinion that he would be best cared for by the team in London, at least for the period of radiotherapy. It is my understanding that Mr Roberts, Neon's father, has agreed to radiotherapy in London. Given the closeness of his parents' flat, it does seem most sensible for Neon to be based there, at least for some of the time.*

Ben agreed it was best Neon should remain living with me, but he had overlooked where we were going to stay. It didn't help it had already been made difficult for me to visit their flat. Ben's mother made her feelings clear from the outset, telling me, 'Michele feels uncomfortable when you come here.'

'It did not seem to bother her one iota when she moved in as Ben's mistress for the final six months we remained in our home in Devon,' I retorted, unable to bite my tongue.

Personal grievances to one side, London was not where I wanted to take Neon. At odds with the NHS, I faced a machine. Although denied the information required, with the legal threats made and matters snowballing out of control, I needed a lawyer.

On meeting up with a local solicitor and explaining my setback in finding a more humane treatment plan and the position I was in as a result of the ongoing delay by the NHS, although she was sympathetic, she was quick to point out the enormity of what I was up against. When I explained to her how whole brain radiotherapy was described to me as "frying his brain", she advised I should report Dr Lucock to the General Medical Council (GMC).

'It is, of course, a matter for you as to whether you report me to the GMC. This would undoubtedly cause me great personal discomfort,' Dr Lucock replied when I contacted him via email and mentioned what the solicitor had suggested.

On Friday afternoon, two days after my meeting with the local solicitor, I received an email from Dr Lucock at 5pm saying that I needed to take Neon to attend a scan at 10am at Bristol hospital the following morning. The timing was terrible. I had just dropped my car off at the garage to get four new tyres and was not due to pick it up until Monday morning. The same email included the DNA aberration results I had been asking for, but it was yet another ambiguous email contradicting what it said in the histology report I had also just received.

As a result of the missed appointment, it progressed quickly. The MDT made an application to the High Court to make Neon a Ward of Court, which was refused. I received an email from the NHS' solicitor telling me if I did not take him to the London hospital by twelve noon the next day, they would go back to the High Court to try again.

It appeared the main problem was due to the time constraints of the protocol. The pressure was building up to begin planning for the prescribed radiation treatment, but I was growing more anxious with all the conflicting information. The mismatched facts were making me question the medical team, who proposed a dangerous and damaging treatment because of a hard-line protocol. I spoke about my concerns with Kevin.

'The histology report says the tumour did not show Myc or MycN amplification. Yet here, the doctor has written the most likely group Neon falls into is group four, but one of the main features of group four is MycN amplification.'

'Even more contradictions,' Kevin said. 'Once you start seeing all the contradictions it makes you question their capability doesn't it? I feel for you, Sal. I know what you're going through. They did it to me when I was going through it all with Bob.'

'But if I don't take Neon to tomorrow's appointment it will be another missed appointment. I've been able to excuse the two missed London appointments due to the weather but with such a short time left until treatment is due to begin, if I take him will they let us go home again?'

The pressure was pouring into my inbox.

Ben's sister Lucy wrote:

> *I spoke to one of the oncologists at length this evening. She said there's a very recent study that pretty much proves a considerable drop off in recovery from radiotherapy if not administered within six weeks. We are now looking at seven minimum. Because of this, they are desperate that you bring Neon to London immediately. If you don't, they are making Neon a Ward, which would restrict your access, which would be horrible for Neon. If you don't give him to Ben or the hospital, they will send the police to get Neon. Without Ben, without you, just poor Neon collected by the police if necessary. I think this would all be horrific, but is the only option you are leaving us with in order to give Neon a chance at life. I implore you not to cut your access to Neon off in this way, and rather cooperate with the medical profession, Ben, myself and everyone who knows Neon and knows cases like this, other than Kevin.*

Dr Lucock wrote: "His operation was, I believe, on 25 October, which makes a deadline of 6 December to begin therapy. There is a great urgency for you to go to London, where Dr Gadd and Dr Stone will meet with you to begin the planning process."

A tidal wave of fear had crashed over me and swallowed me up. Every sales pitch made by the oncology team made it worse. The last thing I wanted to do was make a fear-based decision. Feeling strongly the "unproven to work" but "proven to harm" treatment would cause irreparable damage, my adrenal glands were working on overtime, resulting in acute stress response syndrome, putting me into full-blown panic mode.

With all that had happened in my personal life, worn out after months of living in Devon in a stressful situation, I was at the end of my tether. The only feasible option to deal with the threat was to temporarily flee to safety. I needed to step aside from the immense pressure and have a little more time to set in place a preferred treatment plan.

There was one place I thought I could go: the Advance Centre in East Grinstead. A charity dedicated to improving the abilities of neurologically challenged children. Kevin had spoken highly of the charity's founder Linda Scotson and the remarkable change she had made in her son who had been given a desperate and hopeless diagnosis of cerebral palsy. Having talked to Linda over the phone, it felt like she was an old friend. Linda was studying for a PhD and had developed her own therapeutic technique: a gentle touch that improved breathing, circulation and posture in children with diverse brain injuries and behavioural challenges. The Advance Centre also offered hyperbaric oxygen therapy and was conveniently close to our new home in Brighton.

I wanted to continue with the hyperbaric therapy while deciding where to go next. Not only was it helping Neon to recover from his surgery, by speeding up the healing process, but if there was a floating cancer cell that the medics justified their ferocious treatment with, then the extra oxygen supplied by way of the chamber could potentially weaken it, if not destroy it.

When I called Linda to speak about using her chamber, she kindly offered for Neon and me to come and stay. It was difficult to think about taking Neon to the hospital when he was making such good progress. He had gained a much-needed 3kg in the time we had been in Tiverton. I spoke to Kevin and Jacquie about the treatment options and the consequences of missing the scheduled appointment. Jacquie was sympathetic and supported me with the view that as his mother it was my right to do what I saw best for my son.

'You are well educated on the orthodox and integrated therapies. You just need more time to find the right one for Neon so you can make an informed decision. If everything had been handled faster and in a more professional way by the hospital, you would not be in this position now. I really feel for you, Sally. You are very brave. I don't know how you are coping.'

Nobody had Neon's long-term best interests more at heart, but she did warn me: 'If you do decide to go, Sally, they won't stop until they find you.'

'It's true,' Kevin agreed, 'with them relying on that small study. With you getting past three months, the whole scope for treating medulloblastoma will have to change. They'll stop at nothing to find you. With you demonstrating their protocol is bogus, imagine how many furious parents there are going to be. All children who have been subjected to radiation and chemotherapy suffer from ill side effects. One young boy we met who was diagnosed with medulloblastoma and had been through radiation and chemotherapy can hardly speak and has to wear nappies. He was fine before the treatment. Imagine those parents learning the treatment was misguided and the irreparable harm done to their child could have been avoided.'

'I'm caught up in an entire network of procedures so complex it's mind-boggling. The conventional treatment has been the only way to treat cancer for a very long time but without diet, lifestyle choices and other therapies considered how can we truly know what works and what doesn't? How many other parents have been through this and asked the same question –

will this treatment do more harm than good? How trusting of us to put our blind faith into a medical system allowing them to use deadly treatments on our children. If only the medical establishment acknowledged that our bodies are capable of so much more than they are given credit for. Provided with what it needs, our body is designed to heal.'

'Sadly, it's not that simple. Most parents do not realise cancer is a business,' Kevin explained. 'It's so beyond comprehension for most people. Who wants to think we have been duped? The truth is hidden out in the open for all to see but who wants to believe the exploited fear of this disease stems from the treatment and at its roots is a multi-trillion-pound industry. The profiteers in the big-drug-business get rich. Humanity is its casualty. The cancer cartel suffocates any attempts to use rational therapeutic regimes. What's worse, the very causes of cancer – vaccinations, antibiotics, pesticides, herbicides, GMOs, additives, fluoride, nuclear energy – it's all actively promoted by our governments.'

'Perhaps it's because we have accepted these bogus treatments to be the only treatments used in our hospitals that there is no cure for cancer. Irradiating people in the name of healing is a big part of the problem. We've been led to believe that we have to "fight cancer" by suffering (and hopefully surviving) through modern-day cancer treatments.

'With all Neon's symptoms, I took him back to our GP and pushed for an MRI. From what we have been through I know it would be apparent if something was wrong if his health began to deteriorate again. To take a "watch and wait" approach while implementing an anticancer strategy is more sensible than the nonsense they are offering,' I continued. 'There are ways to recover from cancer. Why do the practitioners in charge of our health not seem to know about any of it, unless it involves pain and suffering? It is well documented how their treatments unleash a string of other problems. Why is nothing done to soften the blow when so many complementary therapies have proven to be beneficial?'

'I'm afraid you've opened up a can of worms there, Sal. A cancer patient can succumb to infections after having been through conventional treatment. One of the reasons that relapsed patients have such poor prognosis is that their bodies are unable to handle further toxicity, their tumours have become multi-drug resistant,' Kevin informed me. 'Science has proven that the cancer cell is the weaker cell. How many people would be out of a job if they told you to go home, avoid microwaves, juice, drink lots of good-quality water, eat well, avoid junk food, be stress-free and take a few supplements?'

Staying at Kevin and Jacquie's had been a respite, but we needed to leave. Although I was anxious and knew there would be repercussions if I missed the following day's appointment, I could not volunteer Neon for something I felt so strongly was going to cause him permanent harm. The situation had spiralled out of control and was fraught with danger, yet I could never have imagined the magnitude of what would happen by missing the third appointment and the fierce storm that was about to break.

CHAPTER NINE

Forest Row

Driving to East Grinstead seemed to take forever and was made longer by all the wrong turnings I took along the M25. It had been dark for a few hours when we finally reached Forest Row in East Grinstead and pulled into the car park of the Swan public house, where I called Linda who came and guided us back to her home, nestled up a narrow country lane on the edge of the woodlands.

The immediate plan was that we would focus on rebuilding Neon's strength and having hyperbaric oxygen therapy would help reduce the effects that the surgery had had on Neon's brain.

'Okay, sailors,' Linda beamed. 'You may disembark. Come in and consider yourselves part of the family.'

It was hard to determine Linda's age. She looked fifty-something with her fiery red hair and petite frame. Stepping into her full household, Neon and I were made to feel welcome. It was a relief to have arrived and to be so warmly greeted. Her partner John helped us in with all of our things while Lily, Linda's daughter, made me a cup of Yorkshire tea and her son

Doran introduced us to Oliver, their black and white fluffy cat. Doran chatted away while I prepared some buckwheat noodles for dinner before setting up the resonant light machine that Kevin had lent me to use. The serene atmosphere in Linda's warm abode was a contrast to the furore that had erupted in the outside world.

———

Early the next morning, a loud knock startled my parents at their home in Strawberry Fields, North Tawton. Two uniformed police officers asked if they knew where I had taken Neon, doing full surveillance of their house, attic and garage.

Later on that evening, my parents were sitting in their living room when they were disturbed once more. 'That must be the police again, only they would knock like that,' Mum remarked when hearing a loud thud at their front door. This time it was two burly non-uniformed Criminal Investigation Department (CID) officers.

'We're looking for Sally and Neon. When was she last here?' the officer inquired, showing his badge and stepping uninvited through the door.

'Sorry, officers,' Mum said, 'you are welcome to come in but could you please take your shoes off?'

The officer scoffed as he lent down to undo his laces and slipped off his shoes before continuing his interrogation.

'We've reason to believe you know where your daughter is?'

'We have no idea where she is. She did not tell us where she was going. We're worried sick. We wish we knew,' Mum replied.

'You must know where she's taken your grandson?' the stern detective scowled.

'I'm sorry we don't, we've got no idea,' she repeated.

'Mr and Mrs Leese,' the officer sneered, 'you are not known to us. Let us keep it that way.'

Mum's eyes widened as she watched the officer sit himself down on the double sofa in the living room. 'We've accessed your bank accounts and have seen that Sally has made a recent transaction. You need to explain this to us. Could you turn on your computer for me, Mrs Leese?'

His colleague picked up the phone and dialled 1471. 'Whose number is this?' he asked.

'Sally's friend Fiorella was worried about her. She sent me a message asking me to call.'

'You must know where she is. Where would she go?' the officer asked again.

'I wish I knew. Sally did not tell me,' Mum sobbed.

'We have not done anything wrong. Could you stop treating us like criminals,' Dad protested. 'Please stop upsetting my wife.'

'Just tell us where your daughter has taken Neon.'

'How can we tell you something we don't know, we are telling the truth. We do not know where Sally is. If we did, we would tell you. We're both worried sick,' Dad restated.

'Trouble is, Mr and Mrs Leese, we don't believe you,' the law enforcement representative taunted in a low growl while shaking his head.

'I am very sorry, officer, we wish we knew more, but Sally did not tell us where she was going,' Dad said again.

The hard-nosed officer showed no remorse. 'It looks like we'll have to take you to London to be interrogated. You do realise that social services are now involved and are going to take your grandson away, don't you? We think you know very well where Sally has taken Neon. I'm going to phone the commissioner in London to ask him what we should do with you.'

Fiorella was resting with her six-month-old baby, Phoenix, when the police descended on her flat in Pimlico, London. Fiorella had told her mother, Gloria, that Neon and I had disappeared, but that did not stop her surprise when she opened the door to see the fourth floor of their building in Dolphin Square swarming with police. Fiorella was equally startled to see several police officers in her flat when she came out of the bedroom to see what all the commotion was about.

After the police had searched the entire apartment block, as the interrogating officer was putting his notebook away, Hunter, my four-year-old godson said quietly, 'I've seen Mummy's friend.'

'Is that right young man?' The officer looked down at Hunter with a humourless expression and took his notebook back out. 'You've seen your mummy's friend have you?'

Hunter nodded.

Not wanting to coerce her son, Fiorella thought she had better interject. 'Yes, Hunter, we have seen Sally, she came swimming with us a few months ago do you remember? Do you think you saw Sally recently, or quite a while ago?'

All eyes were on Hunter while he thought about it. 'I think it was a while ago,' he eventually replied.

'Thank you for the information,' the officer said putting his notebook away again. 'Here is my direct number. Let us know straight away if Sally contacts you. Need I remind you it is a criminal offence if you withhold any information or do not tell us anything you know straight away.'

———

In Tiverton, a police squad was descending on Kevin's home. Two local officers had come to the gate to ask of our whereabouts. Kevin told them we had left while he was out shopping and did not know where we had gone. Unsatisfied, the fully armed police with helmets, body armour and guns forced entry later that afternoon. Equipped with a warrant, they took Bobby's

Health Store by storm and questioned the staff individually, hell-bent on finding out where we had gone. The courtyard was full of police vehicles: vans, cars and motorbikes. There were no less than twenty officers on foot. Police dogs were barking, and helicopters with bright searchlights were circling above. The police officers searched every corner of Tidcombe Hall, including the two-acre garden. With the raid unsuccessful and the hunt still on, the constable asked Kevin to come outside to his van for questioning.

'How can I help officer?' Kevin asked as he sat down in the passenger seat in the front of the police van. 'What are you doing?' Kevin choked. An almighty force had struck out pinning Kevin against the seat. The officer's grip was suffocating, leaving Kevin gasping for air. An arm had been placed firmly around his neck by a thickset policeman sitting directly behind him, who had him in a stranglehold. Another officer came around and put handcuffs on Kevin, frogmarched him to the back of the van, pushed him in and slammed the door shut.

'We're going for a ride to London, Mr Wright,' the constable smirked, climbing into the driver's seat. 'We believe you have some of the answers to some of our questions.'

'You don't have to be so rude. I've told you all I know. You're wasting your time and mine.'

'We shall see about that, Mr Wright, we shall see.'

After an intense interrogation that went on into the middle of the night, Kevin was locked in a cell until the morning and then taken to court for more questioning by a High Court judge.

An urgent application had been made by the NHS to make Neon a Ward of the Court, requiring Ben or me to attend hospital with Neon for assessment and planning of treatment. Photos of Neon and myself were released to the press, and the journalists started writing sensationalistic headlines to accompany the mugshot pictures. Briefed by the National Health Service solicitors, the media scooped up that I was an "irresponsible parent" denying my "extremely sick son" *life-saving* treatment. Lawyers for the NHS and Devon County Council had released a statement saying that "the mother was causing significant, potential harm to her child", mysteriously accessing my passport photo amongst other pictures of both myself and Neon.

Generally, court matters involving children are discussed in *closed courts* with no members of the public or media allowed to enter. The judge, "deeply concerned" about Neon's welfare, ruled that reporting restrictions should be relaxed so that Neon could be identified to improve the chances of finding him.

Making the ruling Mrs Justice stated:

> *I have made an order permitting the identification of the child, Neon-Luca Roberts, who is aged seven. It's thought that he is in need of urgent life-saving hospital treatment. He suffers from a brain tumour and has recently had surgery, and the doctors responsible for his treatment believe he urgently needs radiotherapy. The doctors say that, unless treatment is started next week, the prospects of Neon surviving are dramatically reduced. I have asked for the assistance of the public in looking for this very sick little boy.*

With her well-spoken manner, vivacious charm, flaming red hair and sparkling blue eyes, Linda's presence filled the room. In between working full-time at her treatment centre, Linda had been writing up her PhD, which included statistical studies in support of the therapy she invented.

Doctors had told her when he was born that Doran would never be able to walk or talk, but he could do both because she had approached things differently. It was a pleasure talking with Linda. She listened carefully and pulled out a small folder from her desk and spread the contents on the kitchen table.

'I have a few articles that might be helpful to you. This one points out that Nobel prize winner, Dr Otto Warburg, devoted much of his life to what causes cancer. His work confirmed that normal cells need oxygen to survive, whereas cancer cells can live without oxygen. He found that at the root of all cancer are two conditions: acidosis and hypoxia, the lack of oxygen.

'Warburg discovered cancer cells are anaerobic, meaning they do not breathe oxygen and struggle to survive in the presence of high levels of oxygen. Warburg found that cancer patients have too much acidity in their body and their pH is struggling to maintain the normal level of 7.35. Ask Neon's clinicians if this is recognised and if it is not please can they explain why not?

'If it comes to it, worst-case and you are left in a position where you need to reduce the side effects of radiation,' Linda pointed to another paper, 'I think you should contact Dr Clare Vernon, a consultant clinical oncologist at the Hammersmith hospital in London. She was quoted in the *Lancet* as saying "every major cancer treatment centre should have a hyperthermia unit". Even the American Cancer Society describes hyperthermia as a "promising way to improve cancer treatment".

'And then there is President Ronald Reagan who chose intravenous B17 injections and hyperthermia over the conventional treatments. Perhaps the situation is different for children – if so, you need to ask why.'

'I'm familiar with infrared. I presume hyperthermia is a similar concept to the infrared blanket? Of course, I'm familiar with hypothermia, but it's the opposite. Heat as opposed to cold. Kevin has an infrared mini-tent for Bobby. As infrared increases blood flow and immune response, I'm looking into getting one for Neon.'

'We use infrared blankets at the Advance Centre. It is very interesting, Sally. Various studies indicate hyperthermia to work by not only killing cancer cells but also because it can improve the effectiveness of radiotherapy and chemotherapy. Studies advocate using it as part of the protocol,' Linda explained. 'When we are sick our bodies naturally induce a fever to kill pathogens. That is what hyperthermia therapy does in a controlled medical environment, treating a disease such as cancer by the induction of fever with the application of heat. The principle of hyperthermia, like an infrared blanket, is that the cancer cells are more sensitive to and intolerant to the effects of excessive heat than normal cells. Hyperthermia has been reported to reduce blood flow to the tumour, decreases its ability to spread and can stimulate immune response causing no harm to healthy cells.'

Wanting to explore it further I called a clinic here in the UK to ask about hyperthermia treatment, but due to the restrictions in place, they were unable to treat children.

'How can such poisonous unsafe cytotoxic drugs and inhumane toxic treatments be routinely prescribed and proven safe immune-boosting treatments denied?' I asked Linda. 'Why has modern medicine become so unbalanced, only favouring the pharmaceuticals?'

'A healthy child is always questioning, but as time goes by, we seem to learn that we don't get on if we question those in authority over us and we give way to experts because we are not encouraged to cultivate the robust intellectual tools necessary to test their expertise in a debate. It is a universal social problem,' Linda replied. 'As to your question, one could speculate the answer has something to do with money.'

I was sad when Linda had to leave with John late Tuesday evening. We had been at her house for two days. Linda was speaking at a conference in Leeds and said she would be back on Friday. Before she left, she told me about a toyshop with handmade traditional wooden toys in the East Grinstead town centre. I told Neon about it before going to sleep that night. His eyes lit up in anticipation. We planned to go the following day.

CHAPTER TEN

Snatched

It was coming up to 2am when I heard the sound of banging at the front door, directly below where we lay sleeping. I jumped out of bed to look out the window, the net curtain allowing the luminous glow of the well-lit street lamps to flood the room. There was no mistaking who it was. Several police cars were parked in the ditches and filled the end of the country lane. Red and blue lights flashed in the gathering gloom on the cold winter's night. Well and truly trapped, I was up a dead end with nowhere to run and nowhere to hide. I looked down at Neon sleeping so peacefully in the dappled light. My heart was pounding. I was terrified.

'It's the police. Let us in, or we'll break the door down.'

From the way they knocked, I thought they already had. The light in the hallway turned on. Lily was up. The muffled murmurs of the police officers beneath us reverberated around the room. Through the crack in the door, I saw Lily pulling her dressing gown on and walking towards the staircase.

'I'm sorry my gorgeous boy, I'm so sorry,' I whispered, kissing Neon's soft cheek. My whole body was tense in a grip of silent panic with an urge to escape yet paralysed with fear. My heart was racing rapidly and hammering so hard I could hear my heartbeat in my breath, it felt like it was going to explode outside of my chest. A wave of fight or flight adrenaline mixed with absolute terror had overcome me. Apprehensive about our future, I was drowning in utter hopelessness and was afraid what was going to happen next.

Audible voices floated up the stairs and fell on me like a ton of bricks. 'We are looking for Sally and Neon Roberts. We've reason to believe they are here.'

Next came the footsteps, of which there were many. The staircase was overcrowded. It was impossible to see how many officers there were. They were swarming all over the place. The flashlights were blindingly bright. Even my hand could not shield my eyes from the high beam of the imposing law enforcement superior who shone his torch directly in my face.

'Hello, Sally. At last, we've found you.'

The bald-headed commanding officer dominated the doorway. He had bulk on him and being a clear head higher than the average tall person, he had to tilt his head so as not to knock it. He swaggered when he walked and his knees curved outwards almost parallel to his shoulders, making him so bowlegged he made an O-shape bend. The red light on top of his chest pocket camera glowed brightly, indicating he was recording us. Unable to hide his satisfied smirk he updated the police force on his walkie-talkie about his catch of the day.

'Could you please lower your beam?' I asked. 'You are standing right by the light switch.'

Neon had woken from his slumber and sat up rubbing his eyes in disbelief at all the fuss. He was startled to be woken up in the middle of the night and to be surrounded by the police. 'Mummy, I need to go to the toilet.'

I helped Neon put his dressing gown and slippers on and walked with him towards the bathroom.

'I have to come in with you. You cannot go in there alone,' a hefty blonde female officer informed me and stepped into the bathroom with us, shutting the door behind her and watching our every move.

The police were equipped with various weapons from guns to batons. Whatever happened to the friendly looking bobbies? The uniforms were black, not blue – with all their armour they resembled cyborgs from *Robocop*.

'We're taking Neon straight to the hospital,' the broad-shouldered officer announced.

'You are taking him to a hospital?' I gasped. 'It's the middle of the night. Neon should be sleeping. Why do you want to take us to the hospital?'

'You're not in a position to ask questions. Come on, Neon. You are coming with us,' he declared.

'Can you give me a moment, I have to put some things in a bag.'

'Okay, Sally, you can come along... for the time being.'

His words echoed in my ears. What did he mean... *the time being?*

Neon clutched his toy tiger. When I picked him up, he wrapped his arms around my neck. We hugged each other tightly. 'As if you haven't been through enough,' I whispered.

Doran stood outside our room. He looked traumatised and followed us outside. 'Take care, Neon. Take care, Sally.'

'Goodbye, Doran.'

We slid onto the back seat of the police estate car. The dominating officer who led the raid was driving, and his female colleague who we were already familiar with was in the passenger's seat. How had they found us up a little country lane in the middle of nowhere? Somebody had to have informed them, but who?

'How did you find us?' I asked.

'Because we're good.' The officer responded by singing his own song of praise. 'Because we're really good.'

The drive to Sussex hospital took half an hour. The police car pulled up outside the entrance. The receptionist's mouth fell open, unable to hide her surprise at the sight of seeing a child being escorted into the hospital in the middle of the night by the police.

'This young man is sick. He needs to be seen by a doctor,' the officer declared. The receptionist lent back in her chair. Her facial expression resembled a blank piece of paper.

'This is Neon Roberts. We've been told to bring him to this hospital. He's very sick and needs to see a doctor. Someone should have called through and told you we were coming.'

'This is the first I've heard of it, nobody called,' the receptionist replied scrolling down her computer screen, looking more mystified by the second. 'I'm not sure we have a paediatric doctor on duty right now,' she mumbled picking up the phone. 'I'll see if there is someone here who can see him.'

With nowhere to sit, Neon rested in my arms. We were eventually led up a long, windowless corridor by a nurse. The bandy-legged six foot six officer was in front leading his marine mission, then Neon and myself, followed closely behind by his thickset female colleague.

Neon was allocated a bed and sat up, now wide-awake.

The female officer sat on a chair next to the head of Neon's bed. The robotic officer stood towering above us at the end of the bed. I found him more intimidating with every passing moment. His hands were placed firmly on his hips. His hostile eyes never left us. The red light of his camera still shone brightly by his chest pocket continuing to film our every move.

'There is such a thing as personal space,' I said, standing up and whipping the curtain between us. 'I'm afraid you and your camera are going to have to stand back.'

'I'll turn it off. I'm turning it off… It's off now, Sally… I've turned it off.'

I wished I'd done it sooner. The curtain remained closed.

'Would you like to play triangles Neon?' the policewoman asked. Neon nodded. Unlike her colleague, she had a kind demeanour and friendly face. I was touched by her tenderness as I watched them take turns drawing a line. The objective, to make as many triangles as possible by drawing lines from one dot to another.

When the petite Indian doctor eventually arrived, she was clueless about our circumstances. She started from the beginning and asked what Neon's symptoms were leading up to the surgery. The young doctor looked perplexed as she ran her observations, often raising her perfectly arched eyebrows that framed her charcoal-black eyes. She was expecting to find something wrong. She had been told that he was seriously ill, but all the tests she did indicated Neon was in good health. She was impressed he had recovered so well from brain surgery. After an hour of questioning and various routine tests, the doctor looked at me with a bewildered look of despair. 'I cannot find a reason for Neon to be admitted. He appears to be in excellent health. He can go.'

It should have been a happy moment. We should have been allowed to go *home*. Neon needed to be back in bed asleep. Cuddling up next to Neon I wondered what they were going to do with us. Would we have to go straight to London? The officers were talking amongst themselves and radioing their superiors. It was coming up to 5am.

A little while later the female officer approached our bed. 'Sally, I know you're not going to like this, but we have called social services who are on their way to come and collect Neon.'

'Social services? What have you called social services for?'

'I'm sorry, Sally, they're on their way. They'll be here in about half an hour.'

'Will we stay here?' I asked.

'No, they'll be taking Neon.'

'Taking him where?'

'I'm unable to disclose that information to you.'

'Pardon, what do you mean you are unable to *disclose that information*? Neon is my son, and he needs his mother.'

'Sorry, Sally, you'll not be able to go with him.'

'You can't do this. I have to go with him. Where will they be taking him?'

'You're not allowed to go. Don't make this harder than it already is.'

I had heard of children forcibly taken by hospitals enforcing treatment, but never had I imagined something on this scale happening to us. Through my tears, I attempted to reason with her.

'What about other family members? My mum, Neon's grandma, she will come and take care of him, or Neon's father. Please call someone he knows. They will come straight away.'

'It's not up to us. There's nothing we can do. Social services are on their way.'

'To be taken away by strangers in the middle of the night, Neon will not be able to cope.'

'They are on their way,' she repeated.

'Can I please stay with him?' I begged.

'Sorry, Sally, that's not how it works. You'll make this harder for Neon if you fight it.'

Fear surged through me. I ran to the restroom. I could not allow them to take my son, but *they* were coming. Somehow I had to pull myself together and get back to Neon where he lay sound asleep.

Too soon, two plain-looking people who were members of the child services department came through the double doors. The male wore thick-framed glasses and had a grey beard. The woman was about five foot two and had straight dark-brown hair and a curtain fringe that fell around her face. They both looked like they were in their fifties or sixties. The thought of Neon being taken away by these people was making me nauseous, and

I started to hyperventilate. It was difficult to calm down when I was overflowing with anxiety and frantic with worry.

'Neon, you have to wake up.' There was no stopping the policewoman. She was doing her job. Neon started to stir.

The irrational decision of the "powers that be" to take Neon away from me was making me want to yell, punch, kick and scream. Extreme emotion was pouring out of me. The imminent threat of us being separated made me feel beyond hysterical, but I knew I had to hold it together and remain calm for Neon. If he saw me getting wildly angry and upset about letting him go with the strangers, it would scare him more than he already was.

'Could I please see your identification?' I gasped with my heart hammering in my throat.

The iron lady showed me her ID and then her colleague's. I examined it as much as my shaky hands would allow, but I was barely able to focus through the tears.

'Where will you be taking him?'

'We cannot disclose that information to you,' the poker-faced woman replied.

'Please call his father,' I begged the officer once more. 'He's in London. It won't take him long to get here.'

'I've told you, Sally. It's not up to us.'

In desperation, I went over to the nurses' desk. 'They want to take my son away. Please don't let them. Can't we stay here?'

'Sorry, we can't help,' one nurse replied looking around at the other night workers, who all appeared to be busy doing nothing.

'Don't make this harder than it already is,' the female officer said. 'You can walk with us to the carpark and say goodbye.'

Picking up Neon I burrowed into his neck. We held on to each other as we walked down the corridor towards the entrance. A new day was breaking, but the dawn was still dark, and it was bitterly cold.

'Where are we going, Mummy?' Neon asked.

'To be honest, Neon, I'm not sure.'

I could hardly see through my puffy eyes. The whole world had vanished. All that remained were our trembling bodies that were about to be torn apart. Engulfed in terror, I proceeded to scream in silence.

'It's time to say goodbye,' I heard the policeman say.

'I'm so sorry, Neon; these people have to take you for a little while, but you are going to be okay. Everything is going to be okay.'

Neon shook his head and started crying. 'No, Mummy, I don't want to go with them.'

'I know you don't. I know you don't.'

'No, Mummy, no, Mummy.'

The lady officer handed me a tissue. 'Come on, Sally. They have to go.'

We were stuck together like glue.

'No, no. I don't want to go. No, Mummy.'

'I know you don't want to go,' my voice cracked. 'I don't want you to go with them either, but they have decided for now that you have to. I'm so sorry, Neon. We don't have a choice.' I could barely get the words out. I was doing my best to hold it together for Neon's sake. 'You'll be back with me very soon. I love you. We both have to be brave.'

'That's it, Sally. Your time is up. They've got to go,' the officer echoed.

I was holding Neon's beloved toy tiger Tallulah and placed it in his hand, gathering all the strength I could muster. 'Make sure you take care of Tallulah.'

Neon shook his head and sobbed into my shoulder. 'Mummy, am I ever going to see you again?'

My head swam with unforgivable regret while my insatiable heartache devoured every single part of me. 'Of course you are, Neon, I will find you tomorrow. These people have been told they need to take care of you for a few hours. Anything you need, you just have to ask them.'

Neon was still shaking his head. We both found it impossible to let go. The lady officer somehow pried Neon away from me and put him in the car and shut the car door. It was hard to see through my torrential tears. All I could see were Neon's tears streaming down his face and his hands placed on the window. Before I had a chance to reach out, Neon and his captors drove away.

Torn apart, I collapsed onto the curb and watched the car drive out of the car park and up the road into the distance. Gasping for breath, my broken heart was filled with unlit emptiness. Sitting on the side of the dust-ridden road, my face fell into my hands.

The female officer put her hand on my shoulder. Leaning down she handed me another tissue. 'Come on then, Sally. We'll take you back to Forest Row.'

Unable to stand, the officers scooped me up. My limbs were weak and felt like jelly. Every fibre of my being ached for Neon; with him gone from my arms, I was left with a hollow void. I have never felt such pain.

CHAPTER ELEVEN

Cop to Court

It had gone 6am when the police dropped me back at Forest Row. Linda was away with John at her conference, but her daughter Lily was up and let me in. In no state to talk, I excused myself and went upstairs. Collapsing onto the bed, I nestled into where Neon had been sleeping only hours before. Inconsolable, every part of me throbbed with emptiness. The agonising anguish weighed heavily down on every part of me, and the overwhelming grief consumed me entirely. With not even a familiar smell on the pillow, I sunk deep into the depths of despair and wallowed in my wretchedness. Yes, I blamed myself. Not usually one to succumb to self-pity, I fully embraced it.

At 8am I turned my phone on. It had been quite some time since I had contact with the outside world. I was inundated with messages including from my mother and father who were extremely upset.

"Have you lost the plot? Sally, what do you think you're doing?"

If I thought I couldn't feel any worse, I was wrong. It was like salt being rubbed in my open wound. I phoned Ben. Christine tutted, placed the phone down and went to wake him.

'Social services have Neon. Please find him. You have to find him,' I cried.

'Well done, Sally,' Ben retorted. 'What did you expect?'

'You know I don't agree with the treatment, Ben. I was trying to protect him.'

'Well, you haven't done a very good job have you, Sally?'

'If you agree with the NHS and give your consent there is no reason why Neon can't be with you. You need to find where he is. Please call social services and find out where he is and let me know when you find him,' I sobbed.

'What were you thinking?' Ben asked, not waiting for a reply. Instead, he left me with the dial tone.

I called Kevin, who had been back at home one night after being questioned in court.

'Come to Tiverton, Sal. They've got you booked in for court tomorrow morning. You've already missed one court case on Monday. You're going to have to go. You have to prepare for your case tomorrow. It looks like you'll have to represent yourself. I'll help you. Catch a train and get yourself here. Let me know when you're close, and I'll pick you up from the station.'

On the train sitting opposite me, a lady was reading a newspaper. There I was... front-page news. The headlines were scandalous:

"CANCER BOY SNATCHED BY MOTHER WHO WANTS TO STOP HIS LIFE-SAVING TREATMENT."

"BRING OUR SON HOME SO WE CAN SAVE HIM BEGS FATHER."

I sunk back in my chair and stared out of the window hoping not to be recognised. Life had chewed me up and spat me out in the gutter. It was the treatment I feared… labelled "life-saving". It was difficult to swallow.

Arriving at Tiverton station, Kevin was waiting for my arrival in his classic silver Mercedes.

'I'm guessing you already know that you're all over the news,' Kevin declared handing me a newspaper, 'but I don't think you're going to like it.'

My eyes skimmed over the article. Absorbing what had been written my heart sank even further. I was going through the worst time of my life, and now I had reporters scooping up "the story" and writing a "Chinese whispers" fictitious version of events and fabricating the truth.

'It's very deceptive. The dispute is between me and the NHS, but it says here it's between Ben and I. "Ben and Sally are currently at the centre of a court battle over Neon's treatment." Why would they say that? It's not true. It's the NHS who are taking me to court.'

'Ben is just a pawn. Medical kidnapping is very serious, and it makes the NHS look bad. If the general public knew the truth, that the NHS was treating Neon with radiotherapy without parental consent, it would be far harder for them to get away with it. By the media reporting that Ben seeks treatment and the court case is between you and him, it takes the heat off the NHS. The public then thinks it's a dispute between husband and wife and the NHS get what they want. Luckily for them, Ben is an absolute pushover. You'd better watch out… if Ben sees the article, he might start believing it's him taking you to court,' Kevin joked. 'Good cop, bad cop. It might give the poor excuse of a man a sense of purpose.'

'I guess you are right. Imagine if they printed the truth. "Boy with no trace of cancer gets prescribed standard treatment *just in case* there's a phantom cell". A life-threatening treatment called life-saving,' I sighed. 'That should be the headline. "Young boy forced into overprescribed therapies that will cause irreversible damage". With the truth so outrageous, it makes the lie much easier to believe. What would people think if they highlighted the truth? "NHS uses radiotherapy and chemotherapy on already cured boy".'

'Your wishful headline says it all and is much more appropriate, but sadly the newspapers are often full of shit, Sal. It happens all the time. What you need is a good journalist to understand what's going on and be willing to write about the deceitfulness. There are good ones out there, you just have to find them, or if you're lucky maybe they'll find you.'

'It says here I am a "keen believer" in homeopathic medicine. It's the first I have heard of it. I don't know much about homeopathic remedies. I'm certainly no expert. I wish I'd thought to give Neon some arnica after surgery, but I didn't. The caption below my picture reads: "Mother Sally Roberts believes in natural medicine". Where are they getting this information from? Are the media allowed to say what they want to make better stories?'

'Think about it, Sal. It was probably that sister-in-law of yours. She's a bad egg that one. When she came to visit, I knew something was not right about her. Besides, you're going against the system. They're making an example of you. In the media's eyes, you either have to be stupid, crazy, some sort of health freak, or at the very least, irresponsible to go against the health service. They'll have you meditating with crystals, hugging trees and relying on snake oil next.

'And with your ex siding with the NHS, he'll be made out to be the hero. Mark my words. The more they can make you look wishy-washy, the more it makes you look like you are a flaky parent that does not know what you are talking about. If you were a JW, they'd blame your religion.'

My eyes glanced down the page. 'There's a picture of Neon with the caption, "Very sick little boy". But the Sussex hospital released Neon to social welfare because there was "nothing wrong with him". The doctor discharged him saying he was "in excellent health".'

Back at Kevin and Jacquie's house, my parents were in the kitchen sitting at the dining table waiting for me with a handful of gentlemen I did not recognise. They all stood up and greeted me when I walked in. I was used to many people being at Tidcombe Hall – as the online health shop was run from home there was always something going on – but there were even more people than usual. Kevin had failed to mention my mother and father were waiting for me, and the men I soon discovered were members of the Press Association.

'Hello, Sally, it is good to meet you. My name is Paul Bentley. I'm a journalist and have been looking all over the country for you. I've been trying to track you down since we first heard of your story. I've done hundreds of miles trying to find you.'

Paul wore a long, smart, sandy fawn overcoat, probably in his late twenties, his hair was dark and cut very short, and he was well spoken as well as charming, looking every bit the top journalist.

'How did you find me here?' I questioned.

'I went to your old home in North Tawton and got a lead that you may be here. This is the second time I've been here this week.'

'I do apologise, but with such little time to prepare my case, I have court in the morning, I do not have the time to talk to you at the moment. Maybe after the court case.'

'Sal, I know this is probably the last thing you feel like doing right now, but it's your chance to set the record straight,' Kevin said. 'With us all here as your witnesses you can make people aware of the true story rather than what was reported in today's papers.'

I sat down at the decent-sized rustic kitchen table and kept the conversation focused on the issues.

'After surgery to remove the tumour, Neon has remained cancer-free.'

'In Neon's case, radiation is overprescribed and used as an umbrella treatment.'

'Neon is not being treated as an individual.'

'Better treatment options are available, just not in this country.'

'I would like a safe treatment for my son that is not going to cause him suffering and irreparable harm.'

'Radiation should not be used as a cure on an already cured patient.'

'I do not want Neon railroaded into a treatment that is not in his best interests.'

'The proposed treatment is unproven and experimental.'

———

At 8:30pm I called Ben.

'Neon arrived about half an hour ago, all safe and sound. He has been on quite the journey. The Devon County Council authority had made a mistake because of us recently moving,' Ben explained. 'Neon has been in the car all day. They drove him to Devon before realising they were in the wrong place and then had to drive him to London.'

'But that's over four hundred miles,' I gasped. 'Poor Neon.'

'I know, but he is here now. He's shattered but would like to say a quick hello.'

I crumbled when I heard his sweet voice. 'Hello.'

'How are you, Neon?'

'Good.'

'Were the people nice to you?'

'Yes.'

'You must be so tired from all the driving.'

'Yeah,' Neon replied.

'I'm happy you are safely at Grandma and Grumpy's in London. I miss you. I love you. I'm sorry you've had to go through all of this. I'm about to leave to come to London too. I'll see you soon.'

'Will you be coming here, Mummy?'

'Yes, Neon, I'll be seeing you tomorrow.'

'I'm not going to be in court,' Ben mentioned before hanging up. 'I have been told that I must take Neon to the hospital in the morning for an MRI scan so they can continue planning for the radiation treatment.'

———

It was a mad rush to get everything together. I had to drive into Exeter to buy something to wear to court. With everything packed away in boxes, I had been living in tracksuit pants and Ugg boots for the past few weeks. I did not want to be viewed unfavourably by the judge by turning up in loungewear without even a flick of mascara.

'Ready or not we have to leave,' Kevin advised. 'I'm going to bring my computer and printer. Ian will meet us at the hotel in the morning. He has studied law. Between us, we can build your case. Paul Bentley has organised hotel rooms for us both and rather than us catch the train he has offered to drive us there. It's going to be past midnight when we arrive in London.'

CHAPTER TWELVE

Litigant in Person

My wake-up call went off as scheduled at 6am. Feeling tense and desperately apprehensive I pulled the crisp, white sheets over my head, dreading what was unfolding and what the day would bring. Having just opened my eyes, there was a knock at my door.

'Sally, it's Ian. We've ordered breakfast. Please come to our room. It's three doors down, number 614.'

Quickly getting ready I headed to Kevin's room.

'The food looks lovely, but I've lost my appetite.' All I could manage was a few sips of Earl Grey and a bit of a croissant.

'Here's Paul's article, Sal, but I don't think you're going to like it,' Kevin said, placing the daily newspaper in my lap.

"FEARS: SALLY ROBERTS WANTS TO RELY ON ALTERNATIVE THERAPIES."

'What? I never said that. What do they mean alternative therapies? Yesterday's papers said I wanted to rely on natural remedies without talking to me. After speaking to Paul, it has turned into relying on alternative therapies?'

'It's because we told Paul how you'd been using the hyperbaric chamber to help Neon recover from the surgery. It's somebody else's job in the newspaper offices to think up the headlines. Paul has no control over that.'

'Oh.' I sighed, picking the paper back up. 'Look at this one. "I WAS AFRAID THE CANCER TREATMENT WOULD FRY HIS BRAIN – WHY MOTHER FLED HOSPITAL WITH HER GRAVELY ILL SON, SEVEN."

Which is worse, the article before or after they spoke to me? My attempt to set the record straight has backfired. This says I fled from the hospital, but Neon had been dismissed from the hospital for three weeks. The words "gravely ill" portray a sick child but Sussex hospital only yesterday confirmed he is in "excellent health".'

'Let's worry about this later,' Kevin said. 'You cannot expect them to understand your plight overnight. More importantly, we should be concentrating on how you're going to convey to the judge your position to save Neon from harm. You need to make them see that radiation is a grossly overprescribed treatment, especially considering there is no evidence of cancer.

'You have to explain all the contradictions and delays you have experienced with the NHS. That is why you're in this position now. If the NHS had given you what you needed, you could have had your second opinion long ago. The judge needs to know that you are not averse to treatment if it's proven he needs it. However, you are not prepared to let them irradiate his brain and spine when there's no evidence of disease. Anyone with a few brain cells to rub together can see that this would be classified as over-treatment. In fact, it is the most perverse form of child abuse.'

'The study carried out in Germany in 2005 of children diagnosed with medulloblastoma that did not receive radiation after receiving a full resection is strong,' Ian pointed out. 'Even though they were under three, it makes no difference. These children were recorded to have had a ninety-three per cent chance of survival after receiving chemotherapy alone, thirteen per cent higher than the NHS estimate of *the cure* if radiated.'

'That's something else that needs to be raised with the judge. They say the cure is around the corner, which confirms we have not found it yet. They cannot call it a cure because it isn't one. "The war" would have been won. The halfwits are chanting that without treatment the chances of survival will significantly decrease, going as far as to say that without treatment a person would die, but where is the proof? They haven't been able to show you any because there is none,' Kevin remarked.

'Anything you say in court has got to be backed with any evidence,' he continued. 'Any claims you make need hard evidence. The NHS should have to do the same. If they don't show any evidence, it's only hearsay.'

'Having read the Urgent Application filed by the NHS, it strikes me they have not referred to any studies,' I said. Is this typical of doctors? Perhaps they think that because they're doctors nobody will question them and the validity of what they say? I've got published medical, peer-reviewed papers indicating it would be more beneficial to boost Neon's immune system rather than send him to the torture chamber. It will be good to share it with the court.'

I glanced down at my folder. The autumn 1997 edition of the *Leukaemia Research* journal, reporting the views of scientists: "The intensive therapy given to children to ensure their survival (!)... can result in longer-term side effects such as intellectual impairment, heart damage, growth disorders and even second cancers."

Turning the page, I looked at a PubMed abstract. "WBRT (Whole Brain Radiotherapy) may negatively impact some aspects of HRQOL (Health-related Quality of Life)."

'So many people have died at the hands of the standard treatment. It wrecks the immune system. If someone dies from pneumonia (while being treated), they don't go down in the death from cancer statistics. It goes down in the records they died from pneumonia,' Kevin added. 'It is swept under the carpet how many deaths have been caused by the treatment for cancer. Countless victims are put in an early grave, but it's not recorded and does not show in the statistics.'

'The medical terminology leaves a lot to be desired. The correct phrasing for somebody who has beaten their cancer is being in remission. Remaining in remission by cancer survivors after the conventional treatment is called event free survival [EFS], which is the conventional treatment's definition of the sought-after cancer cure: not having any symptoms and remaining in remission for five years. If the patient dies from cancer or treatment any time after five years, they remain in the cured statistics. Cured and dead,' Ian explained.

'Do you think if people were aware of the truth they would allow it to continue?' I asked. 'The treatment increases the overall toxic burden and being carcinogenic, it can cause cancer. How could anyone think irradiating my sweet little boy would be worth the endless amount of suffering he would be subjected to while going through treatment and then to have to deal with the dire after effects?

'We've been led up the garden path so far, do people think it's normal? If you consider it's the only treatment that has been allowed to be used for seventy years, that's some pretty serious brainwashing. With such a poor success rate I cannot let them use Neon as one of their guinea pigs. There are too many risks involved and with all his tests proving that he's in the clear, how can the medics possibly be allowed to proceed?'

'Cancer Research UK is a massive part of the problem. It's in the name, CRUK, they are a bunch of crooks. They spend countless millions on scientists, funded by the drug companies doing the "research", who research varying doses of administering radiation and chemotherapy, telling us it's safe even if it's not, all while not doing any research into holistic, nutritional or naturopathic therapies.

'People don't realise diagnosis is not a magical event in the life of the tumour. There's no evidence to say that starting radiation later than six weeks is associated with reduced survival. You need them to show you the studies. Without the studies, they do not have a leg to stand on,' Kevin insisted. 'He'll not die without radiotherapy. That is an assumption by people who don't get paid if they think otherwise. What you have to do is show the court that he will be better off without it.'

'My folder is bursting with studies,' I nodded. 'Hopefully, the court will take the 2005 study seriously. It does stand out above the rest. "Treatment of early childhood medulloblastoma by postoperative chemotherapy alone." Its conclusions: "Postoperative chemotherapy alone is a promising treatment for medulloblastoma in young children without metastasises".'

———

My limbs felt like lead being taken to court by the NHS. With my head on the chopping block, I did not want to leave the comfort of the hotel lobby. It felt like I was stuck in a real-life horror movie. Reluctantly I headed towards the circular revolving doors and pushed down on the oversized polished brass handle, only to be greeted by the blistering cold air. Pulling my jacket tighter, I hurried towards the waiting cab.

'Don't worry.' Kevin squeezed my arm as we sped off towards our destination. 'You have better evidence than them. Your folder is packed full of reports and information to show how damaging the radiation is. The NHS lack any *real* evidence to prove radiotherapy is at all beneficial. You've got a strong case.'

Pulling up outside the sprawling Royal Courts of Justice, I spotted a large crowd all huddled together like pigeons at the bottom of the elaborate stairway where I needed to go. It turned into a frenzy as journalists, people with cameras, microphones and notebooks stumbled over each other in an attempt to reach their target. Seconds later I was surrounded.

Walking towards the looming double doors positioned under the sheltered arch at the top of the stairway, it was impossible to overlook the beauty of the building. With all its grand Victorian Gothic architecture, soaring arches, spires, stonework and stained-glass windows it resembled a cathedral more than a courthouse. Although admiring one of the most spectacular buildings in Europe couldn't have been further from my mind.

'Over here, Sally.'

'Over here.'

'Sally.'

Like birds hungry for crumbs, the flock dissipated as I moved forward.

Inside the safety of the extravagant Great Hall, everything stood eerily still, a vast contrast to the chaos shut outside. Standing in line for a security check I could not ignore the splendour of the building, which was as much inside as out reminiscent of a historic church. The attention to detail was outstanding, the interior every bit as lavish and magnificent as the exterior. From the vaulted ceiling right down to the gleaming black-and-white chequerboard marble floor, it had a strong Masonic flavour. The architectural scale of the Law Courts was remarkable. Alongside all its features, including windows ornamented with the coat of arms and Gothic corridors with mile-long passages leading off in every direction, it felt very medieval.

CHAPTER THIRTEEN

My Knight in Shining Armour

Arriving outside the designated courtroom, I caught the eye of an impeccably dressed, tall gentleman who was making a beeline towards me through the crowd. I could tell from his appearance that he was not working for the tabloids.

'Hello, Sally, thank you for coming. My name is Robin Tolson. I was here for Monday's hearing, but it was a bit difficult without you.'

Unable to hide my surprise I reciprocated the handshake with a raised eyebrow. It transpired the solicitor in Devon had contacted him on my behalf. Robin had a sharp disposition and silvery hair, which matched his grey designer suit beautifully. He had a well-spoken English accent articulated in such an eloquent manner I warmed to him immediately.

'Most of these people are from the Press Association,' Robin informed me, casting his eyes around the people filling the hall, apparently there to document my fall from grace.

'They are a bit of a nuisance,' Robin commented under his breath.

'How have they got free access inside and why are there so many of them?' I asked.

'The media have been permitted to attend proceedings for quite some time, but you may have noticed there are no cameras. Filming and photography are prohibited within the court vicinity. Since the publicity order obtained by *the Trust*, it has been apparent this hearing would have journalists present in the light of the legitimate public interest in the case. The court will rarely have seen such a moderate stance in a case of this kind by someone in your position. With the press gaining access they will try to talk to you. A story like this is rare, especially given your disappearance. They are most grateful to have been invited by the judge to report on it. Sally, please come to my chambers where I have put together a skeleton argument. We have very little time. We need to make the best of it without being disturbed.'

'How has he managed to put a skeleton argument together without talking to me?' I asked Kevin, following closely behind the Queen's Council.

'We'll listen to what he has to say. He is a QC after all. You never know, maybe he'll be your knight in shining armour.'

Sitting down at the sizeable conference table in Robin's tranquil chambers, it was a stark contrast to the media madness we had left on the street below. We were offered tea, coffee, juice and bite-sized cucumber sandwiches as Kevin and I concentrated on filling in the gaps while Robin eagerly took notes.

'I object to my cancer-free son being ruled to have cancer-causing carcinogenic treatment such as radiation. I do not want him to be part of a trial treatment that will cause him needless suffering and seriously harm him for the rest of his life.'

'I thought he had a brain tumour and was very sick?' Robin questioned.

'The tabloids have left out important facts the hospital solicitors have not told them; the tumour has been removed, and he has made a good recovery from surgery. The numerous investigations concluded there is *no evidence of disease* and he is tumour-free.'

'Oh really? Then why are they using radiotherapy?' Robin looked puzzled.

'That is exactly my question,' I replied. 'It is what they are trained in and what is prescribed, it's protocol.'

'How can they render obsolete the costly radiological and chemotherapeutic treatments in which so much money, training and equipment is invested?' Kevin voiced. 'Furthermore, there are well-documented risks of radiation such as intellectual impairment, further cancers and death. Sally has a folder full of evidence to show the judge. There is a long list of less harmful ways to beat cancer, let alone for a boy who has already been given the all-clear. Curing an already cured boy, you do the maths. Good for Neon or their statistics? This is the study which the NHS base the whole entire treatment protocol on, post-surgery for a medulloblastoma.' Kevin handed the report to Robin.

Early reports (from as far back as 1942) recognised that survival for more than a few months without radiotherapy was very rare. 17 patients who did not have radiotherapy in one series survived for:

<1 month	*12 cases*
1–2 months	*2*
2–3	*1*
3–4	*1*
4–5	*1*

Because of these very early studies, radiation therapy became an important part of therapy.

Robin looked stunned, staring at the simple document Kevin had handed him. 'Are there any other studies?' he asked.

'No,' I replied. 'The NHS has not shown me any evidence to prove radiotherapy is necessary. The lead consultant told me that there was *"very little information, if any, about children who had not been subjected to the conventional treatment – because the standard treatment has been to give radiotherapy, chemotherapy or both for over fifty years"*.'

'This highlights how out-of-date the treatment protocol is. Even in this study provided by the NHS, the six children who had received radiotherapy did not survive longer than two years,' Kevin explained. 'As for the children who didn't receive it, with his operation six weeks ago, Neon has already outlived seventy-two per cent of them.'

'How can they prescribe such damaging treatment saying it's the only option with the only evidence that it works a simplistic study which involves seventeen children from the 1940s?' I stated. 'The NHS is coming up to seventy years old. Radiation came in as a treatment for cancer when the NHS was formed because of medical research in X-ray treatment largely sidelined during the Nazi regime and World War Two. Radiation and chemotherapy is not the only way to treat cancer. It is the NHS's answer to cancer.'

Robin nodded while looking through the paperwork I had presented him with.

The 1940s study provided to me by the NHS read as follows:

The post second world war paper states on page 375 of the paper by Bodian and Lason, they describe a group of 36 patients with medulloblastoma. Four had survived at the time of the paper, but none had reached more than one year from diagnosis. There were 6 others who had received radiotherapy, and these children survived for up to 2 years. There were 17 who received no radiotherapy, shown in the table, who survived for 1 month (12 children), 1-2 months (2 children), 2-3 months (1), 3-4 months (1) and 4-5 months (1).

'When it comes to radiotherapy it's like we are stuck in the Dark Ages, this antiquated study proves it. The consultant told me there is a possibility of a rogue cancer cell but there are other ways the NHS oncologists are not trained in that could kill a stray cancer cell should there be one. How can we be sure radiotherapy is the only option when no other treatment has been allowed in over half a century?' I exclaimed.

'What's more,' Kevin continued, 'having set eyes on the NBT NR Urgent Application document filed by the NHS, we are struck by there being no reference to any studies. Is this because they are doctors, they think they are above studies and don't need to show them?'

Although Robin's chambers were close by to the main entrance of the High Court on the Strand, our coming and going was being watched and scrutinised by millions, courtesy of the ever-growing presence of the media mob. Notebooks-at-hand reporters were everywhere. It had become a permanent distraction.

'Sally, what do you want to do about all this press? Would you like to talk to them or would you like me to do it?'

Robin was a complete professional, so relaxed and charming. I was grateful for the suggestion and had thought I was better off with a QC than without one. I agreed for Robin to represent me and to speak on my behalf.

'Don't worry, Sally,' Robin reassured me, 'don't worry.'

With the usher giving a five-minute warning I headed over to some familiar faces. Fiorella, Tony and Lucy were all together with Kevin at the top of the grand spiral staircase.

'There are so many journalists here,' Kevin declared. 'I think it's the best thing you could have done running off like that. Cases like this involving a minor rarely get any attention. Most parents go along with whatever their doctor tells them. On the rare occasion parents go against the advice of their medics it all happens in closed courts, where the press is not allowed. The judge's order to track you down through the media has given them the green light and is why they're all over this case and lapping it up.

'Good on you, Sal. Good on you for asking the questions. You're raising awareness. There is not enough being done for children in this country who have or have had cancer. Your case is all about parental rights and making informed decisions about what's best for your child. The majority are oblivious to the government's trickery used to ensnare parents, who proudly ensure their children have a birth certificate. What is happening to you puts a spotlight on how this document relinquishes parental rightful ownership of their children. How can we protect our children from medical abuse when we are unaware of the levels of deception? The National Health Service's rights should not be allowed to trample all over yours and supersede your parental rights. But they can, and they do, and most people haven't got a clue. All parents need to be made aware that this could happen to them too. People need to know what's going on.'

I nodded in agreement. I appreciated what Kevin was saying, but it didn't help me feel any better. I knew what I was up against, and I knew I was in way over my head.

Entering the courtroom, I was struck by its sheer magnificence. It was a dark and dismal day, but daylight still streamed through the cathedral-type windows set high above us. The dramatic high wooden ceiling set off the ornate oak walls, executed with the finest materials and skilled craftsmanship. The whole courthouse was littered with striking fittings and finishings, displaying the coat of arms almost everywhere I looked. Rich in detail this room was no different, planned with precision and intricate designs.

I was beckoned by the usher to sit in the front row, with permission granted to be accompanied by my brother. My barrister sat directly in the row behind me. The NHS QC sat alongside my QC, amidst all the reporters filling up the remaining benches.

Directly above me was "My Lord", who dominated the raised platform at the head of the courtroom. From the moment the judge entered I sat captivated by the theatrical display and legalese dialogue in which the barristers and judge spoke to one another. I listened intently, firmly fixed on every word that was being spoken but even though they spoke English, it was not spoken in a natural way and without me being familiar with law-speak it often was as good as a foreign language. With everything described in a long-winded fashion, it was easy to lose track of what was being said.

Legalese was for people trained in law. They were the most erudite people speaking the most complex pompous English I had ever heard. Points of significance were lost within the terms of art language of the law, which was more often than not unintelligible to a layperson such as myself.

That said, the court order was made clear: 'The Trust claims this child requires urgent assessment and planning for ongoing treatment for a brain tumour which was surgically removed on 25 October 2012 with parental consent. The optimal window to begin further treatment, which includes a six-week daily dose of radiotherapy followed by twelve months of chemotherapy, is for radiotherapy to start within forty-two days of surgery. We no longer have the luxury of time considering this time is almost up, and a decision must be made quickly to ensure the boy has the best chance of survival. Mother has since failed to present her son to the London hospital, requesting the London team refer her son back to the Bristol services. She was strongly advised to remain in the London team's care to ensure the radiotherapy treatment could start within the required timeframe but failed to take her son for an MRI scan. It is the view of the lead consultant in London that NR would need to be living in central London to catch up with lost appointments as agreed by the father.

'It is the view of the clinicians at Bristol and London that M is refusing consent to assessment and planning of treatment as a necessary step in providing urgent medical treatment. The Trust believes that her refusal to co-operate with assessment is causing potential significant harm to her son.

'The court is requested to consider an interim order in the following terms: That Neon-Luca Roberts is made a Ward of Court. That Mr Ben Roberts has day-to-day care of NR, including residence. That Mrs Roberts is ordered to give day-to-day care of NR to her husband, Ben Roberts, for the purpose of necessary assessment, planning and care of treatment. That there is liberty to apply.

'The Trust's duty is first to ensure that NR is offered a chance of survival with treatment and its effects now, rather than leaving him at risk of unnecessary recurrence, with the very much lower chance of subsequent cure and the certain need for more intensive and brain-damaging effect of recurrence and its treatment.'

Law-speak weaved throughout plain language. Without legal training, I persevered but struggled. They occasionally mentioned me, referring to me as "the Mother". Neon, they called "N". The NHS, who were referred to as "the Trust", had submitted an analysis in table form several days ago when they attended court at the beginning of the week. Robin covered this not long after his opening statement in putting forward *my* argument.

'It seems the core balance is a reduction in survival rate from eighty per cent to sixty-seven per cent against a gain of around sixteen IQ points in intellectual functioning by the avoidance of radiotherapy. We appreciate this is an approximation and does not include all the factors in play. It ignores, on the one hand, the trauma of a relapse, but also, on the other hand, the additional damage caused by radiotherapy. Such a significant loss of intellectual functioning is a real impairment to quality of life particularly in the world N is likely to inhabit as an adult. There is no evidence, but even if he were of average intelligence, which is ninety to a hundred and nine, it would reduce his functioning to low average or borderline on the Wechsler scale. Thus, our submissions, even on the Trust's evidence is that the mother's position is reasonable.'

Robin briefly revealed the report we had shown him.

'We respectfully attack the Trust's reasoning at several points. Our first point concerns the figure of thirty-five per cent event free survival [EFS] with chemotherapy alone. It may be too low. Our reasoning is as follows. First, there is no data applicable to children of N's age that postdates the 1940s or 1950s. Secondly, even amongst infants – which is the only data available – chemotherapy only treatments result in an EFS after eight years of thirty-four per cent. Infants generally are, it seems to be acknowledged, at significantly greater risk of relapse and death from medulloblastoma than are seven-year-olds.

'Our next point concerns the survival rate amongst those in the position of N who Dr H estimates will relapse following chemotherapy alone. In the table shown this is given as fifty per cent of sixty-five per cent of patients. We believe this figure is again derived from studies of infants. Dr L, in his statement, refers to the German SKK study. It gave a survival rate amongst infants in the group we are considering as eight of fifteen. Thus we respectfully suggest that Dr H's figure for overall survival following chemotherapy alone may be conservative, and too low. In parenthesis, we acknowledge that patients relapsing after chemotherapy alone will then have radiotherapy – but they will then be older and therefore less at risk of serious intellectual impairment.

'Our third point of attack is that the thrust of medical investigation in the over three-years-old in recent years has been to reduce the dose of radiation within a clinical trial and then to compare event free survival levels. A reduction in radiation from 36Gy to 23.4Gy in the trial relied upon by Dr H did not affect EFS levels. It seems, therefore, highly unlikely that 23.4Gy is, in fact, the safe minimum. A further US clinical trial is currently using a lower level of 18Gy.

'We submit the following remain open questions even on the evidence presently supplied by the Trust, this is written before a further statement from Dr H on the range of medical opinions across the medically advanced world.

'What is the lowest level of radiation that does not compromise survival chances? Might it be zero? In any event, is radiotherapy, when coupled with modern alternatives in particular modern chemotherapy, in the best interests of a patient such as N when set against the known, severe, side effects?'

Robin focused with insatiable intent on the content of the skeleton he had prepared, every word (seemingly) being documented by the ravenous flock.

'At present, one parent seeks treatment and is able to give consent. We respectfully suggest, however, that the only question is what treatment is, in fact, in N's best interests? We understand that the Trust acknowledges this to be the case and will not rely on the father's consent to treatment without the court having first ruled on this point. Moreover, in reality, the mother has had no time here to fully prepare her case whether she has been in hiding or not. In those circumstances, it is respectfully submitted this may be one of those rare occasions in which the court may have to make a decision on treatment but yet not finally resolve the question before it in principle.

'In short, it is submitted that, even if the court were to give the go-ahead for treatment, it should continue to seek independent expert evidence on the point to be considered at a further hearing. Further submissions on this are reserved.'

Dr Harper was wearing his distinguishable dated brown tweed suit and took centre stage. He was a powerhouse at presenting the Trust's trusted protocol. As the clinical professor of paediatric neuro-oncology, he was trained in medical procedures and drug developments. I recognised him from the trip to London. He was the insanely enthusiastic professor with equally memorable attire that matched his personality perfectly. He proceeded to present the pharmaceutically funded data and persuade the courtroom that radiation and chemotherapy were the only acceptable ways to overcome cancer, habitually pushing his glasses up off his nose as he lent over "the bundle".

Having been told this was not Professor Harper's first court case representing the NHS, I could see why… he knew his stuff. He spoke with purpose regurgitating what he had learnt from his years studying at medical school treating symptoms with developmental drugs and working as an oncologist.

The submissions made on behalf of the Trust included the 1940s study, with the professor briefly referring to it; after all, it was the only "real" evidence the NHS had to prove radiotherapy was necessary.

'Because of the early studies from the 1940s, radiation became an important part of therapy. It was recognised that radiation has bad effects on people, but the consequences of not using this treatment were that every patient died of the disease. No doctor would advocate a "wait and see" approach to managing a medulloblastoma.'

After swearing my oath, it was my turn to speak. I had thought being cross-examined would be an opportunity for my voice to be heard, but put in such a defensive position and tactfully led away from anything of real significance it was hard to express my concerns. The questions asked by the Trust didn't make it easy to explain my cause or why I objected to the National Health Service's proposed plan.

'Mrs Roberts, are you completely against modern medicine?'
'No, I am not.'

I have always expressed my gratitude for the surgeons and the caring doctors and nurses. I am grateful for the many advances in modern medicine. My grievances were not with the staff or medicine in general. The problem I faced stemmed from the outdated "one size fits all" cancer treatment. My heart was pounding hard in my chest. I knew I had to get my message across and make the judge understand why I thought radiation was wrong for Neon. Putting my fears aside, I looked directly into the judge's eyes.

'I would not be here if it were not for modern medicine, and my children too,' I said, referring to my pre-eclampsia birth complications resulting in an emergency caesarean. 'My family is registered with the local GP, and if I'm worried about my or my children's health, I would call the doctor. I alerted our GP and insisted something was wrong with Neon's neck, even when the GP told me physiotherapy was all he needed. I pushed for the MRI screening because I wanted him to be seen by medical professionals, which led to him being diagnosed. I am not somebody who is against modern medicine. At times in my life, I have depended on it.'

I spoke slowly, choosing my words carefully while voicing my concerns.

'I fear modern medicine concerning cancer treatments has become unbalanced. There are other therapies available but these are ruled out by the NHS due to lack of funding or because they are not available or allowed in this country. It concerns me parents are denied the right to make informed decisions on what they know to be best for their children. Medics in the Western world are overprescribing drugs and treatment, which is what I am most worried about for my son; being overprescribed radiation as a precautionary measure to treating a tumour that has already been removed. All tests indicate Neon is in the clear and remains cancer free.

'Is modern medicine really that modern when cancer specialists are using a small, outdated study from the 1940s to base the radiation and chemotherapy treatment on? This study appears to have no real significance, and there are no studies to compare with to illustrate that radiation is beneficial. Moreover, Neon has outlived the majority of children from the study that the proposed protocol is based on.

'Modern medicine has advanced in many areas, but cancer is not one of them. The dogmatic umbrella approach is not acceptable. I cannot accept radiation as a cure because it isn't one. The tumour has been removed. My son is more cured now than he will ever be after radiation. There are techniques and therapies that will do a better job than radiation, which would not cause a multitude of health-related problems.

'DNA aberration testing is only just being recognised in the UK of which there are four subgroups. I am told Neon is in group four, which contradicts the other reports I have recently been shown which tell me the tumour was not Myc or MycN amplified. Myc or MycN amplification is a feature of group four. This shows Neon's subgroup cannot be group four like I am told.

'A couple of controlled studies would be sufficient from published medical journals to show me that radiotherapy is a proven success in comparison to any other therapy, but it seems because of the paradox, where doctors' hands are tied, and no other treatments are allowed to be used, no comparable studies exist. There is no proof to show radiation is doing any good. It is all an assumption and not at all scientific.'

It was the NHS next, and the mantra had been set and swamped my argument. They claimed, "without life-saving treatment, N would die". These words rang around my head; the hospital, the court and the press used them again and again, at every opportunity, it seemed.

Mr Justice Bodey adjourned at 6pm and surprised everyone by announcing the court would sit the next day, a Saturday. This was unprecedented and another ordeal. I was exhausted and emotionally drained from the day, and it was not over.

After freshening up at my hotel, I went over to see Neon and Elektra at Ben's parents' flat. Dr Harper said he would call with the results from the scan: the MRI scan showed up what the MDT had initially suggested all those weeks ago, there was "possibly" a one-centimetre remnant in the original tumour cavity. The MDT has been unsure before. Were they certain what they were seeing on the screen was tumour remnant? Or, could it be what they had previously suggested: scar tissue?

Dr Harper told us they would want to operate immediately, but one centimetre was smaller than what they usually considered necessary to operate. Why change the rules for Neon?

CHAPTER FOURTEEN

Medical Landscape

I was awake when my alarm call went off. My body felt heavy with dread, and I wanted to stay curled up in a ball. Somehow, I coaxed myself out of bed to turn the kettle on and opened the curtains. It was quite the view up on the sixth floor overlooking High Street Kensington, next to Hyde Park. The traffic outside was already constant, the noise blocked out by the triple-glazed windows. Watching the ant-like people hurry to their destinations I ached for normality. It was another grey morning, the weather reflecting my frame of mind. The tight knots in my stomach were making me nauseous. At first, I resisted the temptation to look at today's papers that lay outside my hotel door but eventually caved in. I choked on my Earl Grey tea when I read the headline.

"I'M NOT A BONKERS MOTHER".

As I skimmed through what had been written, any faith I had in the reporters ceased to exist. There was no analytical reporting and no quotes of any worth. To say I felt humiliated is an understatement. The editorial bias had generated a manipulation of the truth. Having words put in my mouth and being criticised from false accusations was a lot to contend with.

Rise above it, I told myself many times in the coming weeks.

'Anyone using their common sense can see you are playing the perfect scapegoat,' Linda reminded me. 'The press will enjoy unleashing an unrestrained attack on your character which will sell news more profitably than reporting anything of any importance on cancer therapies. Moreover, Sally, it's a smokescreen. It distracts from the message you are conveying and draws public interest away from the concerns you have about radiotherapy.'

It was an unstoppable merry-go-round, and there was no getting off. A theatrical play I had not signed up for, yet here I was playing a lead role. My chaperone Paul, the wolf in sheep's clothing, had made all the arrangements for getting me to court. Ironically, Paul safeguarded me from all the other pushy press. Ever after the desired "exclusives", Paul made it his duty to *look after* me and fend off the competition. I questioned Paul about the article he had co-written for today's paper, alleging that I had used the phrase "I'm not bonkers".

'Why would you quote me saying something that I did not say? Is that allowed?'

'Your QC, Robin Tolson, issued a statement on your behalf after court yesterday,' Paul replied. 'Perhaps he is the one you need to talk to.'

———

Arriving outside the entrance of the picturesque Royal Courts of Justice on Saturday morning, I wondered if all these people were press. There were so many. Any thoughts were muffled out by questions being fired at me in every direction. I made my way through the hungry pack, dodging past the cameras and microphones feeling much like a wounded gazelle. My self-proclaimed PA Paul was navigating, leading me to where I needed to be. There was no airport-like security check. There were no other courtrooms open. We entered a side wing to the left of the main building. Everything was empty. It was like a ghost town. It was a completely different atmosphere from yesterday's crowded halls.

'How often does the High Court open on a Saturday?' I asked.

'It doesn't,' Paul responded.

Arriving outside the designated courtroom, I was signalled by Robin and led into a small, grey room with no natural light. It closely resembled what I imagined to be a prison cell. The windowless concrete room felt like a refrigerator and was completely bare, except for a wooden table that was pushed against the wall in the middle of the room, where I sat down opposite Robin on one of the four aluminium-framed chairs.

'We don't have long. What do you want to do?' Robin queried.

'I'm upset,' I declared. 'On top of it all, I have now got the media quoting preposterous comments, things that I have not said.'

'Oh, and what comments might they be? Robin looked bemused.

'I don't know if you've read the papers, but I have been quoted saying "I'm not bonkers". I would never say something as ridiculous as that. Why would you say that? On my behalf?'

'It works in your favour,' Robin retorted.

My mouth fell open. 'Works in my favour?'

'You have to trust me on this, Sally.'

'Trust you?' I frowned. 'There is no way a comment like that could do me any favours. All it does is plant in the public's mind that perhaps I am bonkers. It does me no favours at all and makes me look/feel worse than I already did. It does the

NHS a favour, not me. You also did the press a favour; you gave them a fantastic headline, making me look like a prize idiot. Please refrain from making any further comments on my behalf.'

On top of being weighed down with worries and drenched in torment, the media were proving to be an absolute nuisance by creating further obstacles, diverting our attention and interrupting our concentration. In spite of that, Robin changed the direction of our conversation. Fully aware we needed to focus on more important matters, for now, I had to let it go.

'What is your view on yesterday's MRI results, Sally? We are going to be asked to go in soon. I need to know what you want to do?'

'My view is that they are determined to get him back in the system and on the starting block, regardless. Ideally, I need a little time to get a much-needed second opinion, and not from within the UK. All doctors in the UK are singing from the same song sheet.

'The NHS' protocol states they do not operate on growths less than one-and-a-half centimetres. What I need to know is why they are changing their own rules for Neon to undergo more surgery. They say they have located *a possible* one-centimetre nodule in the original cavity that was previously said to be scar tissue. If they decide on more surgery can they not wait until after Christmas? Especially considering it is smaller than what they usually deem necessary to operate on. Christmas is the most exciting time of year for a child. With everything he has been through, Neon deserves to be with his family for Christmas.'

'I see.' Robin nodded.

'Also, Robin, most importantly, I need to make it clear, if surgery is to go ahead, please no biopsy.'

'Oh, and why is that?' he asked.

'Biopsies spread cancer cells. I requested no biopsy the first surgery and will continue to do so. If there is something there, let them poke it and analyse it after the lump or bump is out of his body, not while it is inside.'

The usher made himself known outside our room and Robin excused himself to go and talk to him. Robin had left the door slightly open. My brother Tony and Ben's sister Lucy peered in.

'Hi, Sal,' Lucy said as she walked into the room and sat down where Robin had been sitting.

'Sally, I am so sorry, but I have to ask… Kevin said yesterday that you did all of this for media attention?'

'Oh for fuck's sake, you're kidding me?'

I was astounded by such juvenility and that my day was getting worse. It was difficult to comprehend, how could anyone come up with something so absurd? Then I remembered how the system keeps us confused. If you are so inclined to investigate "cancer research", you need to make sense of the technical and tangled sentences filled with arcane language. Even for those of us who persevere, it can be easy to lose track when research methods are written in exhaustive detail, which often results in inconclusive findings (depending on who funds the research, of course).

At any other time I would have laughed Lucy off, but my situation was anything but funny, and I had lost my sense of humour. Ignorance is a lack of information and Lucy typified that. If you are relying entirely on mainstream medics for your knowledge and advice, your outlook is going to be based on fear and extremely one-sided, leading to an unbalanced perspective favouring the pharmaceutic profession.

Meanwhile, key elements were ignored while "justice" was sensationalised. The media were playing a fundamental role in shaping the perceptions of the public. The benefits of radiotherapy were exaggerated while the dangerous consequences were either overlooked or obscured.

Without Lucy diving deep into the world of cancer care, how could I expect her to understand the multifaceted complexity of what I was facing? After all, her blind faith in radiotherapy was not uncommon; a result of a cover-up of radiation's drawbacks and downplaying the hazards. All while promoting it as part of the package to beating cancer while ruling out safer options.

It was far easier to scrutinise my personal predicament and lay judgement upon that rather than analyse an out-of-control medical system backed by an unjust judicial system. Lucy did not question the radiation therapy's effectiveness or its safety. Without her doing some proper research, it would be difficult for her to understand my viewpoint that using powerful beams of radiation in the name of medicine was an almost century-long mad science experiment that had ultimately proven to fail. Exposure to radiation and poisoning your way back to health with hazardous toxins did not make logical sense.

Moreover, what did she mean by "doing all this"? By running for the hills and hiding and trying to protect my son from harm? By being robbed of my parental rights and dragged to the High Court by the NHS leading to a publicity order so I could be vilified? My life in tatters and under media scrutiny, taunted for seeking out safer solutions? It was getting more surrealistic by the second.

Having attracted so much attention was not my choice and far from what I desired. The intense media glare polarised opinions and made an acutely distressing situation further intensified. Not only was I not getting the space that I needed, but also my main concern was overlooked: radiotherapy would compromise my son's quality of life.

Nevertheless, I felt compelled to satisfy Lucy's irrationality. Picking up my phone I turned it off airplane mode and called Kevin, who had returned to Tiverton to be with his family. Kevin picked up straight away. I had him on speakerphone.

'Hi, Kevin, sorry to bother you, I'm about to go into court and instead of focusing on the ruling I have Lucy sitting in front of me, she said that you said *I did all of this* for media attention?'

'Has she been smoking crack? That girl is either really thick or shit stirring,' Kevin laughed. 'You were there when I said it outside the courtroom, remember? Your brother was there too. Lucy is taking what I said out of context. What I meant by it was what I said; by you running off, it was the best thing you could have done to get all this media attention. It's shedding light on a dark subject. Most people have no idea about childhood cancer until it happens to their child and then you're in so deep, panicking and can't see the wood from the trees. Most people accept whatever their doctors say as gospel.

'Brain tumours receive so little funding. All the money for research goes into drugs, drugs that have proven to fail us. All while the profiteers keep profiting. The media attention is a good thing because of the necessary public awareness about childhood cancer. Times have got to change, and that won't happen without public awareness. That the media is more focused on you and maligning your character is no surprise. Targeting you, ripping you to shreds and undermining you distracts from what you are saying. It's the oldest trick in the book. As for Lucy, how's she ever going to understand the bigger picture, she fried her brain on drugs long ago. Sal, ignore her.'

'It appears you've taken what Kevin said in the wrong context,' I said to Lucy who had heard every word and was looking rather sheepish. 'The judge revealed our identities which resulted in this media showdown unravelling itself. How could I have ever foreseen this? It is a consequence of the NHS taking me to court and the judge inviting news reporters to sit in. It is a *public interest* story at my expense. Right now I should be focusing on more important matters concerning my son's future. I'm in this frightful position because I need to save Neon from harm and have so many eyes focused on me. It is unwanted scrutiny. I get what Kevin says about raising awareness, and yes, I agree that is a good thing, but where is the positive in the media's outlandish courtship for me? They are persecuting me and making me look like a fool. Not only is it an awkward and uncomfortable position, but it's also a distraction. A distraction that I would be better off without. Worldwide, courtesy of the news, people, strangers, are all watching me struggle through the unimaginable and to top it off, just before I go back into court, you've pulled something from thin air suggesting I'm fighting for my son's future so they can write about it and talk about it? Do you realise how shallow and ridiculous that sounds? Think about it if you were in my situation. Would you want people reporting on it, judging you from distorted soundbites and talking about it over coffee?'

'No, I wouldn't,' Lucy replied. 'I'm sorry, Sally.'

'That's okay, Lucy.'

All that aside, it was time to enter the courtroom. Sunshine was pouring through the windows overhead. As I looked around the full room, I caught the eyes of a few familiar faces and gestured a hello to the nods. Soon, Justice Bodey entered.

'It has been my intention today to give my judgement as part of NR's treatment for brain cancer on whether he should receive chemotherapy only or radiotherapy as well. Medical developments have now occurred regarding the possibility to receive said treatment for such therapies at the present time. I am told that the scan yesterday has shown a one-centimetre mass in the area, where the previous brain tumour was removed. This has changed the medical landscape. Nature is no respecter of the courts. This case is adjourned until December 18 to allow for medical records to be updated.'

Robin was invited to speak. However, I had little input, and he did not reflect my position accurately.

'Since yesterday's hearing, Sally Roberts has been told that Neon's cancer has returned. This is obviously very upsetting for her, Neon's father Ben and the whole family. Neon himself of course, who continues to seem completely healthy, does not fully understand what is happening. Mrs Roberts and Neon are receiving a lot of support from their family and friends. Sally is very grateful for this.

'She is also grateful for the efforts of all the doctors and staff at the hospital where Neon is being treated. She understands, first, that there is no evidence that any delay in Neon receiving treatment has caused this cancer to return: this is just very bad luck. She also understands that as the cancer has only been found at the original site, further surgery is possible and that, if it is successful, Neon's prognosis will return to being that of a standard-risk patient, as it was yesterday.

'Sally has never been against surgery for Neon. She agreed to this in October, and she agrees now. She has only been against radiotherapy with all its side effects and the long-term damage it causes. She is still profoundly against that. With *the return of cancer*, Sally has been told that surgery becomes the first treatment and that the hospital will postpone radiotherapy in any event, whatever the court's decision might be.

'So, in these new circumstances, Sally thanks the court for agreeing not to give its ruling today. However, as she is determined that Neon should be cured and lead a full and happy life afterwards, and as Sally believes he will again be a standard-risk patient, she does ask that *the court give its ruling as soon as is convenient* in the course of the next few weeks. This is so that she and Ben can know what will happen to Neon and *so that other parents in their position can know what the law has to say*. In the meantime, as any parent would want in the circumstances, Sally will continue to seek a second opinion both on Neon's present position and in the question of radiotherapy. I ask the judge for sympathy, the mother's position is principled, reasonable and in the best interests of Neon.'

"*The return of cancer?*" It was described to me, by Dr H, as being a *possible* remnant of the original tumour previously confirmed as scar tissue. The possibility of a remaining nodule is *not* a recurrence.

"*The court give its ruling as soon as is convenient?*" I needed more time Robin… not less. Give me the proverbial shovel, and I will dig deeper.

That Robin Tolson also stated "*so that other parents in their position can know what the law has to say*" set alarm bells in motion: all in all, they had me playing the role of a perfect scapegoat, and it seemed Robin Tolson, *my* QC, had other motives. He was helping me lose the case, not win it.

Outside the courtroom, Lucy approached me. 'Sally, you are trying to do too much on your own.'

I looked at Lucy who had changed her tune since the last time we spoke. 'What do you mean?' I asked.

'I have a friend who can help you. Her mother has cancer, and she has done a documentary about cancer and is interested in Neon's story and would like to meet you. Ben has met her recently. He did a job networking her computers. Her name is Sarah, and she has a production company called Smoking Pony. Sarah has access to a team of researchers who can help you. Can I give you her number or is it okay if I give her yours? I think you should at least talk. We call her Burkers. She's really nice. You will like her.'

'A team of researchers?' I echoed.

'Yes, Sally, that is what you need isn't it?' Lucy smiled sweetly, exuding warmth and kindness.

———

Exiting the courthouse was surreal. Flashlights were going off, reporters were scrambling everywhere, cameras were pointed at me, and microphones held out. Robin advised me to thank the media for their interest, and so, with my heart pounding, I stepped in front of the world's press.

'Thank you for all your interest in the case... and all the support. I have nothing to add to the judge's statement.'

How I managed to say anything was beyond me, my heart felt like it was going to burst out of my chest. I felt like a lamb to the slaughter. That one sentence felt like an eternity. I immediately regretted not saying "no comment".

Clicks and flashes were going off in every direction.

'How's Neon getting on?' one journalist asked.

It was a fair and simple question, but I stumbled on it. 'No more comment thank you,' I answered. It was an automatic response, but even as the words were leaving my mouth, I realised I wanted to be more positive. 'He's good. He is very good in himself, and yes, we will speak early next week.'

The clicking camera shutter sound rang in my ears. Breaking through the wall of light, I swam through the swarm who were clambering all over each other determined to get one more shot. I stepped into the safety of the waiting taxi with cameras pressed against the window. It was mayhem. There was one young lady who was not taking no for an answer. She climbed into the black cab with us, pulled the extra seat down, sat down and shut the door.

'Sorry about this, Sally, but I have to talk to you. I don't know if you remember me? My name is Georgie.'

'Excuse me could you please get out?' Tony objected but the door was shut, and with the hungry horde pressed against the taxi, the driver had started to pull out onto the Strand, leaving the impressive Courts of Justice and animated frenzy behind us.

CHAPTER FIFTEEN

Dodge the Bullets

Georgie looked like she was in her early twenties, her blonde bob-length hair was tied back in a high ponytail accentuating her pretty face. Georgie spoke with such overwhelming enthusiasm and, although verging on brash, her upbeat manner lightened the atmosphere. There was no space for silence with her charismatic chatter filling the cab as we sped through the City of London towards Kensington. If the media were a pack of wolves, Georgie was the cute pup of the pack.

'Thanks so much, Sally. I really appreciate you giving me a moment,' Georgie gushed. 'I think what you are doing is incredibly brave. So many mums understand what you're going through. I want to offer you an opportunity for your voice to be heard and to share with our viewers what's been going on behind the scenes.'

My big brother jumped to the rescue. Tony saw it his duty to protect me. 'We appreciate your efforts... Georgie, was it? Sally has got enough on her plate right now. I'm afraid you are going to have to get out of the cab.'

'Sally, so many people are supporting you. Do you know who Lorraine is?' Georgie persisted ignoring Tony's requests. 'Lorraine is lovely and is so interested in your story… she'll be really understanding… she really wants to interview you. So far you haven't had a voice, many of our viewers are mums just like you. It's so important to have your voice heard. Please, Sally, could you just consider it?' Georgie pleaded.

'I've been in the courtroom and really sympathise with you that you have rarely been given an opportunity to speak and when you have had a chance to talk you've been incessantly put into a defensive position, bombarded with contemptuous questions and cut off. We promise we'll take good care of you, Sally. I think it's so important to get your message across. If there's only one interview you give, it should be with Lorraine.'

Georgie picked me up several days later at 5:30am to be taken to the ITV studio. The date was 12.12.12… to appear on the *Daybreak* show. The moment my wake-up call went off at 4:30am, I was swamped with a deep sense of regret. Then I reasoned with myself: *what could go wrong?* Unlike at court, at least we would be speaking directly to each other and in the same language.

Georgie was her upbeat friendly self and chatted the whole way there in our executive Addison Lee cab.

'Don't worry, Sally. You'll be absolutely fine. I'm so pleased your voice is finally going to be heard. You'll be able to explain your reasoning for absconding with Neon. Lorraine is so pleased about interviewing you. I'm sure you'll be able to discuss the treatments you would rather Neon have.'

'I hope so, Georgie. It will be great if Lorraine gives me the opportunity to raise awareness about the 1939 Cancer Act. We need to ask the question of why there is a reluctance to update such an old law. Apart from Britain having one of the worst cancer survival rates in Europe, it's my duty as Neon's mother to find him the best treatment. Children's medical ethics require accepted treatments. The only accepted treatments by the mainstream are radiotherapy and chemotherapy.'

'Well, good luck, Sally. You are very knowledgeable and always so composed. I'm sure you are going to do really well and thanks again for agreeing to do these two interviews. I'm not sure when the next one will be, probably after the verdict. Five thousand pounds is quite the fee. It shows how much they want you. I've only ever known one other person to get that amount, and they were royalty.'

Arriving at the ITV studios, Georgie took me to the make-up room where everyone was lighthearted and lovely. Georgie then led me to a yellow and orange waiting room filled with bouquets of flowers and a television on the wall screening *Daybreak*. The cheerful lady who stood behind an L-shaped breakfast bar countertop pointed towards an assortment of fruit and pastries which lay beautifully presented in a large wicker basket and a silver platter. Any other time it would have looked appetising, but not today. Accepting a cup of tea, I sat down on the oversized red corner sofa and looked up at the big screen I would soon be on. A surge of panic-filled emotion washed over me. Scared stiff, I turned to Georgie almost in tears.

'I don't want to do this, Georgie. Your powers of persuasion are unreal. My heart is about to explode. I can't believe I agreed to this.'

'It's okay, Sally. You'll do great. Focus on what you want to say. You have come with a message. You're going on in the next ten minutes. The interview is only for a few minutes, and it will go very quickly. Just be yourself. Everything will be fine.'

Excusing myself, I raced to the bathroom to pull myself together. All too soon, Georgie called for me. 'Sally, you're on next. When you are ready, I'll take you through.'

Lorraine complimented me in her Scottish drawl as I approached the sofa. 'Gosh, look at you, haven't you got lovely long legs, like a supermodel.'

'Thank you,' I replied.

"Lights, action, camera." Lorraine barked questions at me, barely giving me time to answer:

'How could you be playing with your son's life?'

'Why would you deny your son life-saving treatment?'

'Don't you think the doctors know what they are doing?'

'Don't you think you're acting selfishly?'

'Don't you think it's incredibly irresponsible of you?'

'Don't you think you're playing Russian roulette with your son's life?'

'Do you not realise your son will probably die without radiotherapy?'

I could not dodge the bullets. I thought she was just the lady who asked the questions, but it felt far more personal than that. Lorraine Kelly thought the conventional treatment was the God-given almighty cure and I was crazy to question it. Being put on the defensive, I was not given an opportunity to answer any analytical questions. It felt even more brutal than court under the intense lights of the studio, along with millions tuning in while they ate their breakfast.

It must have been uncomfortable viewing watching me wriggle and squirm. Sitting on the bright red sofa surrounded by orange cushions and orange walls, orange mugs and Lorraine Kelly who also looked a little bit orange in between the orange onscreen graphics, I took a verbal beating. Lorraine resembled a Rottweiler with a meaty bone. Gone was my impression that breakfast show presenters were briefed to smile no matter what. Through gritted teeth, Lorraine hammered me with questions driven towards dragging me into a heavy state of the guilt factor.

With Lorraine not wishing to discuss the dangers of the one-size-fits-all protocol, all while calling the radiation treatment "life-saving", I just wanted the interview to be over. It was an act of sabotage with Lorraine beating down on her drum that it was "radiotherapy or death", once again like the court, not only downplaying but blatantly ignoring the side effects of the radiotherapy. It was impossible to discuss the true dilemma: was radiotherapy going to do more harm than good?

In Lorraine's eyes, I had committed a crime, her contorted view masterfully moulding the views prevalent among the public. I had hoped we would discuss like adults my reasoning for wanting to avoid radiation treatment for Neon. I had signed up for the show to highlight the limited treatment options and to discuss the drawbacks, but with Lorraine leading the interview and convinced that radiation and chemotherapy were crucial for survival, it was difficult to answer her questions which centred around why I would question the professionals and their chosen *curative* treatments.

Lorraine showed no warmth. It was like being in a freezer works. It worried me I had signed up for another round. I did not fancy another beating. Feeling shellshocked, I wondered if I could terminate the contract. It crossed my mind as I sat burning up in orange mania, what would happen if I got up and walked out? However, I was frozen to the spot and very much like a bunny in the headlights. After receiving some fierce punches from Lorraine Kelly, talk show host/heavyweight champion, I was, at last, allowed to leave. I would rather have been thrown in the ring with Mike Tyson. It would have been a fairer fight.

––––––

With it being a rare high-profile case and the media allowed coverage and following me like a hawk, it was impossible to escape them. Along with an offer of £25,000, I was presented with a contract from Paul. The newspaper he worked for wanted exclusive rights to Neon's story. He said it would be for one month and they would want to talk to me once before and once after court.

'You need to make a decision this evening,' Paul told me. 'The offer will not stand tomorrow.'

I called and asked Ben what he thought. 'They are offering a large lump sum. It means I cannot talk to any other press, meaning I'm off-bounds. They should then all leave me alone, and I can sign the full amount over to KICT, a children's integrated cancer charity. The articles are being written anyway. Why not put some money towards a good cause?'

'I think you should go for it,' Ben replied. 'It is a lot of money, and it's only for a month.'

The agreement extended to an apartment in central London. Paul said it would take them a while to find a suitable apartment, but just days later one of his colleagues found a place for me in West Brompton.

I was lost for words when we went up the dark and narrow flight of stairs. Opening the door, I felt like I was back in Tokyo. It was worlds apart from the five-star chic room I had become accustomed to at the Royal Garden Hotel in Kensington.

'Great. It's got wooden floorboards,' I commented. 'It's very cosy.'

The apartment was tiny, and it looked directly out onto the Metropolitan Police station.

'Is that deliberate?' I asked Paul.

'Er… no,' Paul replied, his eyes firmly fixed on the floor.

————

Enticed by the idea of setting the record straight, raising awareness on childhood brain cancer and emphasising the limited treatment options as well as a tantalising offer of a team of researchers who would help me find other ways to treat Neon, I met up with Sarah for lunch on the fifth floor of Harvey Nichols in Knightsbridge. Despite the hostility I had been facing in every direction, I was hoping to resolve the situation. Sarah appeared friendly; sitting wide-eyed and sipping on her Diet Coke she spoke zealously and gave the impression she understood. Although ambitious, Sarah came across as passionate and intrigued to learn about a more holistic approach to treating cancer.

'People want to know why you disagree with the experts. This documentary can be your platform to educate the British public on what you think are safer ways to treat cancer and discuss what you understand the dangers of radiation to be and why you don't want it for Neon. It will be me doing most of the filming, so it won't seem too invasive.'

Sipping on my bottled spring water, I nodded but felt the fear and could not hide my hesitation. 'I appreciate what you are trying to do, Sarah. However, the thought of a camera following me around puts me off.'

'My mother is suffering from cancer and going through chemotherapy. With such powerful subject matter affecting so many of us, the film will be of great interest and will reach out to so many people. I aim for it to be taken seriously in Parliament. If you want to raise awareness, Sally, what better way to do it? I'll be discreet and only film when appropriate. The documentary will not be coming out for three to six months. We can work at a speed that suits you. I can fit around your schedule.'

'So far my contact with the media has gone horribly wrong, how can I guarantee you are not going to edit me unfavourably and put forward another biased view?' I challenged.

'You must appreciate disagreeing with the doctors' decision is not the norm, Sally. People want to know why you think radiation is not the cure for cancer and why you do not want it for Neon, especially when the team treating him are so sure he needs it and say he probably would not survive without it. You will be able to see the film before it is aired.' Sarah paused. 'Can I ask why you are so against radiation?'

'Firstly, in Neon's case it is overtreatment; with no tumour, they are treating something that is no longer there. Secondly, I think that in years to come we will look back on these times when we were stuck in a rut and think of radiation and chemotherapy as a primitive, primeval time when we killed people in an attempt to cure them.'

'That's perfect. I think that's brilliant.' Sarah's eyes twinkled. 'If that's what you think, Sally, people want to hear it. This documentary will be the perfect platform. I promise I shall treat you fairly.'

'It does sound promising. So far no reporters have done any investigative journalism, focusing more on belittling my character than wanting to discuss any other ways of treating cancer or considering for a moment why I do not give my consent for radiation. Apologies, Sarah, I cannot help being wary though. As much as I'd like to think a Channel Four documentary is a fantastic opportunity to educate the British public on the prehistoric treatment currently being offered, I cannot help but wonder, will they want to explore the advantages of lesser-known, less invasive, unpatentable, more humane therapies? If you were able to air such an informative documentary, there are billions at stake. Vested interests are running rampant with cancer research its very backbone of deviousness. With all due respect, Sarah, I'm not sure who I can trust.'

'You can trust me, Sally, my mother is receiving chemotherapy too. If there's anything I can do to help her overcome the side effects or cure her cancer, I want to know about it. The documentary can show a view of both orthodox and alternative therapies.'

'Thank you, Sarah. Finally an opportunity to share a balanced view which is not going to be distorted in the process.'

'Rest assured, Sally, this documentary will be very different from anything you have experienced with the media already. We won't rush it. You have a powerful message. I'm sure mothers will understand and sympathise once they learn the reason you ran from the treatment. Nobody knew Neon was in the all-clear. You will be able to present an all-embracing view. I would like to start filming soon. Please, could you sign this waiver?'

Linda, however, was not comfortable with the proposal.

'It could make or break your case depending on the way it's edited. Even with such a strong message, edited badly, you could come out much worse off and scarred for life. It is much easier to edit someone to look bad than good. Make sure you do not sign anything until they have agreed in writing to give you full editorial control. Without that, they can edit you however they like, and you should not do it. Be careful, Sally, just be careful.'

———

With her keen to earn Linda's trust, I agreed to allow Sarah to drive with me the next day to meet Linda at the Advance Centre. Sarah was hungry to hear Linda explain the history of hyperbaric oxygen therapy (HBOT) and why something so cheap, safe and apparently simple had been found to have such wide-ranging health benefits.

The normally overcrowded car park was empty. The Advance Centre was usually closed on Sundays, but Linda had agreed to meet us there and was busy working at her desk when we arrived. After introductions were made, Sarah eagerly looked around the room.

'It is amazing what you do here, Linda. I was looking online last night and found it intriguing learning about the Scotson technique you have developed. Presumably, that is what all these beds are for? Do families bring their children here to learn how to do your massage therapy?'

'Yes, Sarah, they do. Abnormal breathing can interfere with the course of normal development including functional abilities, muscular-skeletal structure and the long-term health of the child. I have found when this is addressed they can begin to improve physically, neurologically and psychologically.'

'So the massage therapy you developed helps children to breathe normally?' Sarah asked.

'It has been found the work of the breathing muscles also affects heart rate, circulation, posture, speech quality, stamina, general health, digestion, sleep, emotional state and more since all of these systems dynamically interact with each other to drive forward health and development.'

'You really are a fountain of knowledge, Linda. I'm so intrigued. Sally has told me about the hyperbaric oxygen chamber, and I have been looking forward to seeing it. I see you have two – they are quite large. Can you tell me more about them? Do they work alongside your technique?' Sarah asked.

'In the large ten-person chamber the children wear oxygen hoods with free-flowing air, or the smaller "Thomas the Tank Engine" chamber fits an adult and child comfortably. In this chamber, the child can breathe the oxygen freely without needing to wear a mask. Hyperbaric has gained recognition as a complementary therapy for many conditions. It has many benefits including increased oxygen absorption when blood flow is diminished or blocked.'

'I find this all so fascinating. As I brought my camera, would you mind if I film?' Sarah asked.

Linda paused for a moment to study Sarah's face. 'Look, everything I am saying is factual, Sarah, so I have no problem discussing it, but maybe it's best to discuss things a bit further before we film. By the way, there are many published studies now confirming hyperbaric is helpful to reduce the destructive side effects of radiation therapy, a view Macmillan had put forward for some years. It is a puzzle why hyperbaric poses such a problem to the NHS.'

As time went by, Sarah asked again if we minded her filming this or that comment because it might be helpful to me. Gradually I realised she was filming everything. 'Sorry, Sarah, do you mind turning off your camera until we have come to an agreement? I feel very vulnerable at the moment and want to be sure of what footage will be used before we move forward with the camera rolling.'

'Sure, Sally, no problem. It's important you feel comfortable. How about we discuss these scientific studies Linda has printed out for you and talk a bit more about the HBOT?'

Not media-savvy, it crept up on me quickly. In short, I was naïve in my approach and should not have allowed her to film. Eventually, after promising me the camera was turned off, Sarah assured me that Linda and I had articulated my side of the argument clearly and passionately. However, riddled with stress, I was a bundle of nerves, and I was aware of how this knotted-up tension would look on camera. I was way out of my comfort zone and had stumbled on my words and was overflowing with doubt. More than ever, I needed to be sure Sarah would not be able to use any footage of me that was not in my favour. As we were leaving, Linda sensed my discomfort and put her hand on Sarah's arm.

'We both accept you have a genuine interest and seem to have good intentions, but Sally would be foolish to allow filming with no editorial rights over the content. The documentary needs to be a collaborative effort. I cannot see how she could be part of your film without any rights.'

'Absolutely, Linda, I couldn't agree more,' Sarah replied as she waved goodbye. 'You can trust me.'

Refusing to be browbeaten until I was sure I was doing the right thing, I refused to sign the waiver. However, that did not stop Sarah from persisting. I agreed she could accompany me back to court on 18 December. Sarah persuaded me to film on our way there.

'Please, Sally, it is so important I have footage throughout the court proceedings. We can decide if it goes in later. Let's just see how it goes. We will be outside the court soon. I'll only ask you a few questions.'

With the cameras rolling, Sarah's sympathetic view disappeared. It was replaced with the common media perception stated by the NHS' legal team that I was denying my son life-saving treatment. All the questions asked before. Sarah fired them out one after the other:

'Don't you think the doctors know what is best? Why would you deny Neon the best treatment available? Don't you think it's a gamble that could cost you his life?'

It upset me, and I was glad to get out of the cab. Once inside the courthouse I called Linda at the first opportunity.

'It feels like I've already been put in the box, Sarah has done a good job of cross-examining me on my way to court. It's like I'm swimming with the sharks. I'm not going to do this documentary. I cannot see how I can continue filming with her. Lucy said that Sarah would provide me with a team of researchers and that has come to nothing apart from luring me into agreeing to allow her to film in the first place.'

'We have had to live in hope, but in truth, it was unlikely a TV producer would be able to raise awareness on the restrictions of the 1939 Cancer Act. As there are no written agreements and you did not sign anything, surely this means Sarah cannot release any footage without your permission?'

'That would be an infringement on my rights,' I answered. 'Thank God I never signed her waiver.'

CHAPTER SIXTEEN

Dismissed

The National Health Service has at its back an army of lawyers. I did not have the same privilege. However, my QC provided me with the email trail that documented my dire straits position in "skeleton arguments".

'Whereby the Trust seek to limit (i) the scope of disclosure to the mother; and, (ii) the mother's ability to instruct expert oncological evidence.'

"Experts" are subject in the modern era to a comprehensive code, which requires transparency, yet I could not properly formulate solutions to propose when I was being denied material/information that breached my rights.

My QC, in part, set out my argument.

'In medical terms, this is now a case in which the Trust claims the right to keep secret from a parent the views of a doctor expressed on medical matters in respect of her non-Gillick competent child. Secondly, in forensic terms, the Trust claim the right to introduce expert evidence of their choice without any duty of disclosure. Even if the Trust is somehow entitled to ignore twenty years of development in the law of expert evidence in every case and return to the idea of "secret" expert evidence, it would be a serious infringement of the right to a fair trial and equality of arms if the mother was not entitled to do likewise. We risk the submission that the Trust wish to have all the cake, eat it and deny the mother a slice.

'We respectfully repeat our submission that the Mother makes, now, a principled stand. The medical profession's adherence to the need for and benefits of radiotherapy for children such as Neon is misplaced. This is the only point she takes. This is a serious issue to be tried. We do not understand why the Trust now seem anxious to distance themselves from this issue.'

———

Day three at the High Court, there was even more interest on the pavement than the days before. However, the media's perception was far distanced from the truth and with such fabricated reporting, it was complicating matters.

I picked up my pace hurrying towards the huge double doors, though not quickly enough to stop the onslaught of questions the press were compelled to ask.

'Sally, is it true, is Neon back in hospital?' a reporter called out.

I had never been overly loquacious with the press. This particular time I was lost for words. It was true, and I should have been with him.

Robin was waiting outside the courtroom and on my arrival dropped a bombshell.

'Sally, I am afraid you are going to have to prepare for defeat.'

'Pardon, Robin?' It was not what I wanted to hear from my legal representative. 'Prepare for defeat? I have been dragged to court by the NHS. I am fighting for my son's life, and the heart of

Neon's case is centred around parental rights to make informed decisions for their children. Giving up and preparing for defeat would be allowing unnecessary and permanent damage done to my son. I will do anything and everything to protect Neon. A mother's love and knowing what is best for her child runs far deeper than any legislation put in place by a government body and you Robin, as my QC, are the one in the position to fight the battle.'

Robin looked at me with a blank face. A silence fell upon us.

I called Linda while pacing up and down the masonry maze of Gothic corridors in the deserted wing next to my designated courtroom.

'What can I do, Linda? I'm about to be called back into court, and my hired gun is telling me to prepare for defeat.'

'Telling you to prepare for defeat? What do you mean? You're going to have to dismiss him.'

'But it's the eleventh hour, Linda, how can I possibly dismiss him?'

'Do not give up, Sally. I think it would be a good idea for you to engage with the human rights lawyer Imran Khan. As a human rights lawyer, he should be able to assist you with the parental rights issues you are up against. Imran Khan is an expert in his field. I'll give you his number.'

I needed someone who understood. Imran Khan gave me a glimmer of hope when he said he would drop everything and come to the High Court immediately, but I only had a moment to brief him before re-entering the court. Our meeting was fast-paced, surrounded by the constant hum of hustle bustle and was not without interruption as we sat outside the courtroom, aware that any moment we were to be summoned back in. It helped that Imran Khan had a very calm demeanour, which rubbed off on me while I rushed to fill him in.

'I've uncovered unprecedented evidence on a wide range of less invasive therapies, but have not been able to present them in court. With the NHS comfortably in the driver's seat, they have led the court in an entirely different direction. The main focus is trying to find children who have not been irradiated. Although I have not found any comparable studies with children above three years of age, there are adult cases reporting event free survival without radiation.

'My friend Linda has spoken of studies done in Russia and China on children who did not receive radiation and had survived and having informed the judge, I have been asked to locate and produce the studies. My desperate search for a study to present to the judge indicating that children diagnosed with medulloblastoma have been shown to survive after surgery without the use of radiotherapy has come to nothing. It has been a wild goose chase and is proving to be an impossible task.

'The main trouble I am having is locating any comparable studies when radiotherapy has been the only option for treating children diagnosed with medulloblastoma since the 1940s. There is much to be said about children having other successful treatments but only after the radiation has failed them and they have been sent home without hope, and their parents have refused to give up. Also, children under three as they, in recent years, have proven too young to irradiate. This is a valid point though; babies and very young children can survive without the radiotherapy. Scientifically this proves my case: older children too would be able to survive without radiotherapy, as do adults.'

The dismissing of Robin had caused a mere ripple. However, the court had its agenda and the core of today's case was focused on Dr Harper having another opportunity to express his mainstream view and explain how "it would be unethical to not give Neon the best chance of life" by irradiating him, followed by the chemical cocktail *cure*.

'It is too great a risk not to use the conventional treatment. Radiotherapy and chemotherapy have been the only accepted and used treatments since World War Two,' he told the court.

Instructed by the medics, Neon had been taken to hospital by his father to prepare for second-look surgery. The NHS was railroading Neon towards a treatment that had no solid evidence at its foundation. Whereas I thought it ludicrous the treatment had remained the same for so long, the NHS used it in their favour as one of their strong points.

I was eventually given the opportunity to express my view on why I opposed the operation scheduled for the next day.

'The medics usually choose not to operate on anything smaller than one-and-a-half centimetres. All of the reports and the medical notes are very vague, stating that the appearances are *most likely* those of a medulloblastoma. *If* it is what the medics assume, then the one-centimetre microscopic nodule is smaller than what they usually consider necessary to operate on. I am not saying they are always wrong, but they are not always right either.

'The medical team have made mistakes before, having previously assured me what was showing on the images was nonsignificant residual and that no further tumour could be identified. *If* what is showing on the images is a medulloblastoma nodule, has it been left behind from the original surgery or is it scar tissue from post-surgical change? One more week is not going to change anything except it will give me the time to get my much-needed second opinion with the added benefit of Neon being able to enjoy Christmas out of the hospital.'

The news reporters wrote their version:

"Not only is Sally Roberts denying her son life-saving treatment but she is also attempting to prevent life-saving surgery."

Justice Bodey declared, 'In such circumstances and with such extreme urgency I must and I shall decide today.'

The order stated that it was:

... in NR's best interests for second-look surgery to take place and that it was lawful for doctors to carry out the procedure notwithstanding the refusal of the mother to give her consent.

This is a case where there has already been a delay in treating N. Ideally, radiotherapy and chemotherapy, the gold standard on current evidence, should start within forty-two days of the original surgery. Unfortunately, however, a number of delays arose from the parents' desire to transfer N's treatment from one city to another and partly due to N's mother missing two or possibly three appointments (depending on bad weather being an explanation). Then M and N went missing.

The consequence is that there is an increased need now to move forward with as little delay as possible and for surgery to take place if deemed appropriate and subsequently with treatment. That decision may well be made this week, or at least a default ruling that radiotherapy should be given, in the absence of any further evidence.

It was said, "If there was any uncertainty about what the scan shows, the most certain way of revealing the answer is by second-look surgery."

To get Neon back on the starting block, whether or not residual tumour was there, the NHS demanded that more surgery needed to take place. Beyond what I could deal with and said to be "putting N's health at grave potential risk", I had to back down. Without expert legal representation, it was impossible to convey my message to the court without seeming unreasonable.

With judgement going in favour of the NHS that Neon had to be operated on immediately (19.12.12), the court was adjourned until the end of the week, three days away on 21.12.12. What mattered was that I was there for Neon. I had to be at the hospital. The judge acknowledged this.

My brother was being supportive and drove me to the hospital, where Neon was surprisingly cheerful.

'They've given me a secret agent name.'

'Oh have they, Neon, and what's that?' I asked.

'Nathan Richards.'

'Nathan Richards?' I echoed.

'So nobody knows who he is, thanks to you,' Ben muttered.

We had not discussed with Neon the publicity. He knew nothing about the media or the news coverage he was getting.

'Whose idea was this?' I asked.

'Sarah Burkeman came up with the name, the hospital insisted. It was Dr Harper's idea to protect Neon from the media,' Ben replied.

'You're joking?'

'No, Sally, I'm not. Let's not forget this is all your fault,' Ben snarled.

'The nefarious activities of a journalist, stalking Neon in the hospital aisles all for a good story. Really? You've got to be kidding me. Changing his name, isn't that going a bit far?' I disputed.

'Come on, it's getting late. We've got to go to Brighton now and get your documents for your lawyer,' Tony interrupted. 'We will be back tomorrow morning for the operation.'

Due to hospital policy, only one parent was permitted to stay overnight.

———

'Hello, I'm trying to locate Neon Roberts, he's having second-look brain surgery,' I reported to the receptionist on the jungle-themed ward the next day. There were several other staff behind the desk. The ward was buzzing with activity.

'Sorry, there does not seem to be anyone here under that name.'

I looked at Tony, confused.

'That's weird.'

'What about a Nathan Richards?' Tony suggested.

'Oh, yes, he's just waking up now, but there are only two people allowed in at a time. Do you mind waiting? His mother and father are in with him at the moment.'

'Sorry?' I glared. 'But I am his mother.'

A nurse behind the desk had overheard our conversation.

'Oh, hello, you're Nathan's mother? I'm so sorry for any confusion. We were under the impression that the woman in there with him now was his mother. You have our sincere apologies. I'll take you to him.'

'His father did say he would call me, I was supposed to be here before he woke up.'

'Don't worry, Nathan is doing well. He's only beginning to wake up now. It's perfect timing; the anaesthesia is only just starting to wear off. They've not been in there long, only a few minutes. He's still very drowsy. You can come in... but is that your girlfriend, Mr Roberts? There are only two people allowed in at a time. I'm afraid your girlfriend will have to leave.'

———

'Nathan, can you squeeze my hand?' the nurse queried as she held out her palm. 'Nathan, can you open your eyes?' The nurse leaned forward and shone a torch towards his face.

'It's okay, Neon, mummy is right here,' I whispered in his ear.

'Nathan, squeeze my hand once if you can see one finger or twice if you can see two.' The nurse pressed on with her observations.

'I can talk you know.' Neon made everyone laugh. His warrior spirit shone through. With his sense of humour intact, he put a cup on his head pretending it was a hat. I was amazed at what he was able to do compared to the last surgery, which had knocked him for six.

Neon was thirsty, he wanted to drink; he could swallow, talk and even smile. All milestones that Neon could not do after the first surgery until out of the high dependency unit. After the second-look operation, he bypassed the HDU altogether. It was a completely different experience.

His bed was buzzing with activity as nurses went about their duties, administering the vast amount of concoctions prescribed post brain surgery.

'What is that you are about to give him?' I asked.

'Anti-emetics,' the nurse replied. 'It has previously been agreed that we would give Nathan anti-emetics per usual protocol.'

'As a preventive?' I enquired.

'Well, yes, the site of the surgery may induce sickness and anaesthetic agents may increase nausea and vomiting. We use a *prevention rather than cure* approach.'

'What about the antihistamine?' I asked.

'We give Piriton in case of a rash,' the nurse replied.

'But he doesn't have a rash, another preventive?' I questioned.

'Yes, is there a problem?'

'Not if he needs it,' I responded. 'I am in agreement they should all be given if needed but can't we see how he goes with the rash rather than just dosing him up? If he does need it, can he have Piriton syrup without the synthetic sweetener aspartame? He's having so much already with it in all the *sugar-free* painkiller syrup and everything else he is being prescribed.'

'Sorry, it's all we have,' the nurse replied. 'I'll keep a close eye on Nathan and only give the Piriton if needed.'

'Oh, and my son's name is Neon. Could you please call him Neon?'

I checked the chart attached to the end of his bed. It read "Nathan Richards".

'I am concerned about the impact on Neon with the name change. How would you like to wake up from brain surgery and not be called by your real name? It must be very disorientating, you are confusing him. His name is Neon... please call him Neon.'

Much to my dismay, my repeated requests fell on deaf ears. Everyone except me (and my family) continued to call Neon, Nathan.

CHAPTER SEVENTEEN

The Starting Block

To most people, it was the end of another week, a Friday. To scholars and historians, this hyped-up date was one of – if not the most – prophesied day in our modern times, 21.12.12. This date signified the end of the Mayan calendar. The end of a "great cycle". The Western media had dramatically steamrollered the *dumbing down* meaning to this date towards the end of the world and argued between themselves about it.

With the judgement ruled today, it was said to be the end of the case. I was a mother who stood against the tyranny while searching for more effective and humane treatment options for my child. However, my fight for the right treatment was under siege. Justice Bodey made it clear that without evidence to prove radiation was *not* necessary (asking me to present a paper indicating that children, above three years of age, diagnosed with medulloblastoma have been shown to survive after surgery without radiotherapy), I would have to accept the treatment prescribed by the NHS Trust.

The Trust wished to interrogate me further before the judge made his ruling. I had hoped to discuss the dangers of radiation and was challenging the radiotherapy to avoid the need for lifetime medical surveillance due to toxicities from treatment-related complications. One PubMed abstract from the medline database in my folder suggested "very few late effects were evident among those treated with surgery only, but risks were consistently elevated for those treated with radiation and surgery, and higher still for those who also received adjuvant chemotherapy". However, the court was led in another direction.

'Mrs Roberts, where are you getting your evidence from?' Before I could respond, the sullen-faced barrister continued, 'Are you getting your information from the Internet?'

'My information comes from published medical journals and other reputable sources. I am aware of the vast amount of misinformation on the Internet and would most certainly not rely on it. I am careful where I source my information from,' I replied cautiously so not to slip up on my words. 'My folder is packed full of peer-reviewed studies.'

The blatant blockage of getting me what I needed to obtain a second opinion was barely acknowledged, let alone discussed. Tactfully swept under the carpet, anything of true importance became shrivelled up and thrown away like a screwed-up piece of paper as the barristers bantered between themselves about matters that did not go anywhere and had very little relevance.

It was yet another theatrical performance and the content far from what I had anticipated. Completely powerless, I could only sit and watch what unfolded. There was a brief opportunity to mention how many delays I had encountered when cross-examined. I told the court I was unhappy with the many contradictions, including the conflicting information I had experienced while dealing with the NHS but with nobody picking up on it, including my new unequipped QC, as much as I had all the evidence with me, it was all overlooked.

On one hand, I was faced with the savvy skills of the NHS' legal empire focusing on their "life-saving treatment" *and* belittling my character, and on the other hand, I lacked a strong legal companion. Anyone representing me saw no other option than what was offered by the National Health Service, literally bowing before them. Everything was happening so fast and I was being chaperoned to the finish line.

I was in the High Court because I feared the consequences of the prescribed nightmare for my seven-year-old son and could not agree to it. Although briefly acknowledged, the dangers of the treatment were overlooked while the campaign to ostracise me took over. I was already aware of the tactics and extent of the media's limitations. By being the centre of an attack, it gave me a rare opportunity to experience how brutal the press can be when it comes to protecting an institution of their own ilk such as the medical establishment. Winston Churchill once said, "a lie gets halfway around the world before the truth even gets its pants on." With the media portraying a slanted story, on the news back in NZ, I was the Kiwi mother denying her son life-saving treatment when the truth of matters was that I was in search of a more suitable treatment that would save him from harm and not compromise his well-being.

'The press will never let the truth get in the way of a good story.' Mum summed up the situation perfectly. 'Even if it is at the expense of a young boy's health by making an example of him – and his mother.'

The ever-growing media interest had been reflected on the pavement outside when coming into the High Court and inside the courtroom, there were even more unfamiliar faces. One new face was Ben's recently appointed barrister. Until now, I had found the legal representatives, overall, to be professional and respectful, but the air changed dramatically with Sophie Badley, who had shorter hair than any man and a fierce face with mean eyes. It soon became clear that this bad-ass bully was here to tarnish any credibility I may have had, employing covert methods such as false accusations to achieve her goals.

Planting malicious accusations in front of the court, I could see Sophie Badley had no other duty but to lead a campaign of deliberate destruction. I did all I could to maintain my integrity as I became the target of a vicious verbal attack, subjected to Ben's representative manipulating facts to present an untrue picture, pummelling me with "child-like" questions hard and fast.

'Mrs Roberts, are you doing this for Neon or are you doing "all of this" for media attention?'

I looked at the judge wondering if he would put a stop to it. Surely he would not allow this nonsense to continue. Instead, he indicated I should reply.

'Neon is my only son. I fear the radiation will do more harm than good. I am searching for a less aggressive therapy,' I replied.

I looked helplessly down at my brother, and then around the room at the media's eyes all on me. The words "all of this" ringing in my ears. How could anybody think a living hell could be in the slightest bit desirable? Lucy had momentarily stopped examining her individual strands of hair and picked up her pen. Our eyes met in-between her eagerly taking notes.

The awkward atmosphere persisted. Sophie Badley's words clamouring in my ears telling me I was "an ignorant, perhaps self-obsessed woman determined to press unscientific quackery on her suffering child." She also suggested I was "an irresponsible parent, not to be trusted and Neon should be in Ben's care for the full duration of treatment."

Sophie Badley focused on the media. After all, it was her strong point.

'Why did you release pictures of Elektra?'

'I didn't,' I disputed.

'Why are you making any such approaches to the press and other media organisations? Are you not concerned to protect the children from any further press intrusion triggered by your actions during what will undoubtedly be a particularly difficult time and where a sensitive approach is required?'

'I'm unsure what you are implying. I have not approached the media. They've been sitting in the courtroom as it has escalated into a high-profile case. That it is a public interest story is out of my control.'

I felt some relief when I sat back down. With the barristers picking up where they left off with their long-winded legalese discussions, the attention turned away from the direct mudslinging. I had never been subjected to such an extreme act of scandalous slandering.

Shaken up, I called Linda in the break.

'I can see why Ben had a QC. I have just been through the most humiliating experience in my whole life dished out by Ben's barrister. He's not even here. He's in the hospital with Neon. As it transpired, he is going for temporary custody of Neon. Sophie Bad-ass has just finished with me. It was awful. She crucified me while Lucy sat there unable to hide the smile on her face. She must have briefed the QC with her childlike antics. I was put on the spot and asked if I'm doing "all of this" for media attention? How could I possibly turn down radiation and be in court fighting it, I must have ulterior motives. Having cameras shoved in your face and people writing crap about you is such fun,' I vented.

'Sally, close your eyes and take a few gentle breaths and imagine the fragrance of blossom on a summer's day.' Linda paused. 'Did you have a chance to bring up the 1939 Cancer Act?'

'No, I did not. It's like I am prevented from discussing anything of any worth including the dangers of treatment. The barristers are driving the case in completely the other direction. They are currently focusing on maligning my character and not much else. The court does not want to know about choice. They leave it to the experts who know nothing whatsoever about an integrated approach to healthcare or how it would increase the chances of recovery in people and improve their quality of life. Nothing is said of my limited choices and how I am prevented from getting a second opinion. It seems Neon is being made a political example of and I am prevented from discussing the legislation that prevents innovation and safer treatments.'

'How so?' Linda queried.

'I asked my QC, who briefly mentioned it, but the judge shirked any responsibility, quote: "The 1939 Cancer Act is a matter for the government, not the court." How can I make people aware of the 1939 Cancer Act and how it limits freedom of choice? I feel so out of my depth.'

'The difficulty you are always facing is you have to learn things as you go along, each new experience comes in on you fast, just as you are getting to grips with the previous one. I think you have done extremely well so far. The water is very deep. From the evidence, it appears that the British government on the directive of the pharmaceutical industry was persuaded to put its money behind X-ray radiation and by doing so it decided to protect its financial interests by outlawing all rivals. Perhaps at the time, this seemed like acceptable business practice to help fund the NHS, who knows, but why in heaven's name can't we talk about it? You need someone with a lot of experience in this somewhat unnerving world... what about Imran Khan? As a human rights lawyer surely he can help?'

'In a perfect world maybe he could, but it's like the court is following a programme and ignoring the elephant in the room. Everyone is looking the other way. Nobody seems to understand the restraints of the Act. Imran Khan, although interested, could not answer me when I asked him why there was a reluctance to update such an old law which prevents other safer and more effective therapies from being used. I want to make a song and dance about it, but I've got no choice except to sit in silence and listen to them rant on. To be honest, I'm just glad to be out of the box. It's all so utterly hopeless, Linda.

'The poetic, nonsensical banter of the court folk just floats over me. My folder is packed full of studies but how do I present the court any valuable information if I'm not given a chance? I've not been given an opportunity to discuss important facts; if cancer returns on any cancer patient who has gone into remission after five years, it is more likely to be as a result from the conventional treatment than a resurgence of the original cancer.'

'Sally, good people keep funnelling billions of pounds into cancer research for a cure that is always said to be just around the corner. In reality, studies show the UK has some of the worst cancer survival rates in the Western world. Doctors here do not have any flexibility for innovation. Where are the scientific studies of so-called natural, meaning non-patentable and therefore non-profitable treatments? They don't exist because nobody will fund them. Germany uses a more holistic approach to treating cancer, with great success. You would think it would benefit us all if scientists and doctors would be allowed to move forward and explore safer therapies.'

'I'm certainly not the only one to think how the conventional treatment is outdated and a risky business but how do I make the court understand that it's time to pour money into clinical trials of treatments that are not going to damage our bodies beyond repair with long-lasting injurious side effects? Einstein once said, "doing the same thing over and over and expecting a different result is the definition of insanity". Yet this is the current cancer healthcare system; giving our beautiful bodies over to an industry, a business which cannot cure cancer and profits hugely at our expense. Look at the damage and the ongoing deaths from the treatment, but we keep allowing it,' I sighed.

'You need a cool head for this, Sally. You have to have good evidence for every word. Perhaps a university will one day offer the subject to a PhD student. Perhaps an economics student would like to investigate whether tying the NHS so closely to the pharmaceutical companies still makes good economic sense. My heart is with you. Try to stay detached and don't hurry with your answers. Oh and good luck, may you have lots of it.'

'I am going to need more than luck, Linda, but thank you. I'm being called back in. I'll call you after the hearing.'

The hearing continued in much the same vein.

Dr Lucock, the lead clinician in Bristol had admitted that they have little evidence to show that using radiotherapy at this time would be benefiting Neon, yet bound to the protocol, Dr Harper the expert representing the NHS stated *without real evidence* that it was the only option. There were no clinical trials to prove the efficacy of radiotherapy. It most definitely was unsafe, and all the research I had in my folder from published medical journals indicated it would cause irreparable harm.

This highlighted one of the main issues: the extent to which the evidence-base in evidence-based medicine has either been scrubbed out or distorted by scientific fraud.

"The limits of its usefulness and the extent of its effectiveness have never been clearly established through clinical trials. There is very little solid evidence comparing the effectiveness of radiation to other treatment approaches," says top oncologist, Suresh Katakkar. "The lack of clear and unequivocal information regarding the question of exactly what benefit radiation treatment confers on cancer patients has been a longstanding concern."

Naturopathic physician, Daniel Rubin, comments, "While the benefits of radiotherapy are often discussed, its pitfalls are less well known but can potentially cause harm to people with cancer."

The doctors, the court and now the press ignored that Neon's surgeon achieved a full resection of the tumour with excellent tissue margins. Out of the 120 different types of brain tumours, surgery on medulloblastoma had a very high success rate. This success rate was *not* because of the radiation. If it was, there would be studies to prove it. That the histology report showed that the tumour was neither Myc or MycN amplified was also significant. In the USA this would put him in the excellent prognosis group, but this was too complex for the NHS, court and the media. Moreover, it was not yet part of the protocol within the medical establishment in the UK and therefore not justified.

The United Kingdom was not at the forefront when it came to treating children with medulloblastoma. I was seeking the best possible outcome for Neon and a tolerable way to care for my seven-year-old child post removal of a brain tumour. I have the right as his mother to pursue the best treatment available. It is my duty.

Yet through the mainstream media, instead of a rational mother concerned about the consequences of damaging treatment, I was being portrayed as an irresponsible parent. What was lost in the press reportage while struggling to obtain a better clinical deal for my son is the documented severity of the long-term effects of radiation to the brain including stunted growth, deafness and necrosis.

Fighting a losing battle, on top of being persecuted, I grew weaker. As with many court disputes, the most significant issue was the status quo. We had been at an impasse since day one. With no capable legal companion and the continual downplaying of the dangers of radiation, the judgement process was rushed and made in favour of the NHS, who then attempted to make an application to the High Court for me to pay their legal costs.

It was ruled that treatment should go ahead and that for the duration of treatment Neon should live with his father. Mr Justice B 'had to approve the treatment plan of the hospital as it stood up to scrutiny and there was no precisely defined alternative'.

It was said by Mr Justice Bodey 'the mother's judgment had gone awry', and that 'Sally Roberts had set her face against all treatments in the UK'.

I continued to listen to the verdict in anguish.

'The underlying issue is, as I said at the outset, whether radiotherapy and chemotherapy are in N's best interests? The advantages have to be balanced against the disadvantages. The gold standard orthodox approach contained in the CCLG guidance [the Childhood Cancer Leukaemia Group to which oncologists in this country belong] is that a package of radiotherapy and chemotherapy is necessary to produce optimum survival rates. Much research, investigation and deliberation by cancer experts over decades have determined the minimum dosages to produce maximum survival rates, with the minimum possible detrimental consequences as regards quality of life. Before radiotherapy was developed during the course of the last century, patients who had N's cancer invariably or almost invariably died in spite of surgery.'

In spite of surgery? I would have loved to ask the judge. What had become clear to me from looking at the 1940s study was that in days gone by many patient's deaths occurred from less advanced surgical procedures. In that respect, we have come a long way. People dying from surgery-related causes (back then) should be taken into consideration when looking at an outdated simplistic study so strongly advocating post-surgery *modern-day* treatment procedures. If the NHS depends on a shady study like this to show an inquisitive parent like me the worth of the treatment (and the High Court), we need to examine them further. Many children in this particular study did not make it as far as being administered the treatment (radiation + chemotherapy) and go down in the statistics, dead within one month. This was because of less advanced surgery *not* because they didn't have radiation.

Without being equipped with a legal representative who understood the intricate details of what I faced, my case was lost. My attempts to reason with the court had been short-lived and swamped with the repeated mantra of the medical mafia, echoed throughout the proceedings by the judge, legal representatives of the NHS Trust and chanted by the media mindset: "If action is not taken this boy will die."

The court order stated Neon would remain with Ben and "in respect of all further treatment for NR's brain tumour and any related disease or illness, the treating clinicians at any NHS hospital are permitted to rely on the consent of BR alone."

'I thought you did well, Sal. That one barrister tore into you at the end. It can't have been easy her saying all that,' Tony said as we exited the courtroom. 'I feel for you. I know you never said once that you got your information from the Internet, but they put words into your mouth and made out as you did.'

'I noticed that too. You've mentioned before about not getting your information from the Internet,' Sarah, who had joined us, commented. 'I'm sorry, Sally, I know how you had so much to say and you got to say none of it.'

Outside the courtroom was buzzing with journalists.

'How do you feel about the verdict? Will you appeal?' one reporter asked.

'Don't answer him,' Paul urged. 'Just ignore them.'

As the circle of reporters closed in, Paul swatted them off like flies.

One female reporter stepped forward, not taking no for an answer. I recognised her, she had introduced herself in the first court case and had slipped me her card. She was one of the ITV news reporters who had been at the first hearing and all that had followed. I had seen her on television talking about the case.

'Sally.' Sejal Karia caught my eye. 'Could you please give me just one soundbite?'

I looked at Paul. Even if I did have something to say, Paul was being very protective and not having any of it.

'Sorry, Sejal, you are just going to have to wait,' Paul grinned.

'Wait? What do you mean wait? It's the end of the case, Paul. You know it can't wait. You know I need it now. Please, Paul, just one soundbite?'

Already feeling bruised and beaten, I stood glued to the spot. Tony and I looked at each other in disbelief listening to Sejal desperately trying to reason with Paul. She was begging.

'Please, Paul. You know how important it is. This is our biggest piece right now. I need one small soundbite. You know how much I need it, please, Paul.'

'You know how it is, Sejal, and you know it's just not possible.' Paul smirked triumphantly linking arms with Sejal and escorting her away. 'You can speak to Sally in a few weeks.'

'But nobody will care in a few weeks,' Sejal retorted. 'We need it today, Paul. You're being unreasonable. You know how much I need it now.'

Nobody will care in a few weeks. Her words reverberated in my head like an audio effect. I stood only metres away still in clear earshot from Sejal who had her hands placed on both hips, her powers of persuasion failing miserably on Paul's boyish charms. Until now, I had thought she was one of the nicer ones. Her insensitive, callous comments exposed her thick skin from working in such an emotionally hardened industry. Human tragedy to one side, to the press, it was all about today's news. I felt like fish and chip wrapper, just another story, today's news tomorrow's rubbish. I had heard enough. I had to leave this trivia. I needed to get back to the hospital.

CHAPTER EIGHTEEN

Hope on the Horizon

The court case had been rushed through and was over as quickly as it had started. If I had been trying to prevent my son from having a virtuous treatment that was proven to be necessary, it would have seemed reasonable for a hospital backed by the High Court to have intervened on my son's behalf, but this was far from the case with Neon.

Nonetheless, it was a case of "you cannot fool all the people all the time". I had members of the public contact me, my inbox was inundated with messages, and ninety-nine per cent were positive and supportive.

"Sally is a beacon of light for so many thousands of people. This is a REAL TEST case!" one supporter wrote. Kind words lifted my spirits. Many people could see it for what it was; a battle between a mother and the forces of the Pharma Cartel.

One message stood out:

Great to see someone standing up against a corrupt system. Well done Sally, you have helped awaken so many that were sleeping. You showed love and compassion for your son and stood tall above those that would much prefer you to keep quiet. You entered the media and were blasted with negative questions and accused of being a bad mother live on TV yet you kept your nerve and answered each question with balance and honesty. This world will only become a better place to exist within when more like you stand up and make up the numbers. I hope your son is doing well and that you never give up the fight.

In an attempt to win my appeal and not have my defence council run roughshod over again, I was looking towards Germany who for the treatment of cancer is among the leading countries worldwide and has some of the highest cancer survival rates, where many doctors are dedicated to a more holistic approach. Immune system stimulating therapies (not allowed for the treatment of children in the UK) are used as standard practice in complementary clinics in Germany.

The same day as the verdict, within a few hours of leaving the High Court, I learnt about a German oncologist called Dr Herzog. Dr Herzog ran a clinic in Germany that specialised in complementary therapies that supported the immune system of patients while they underwent individualised doses of conventional therapy. Dr Herzog supported his patients with hyperthermia and a whole raft of different supportive therapies to reduce the related side effects and to improve quality of life: high doses of antioxidant and vitamin infusions, homeopathic medications for detoxification, immunomodulation with hymns peptides, magnetic field therapy, ozone therapy, oxygen therapy and orthomolecular therapy.

German complementary therapies are groundbreaking. Why are they not offered as part of an integrated protocol and incorporated into the "gold standard" package if they improve cancer patients' chances and their quality of life?

Dr Herzog catered to the needs of each patient and would treat Neon as an individual by using an integrated approach. Nothing even remotely similar is being done here in the UK. After speaking to Dr Herzog personally on the telephone, he confirmed he could treat children and quickly began to seem like my best hope. All I had to do was get back to the High Court and have the judge agree.

It was 23 December, two days after court, that a proton representative contacted me. Proton beam therapy (PBT) was a more advanced form of radiation because therapists had more control where the proton beam released its highest concentration of energy. Affecting less healthy tissue results in fewer side effects than traditional radiation and was said to be far more beneficial for children as it does not impact on growth and other critical areas in children's development; 96,000 patients had already been treated worldwide with proton therapy and with a very high success rate. The NHS paid for travel and accommodation for children to have this treatment but not for medulloblastoma.

The hospital withheld this information from me (and the court), and it was not offered to Neon. Tooth and nail I had fought the NHS, unwilling to allow Neon to suffer needlessly from the consequences of the photon X-ray radiation and as it turned out the more advanced technology was already available by NHS standards. It was just that the NHS was not yet committed to providing all patients with proton therapy services.

At length, I spoke to the proton expert who contacted me through my lawyer. He assured me they had experience in treating children providing me with articles, reports and statistics to prove it. They had the infrastructure to do so and were willing to take on medical responsibility for Neon. The efficacy of the proton particles was supported by peer-reviewed research and not only did proton beam produce a quality of survival rate to match the NHS treatment plan, it was significantly better because it did not have the long list of dreaded side effects. By reducing collateral damage, there would be less adverse effects, which can occur months to years after standard radiotherapy. If Neon were to have radiation it would be in his best interests to have the newer technique – to me, that was obvious.

At the same time, the Alliance for Natural Health contacted me.

'We are looking to help you find other options that might reduce the neuro-cognitive, psycho-social and other long-term side effects that you are aware of that are associated with whole brain radiotherapy,' Dr Robert Verkerk, the Director of ANH said. 'We moved things forward over the weekend talking to various specialists and building a list of contacts for viable options rather than whole-brain radiotherapy/adjuvant chemo.'

The list (including proton beam in Switzerland) looked very promising.

It was the day before Christmas Eve. Even though Neon was recovering well, I wondered if it was too soon to be let out just a few days after the operation. After the last surgery, it had been almost one month until he was able to be discharged. The hospital said they needed to free up a bed and had decided to discharge Neon on the condition that he went home to rest. Having arrived at the hospital to find Neon gone and his bed with another child in it, I called Ben.

'Oh, hi, Sal, sorry to not have called. It's good news. Neon has been discharged. We were on our way home from the hospital and thought Neon must be hungry, so we have brought him to the organic restaurant in Walton Street around the corner from the flat.'

I called my mother to tell her the news. She had just come out of Euston Square train station and was walking towards the hospital.

'Mum, Neon's been discharged. Ben has taken him to a restaurant.'

'He's what?'

'He has taken him to a restaurant.'

'Is he mad?' Mum fretted. 'The nurse said Neon needs to be resting. I saw how deeply asleep he was for the whole time I was there yesterday afternoon. He has just had brain surgery for Christ's sake. He needs his own space preferably with a bed. If he has been sent home to rest then he should have been taken home, why has Ben taken him to a bloody restaurant?'

'Ben was quite proud of himself. He chose an organic restaurant. We have to accept we have different views to Ben and his family and even though we will never understand why they would behave so thoughtlessly, what can we do?'

'He needs his rest,' Mum complained. 'I know they usually go out for Christmas lunch. Surely just this once they will stay home? Otherwise, they should let Neon be with you. We will take care of him. He needs a low-key Christmas focused on allowing him to rest and having the freedom to be in bed or to get up and join in if he has the energy. You can't let them do this, Sally. You have to get Neon back. You are his mother. He needs you.'

———

I did what I could to ensure Neon had all that he needed and delivered various supplements, an infrared blanket, EMF canopy protection, air and water filters and a brand new cold press juicer to Ben's parents' flat.

Ben's mother was contemptuous of my "carrot juice cure" as she put it and with the continuous chocolate ice-cream on offer and a constant stream of cigarette smoke from Ben and his sister, together with Christian's cigar smoke, I could not hide my dissatisfaction when coming to visit the children at their flat. It didn't help matters that Michele would always scuttle off to their bedroom on my arrival. Overall, I was not a welcome guest, and the ice was starting to crack.

Deep down I knew that Ben also wanted the best for Neon, or what he thought was best but we had very different standards. Whereas Ben saw it acceptable to take Neon out to restaurants and order in pizza as well as buying him ice-cream whenever he wanted it, I didn't. Given our health scare, I wanted to avoid overly processed foods and give him nutritious and delicious food made from scratch at home.

I provided Ben with the "fight not feed" anticancer programme that I had been following. However, as much as Ben might have once appreciated my efforts, surrounded by his family who did not want to attempt to understand my healthy living approach, he was struggling. Although I begged them to continue juicing daily, it was more like weekly and, when they did get around to juice for him, they would freeze it for convenience.

When Neon had been with me, he would willingly eat thirteen apricot kernels every day, but Ben and his clan thought they tasted bad and told Neon he did not have to eat them if he did not want to and offered him chocolate biscuits instead. My presence was interfering with their ideas and lifestyle. Once again I suggested putting on a united front for the sake of our children, Neon needed us all but having such healthy tendencies seemed to be my downfall in a household that faced entirely in the opposite direction. They were all like-minded and prepared to blindly accept the radio/chemo *cure* combo and follow the advice of the hospital dieticians, quoted in the CCLG Helping Your Child to Eat (Children Coping with Cancer) booklet, "sugar, honey, syrup and sugary foods, for example, chocolate, cakes and sweets are all good sources of energy." It was easier for them to show me the door and from then on shut me out.

Since having children, it was my first Christmas alone. I called Ben so I could speak to Neon and Elektra, but it went straight to voice message. Ben knew I disapproved that they had booked into the Charlotte Street Hotel for Christmas lunch telling me that while the children were with him he could do as he pleased.

I had been to the Charlotte Street Hotel. As lovely as it was, I was concerned about Neon going to the busy hotel so soon after his operation. It was only the day after getting out of the hospital.

Finding it impossible to bite my tongue, I had voiced my concerns that Ben's family were behaving selfishly. 'It's only a matter of days since he had brain surgery. He needs to be at home in a safe environment not celebrating Christmas in Soho at a frigging restaurant.'

Having spoken my mind I was now paying the ultimate price, and completely cut off from being able to talk to Neon and Elektra. The last place I wanted to be was my shoebox flat. I had been there for almost two weeks and still not purchased any tea bags. It did not feel like home. Opening my bedroom curtains in the morning and seeing the Metropolitan Police station staring back at me, I soon headed to my favourite cosy space in Earl's Court, The Troubadour. It was a few minutes away from where I was staying on the Old Brompton Road. There were hardly any cars on the road and nobody on the streets. Everywhere was closed for the holiday, including The Troubadour. Across the road, I saw a café sign in the distance, a place I had not noticed before. I was sure I saw a light on and headed towards it. When I got closer, I could see the café's flashing fairy lights draped around the window. Wrapped in a blanket of freezing wind I walked faster, eager to get inside.

A little bell tinkled above my head when I opened the door. The warmth was welcoming. The café was small and had pale yellow floral wallpaper. A woman pulled her seat closer to the table so I could squeeze past and get to the counter where a petite middle-aged lady with a nice smile greeted me; she wore bright red lipstick and had jet black hair which she had tied up in a bun. The ingredients were on display in white plastic tubs under a large glass panel. It was mainly baguettes, and paninis on offer or a hot English breakfast.

'What do you fancy, you sit?' She gestured to a table behind me.

I nodded glancing at the menu, fancying something warm and comforting. 'Could I have a tuna melt panini please with onion and sweetcorn?'

'Would you like salad?'

'Yes please and a cup of Earl Grey tea.'

I sat down at a small round table with three empty seats. It had a PVC red-and-white checked tablecloth, and the knives and forks were all pre-wrapped in white paper serviettes and stood in the middle of the table in a pint glass. Each table had a red carnation. There were one too many tables but it was warm, the lady was lovely, the food looked fresh, and the coffee smelt good.

An unshaven man on the table next to me sat staring off into space. An older lady sat at the next table clicking her pen while doing a crossword. Another man with a long grey beard was talking on and off to another old lady about the weather. I stared blankly at the picnic-style gingham tablecloth with no desire to flick through the magazines or yesterday's tabloids that were on offer.

"Happy Xmas (War is Over)", John Lennon sang. The only reminder it was Christmas Day was the tinsel and fairy lights lining the window that blinked on and off. My eyes returned to my hot cup of tea. I remembered the old cliché saying, "Is my glass half full or is my glass half empty?"

Until now it had always been half full.

CHAPTER NINETEEN

Changing the Goal Posts

The radiotherapy at the central London hospital was scheduled to begin on 9th January 2013. With the High Court ruling in favour of the conventional treatment, I was desperate to launch my appeal and present the safer ways I had found to treat Neon. Moreover, if the court saw no other choice than the "gold standard" protocol, I wanted him to have access to supportive therapies alongside it.

A bulk of the evidence I had ready to submit showed the benefits of complementary therapies such as hyperthermia: many of the harmful side effects of the chemotherapy and radiotherapy would be dramatically reduced, while enhancing any beneficial effects they *may* have had.

Having come to terms with the restrictions in place as a result of the suffocating 1939 Cancer Act and understanding there was no choice except for Neon to have the mainstream treatments, proton beam therapy (PBT) seemed the logical solution considering the severity of the long-term side effects would be reduced. PBT was an advanced radiotherapy technology and less aggressive. I had been sending out the information I had been provided with to get my family on board to help pay. As a result of talking regularly to the SAH Care Proton specialists, everything was set in place at the Hampton Proton Therapy Institute in Virginia. All I had to do was get him there. My parents offered to sell their house. Ben also agreed and said if the NHS would agree to it, he would allow it.

Unlike the conventional radiation, PBT delivered the radiation precisely, minimising the amount of radiation that is received meaning less damage to healthy tissue. PBT had already taken over as the preferred method of delivering radiation for paediatrics in the United States for a child diagnosed with medulloblastoma. Proton beam would reduce the risk of secondary cancers and minimise the risk of damage to the spine, heart, lungs, abdominal organs and brain. This is especially important for children as their bodies are growing and their skulls are still developing and more sensitive to radiation. Children are the most susceptible to the development of secondary cancers as a result of orthodox cancer treatment methods.

My solicitor Imran Khan planned to lodge my appeal by 2 January 2013. Imran asked me to fill out legal aid forms to finance the appeal, and although it was a matter of great urgency, he said he could not move forward until legal aid was granted. He assured me that I was eligible for funding and persevered accordingly.

I needed the judge to agree that Neon could have proton beam therapy in America and then be treated by Dr Herzog where I would take him to stay at his clinic in Nidda, Germany. Given the mountain of evidence proving the benefits, how could Neon be denied a less damaging procedure embracing a therapeutic approach that included a full package of integrated therapies offsetting the toxic side effects from the traditional treatment?

Hyperthermia was an accepted practice in Germany when treating children, alongside various therapies including metabolic therapy: the use of natural food and vitamins to prevent and treat disease by building a strong immune system. Intravenous antioxidant therapy with vitamin C, selenium and B-complex. Infusions with high doses of antioxidants to quench the free radicals that would otherwise run free in the body. There was also immunomodulation, magnetic field therapy, ozone therapy, oxygen therapy and orthomolecular therapy. It was all so much kinder while focusing on nursing the body back to health. Even bicarbonate of soda can have amazing results. Hydrogen peroxide, cannabis oil (CBD) – there are many powerful anticancer approaches, the list is long, and cure strategies can be simple and effective, yet none of these non-patentable therapies is embraced by the NHS. How much longer will we allow our healthcare system to demonise natural treatments in favour of pharmaceutical medication? Bringing back an honest balance can only be beneficial. With nobody funding the much-needed double-blind studies, the paradoxical dilemma continues.

The basic philosophy of complementary therapies incorporates holistic care. Even when intertwined with conventional medicine, integrated treatment regimes treat the whole person. Naturopathic medicine is a medical system with deeply embedded roots in Germany that has been further developed in America. You are hard-pushed to find something similar in the UK that focuses on facilitating the body's innate healing response. Because of legislation, clinics in the UK prevent children from receiving such therapies. German integrative clinics do lesser doses of the conventional treatment and only if required. The basic principles of integrative medicine are sensible; a philosophy that neither rejects the conventional methods nor accepts complementary measures uncritically.

Focus begins with detoxification and a healthful diet helping to move toxins out of the body, rather than adding to the body's toxic load. Complementary clinics recognise that cancer thrives in an acidic body. One of their main strategies is to support the body in maintaining homeostasis by providing the right tools and encouraging an alkaline environment through consumption of a proper diet. It is recognised an underlying cause of cancer is low cellular oxygen levels. Using oxygenating methods/therapies has shown to be beneficial to combating cancer.

This has been proven by research at Nobel Prize level. Why are our healthcare practitioners not taught this and incorporating it within the healthcare service?

If cancer struggles to survive in an oxygen-rich alkaline body, why is it not a routine procedure to use supplemental oxygen therapies as part of the protocol as well as ozone therapy? This is greatly enhanced with a healthy diet/lifestyle and nutrition is of crucial importance. What we put into our mouths can slowly heal us or help feed cancer. We have to ask the questions and wonder why our healthcare providers have put all their eggs in one basket and rely entirely on highly toxic pharmaceutical methods. To move forward successfully, we must review the whole ethos of cancer treatment and leave no stone unturned.

Imagine the improvement to our healthcare system if we embraced a balanced approach by incorporating natural therapies and were told by our physicians to *fight cancer by increasing cellular oxygen levels*. If nutrition was part of their training, they would tell us to *support your body and provide it with living nutrient-dense foods and avoid dead nutrient-devoid foods*. How are we going to conquer cancer when our approach is not integrated and opting only towards harmful (deadly) measures?

David Wolfe says, "success is a refined study of the obvious. Everything is about getting in tune with the obvious." When it comes to treating cancer, how can something so obvious be ignored? Outlawing natural solutions is not only scandalous, but it's also unlawful and a crime against humanity. Until we achieve a balanced and fair healthcare system, we are up the creek without a paddle.

While building my case, supportive emails continued to pour into my inbox. The name, Burzynski, kept popping up. A few people sent me DVDs with details about his advanced cancer treatment available in America. Burzynski had developed a biochemical defence system that activates genes in cancer cells reprogramming them to self-destruct. The high success rate over thirty years which Burzynski demonstrated, prompted the FDA to run a study on children where the conventional treatment had failed. The studies confirmed his treatment worked with no ill side effects.

Antineoplastons are based on what stimulates the patient's cancer. Their goal: to use the most sophisticated approach to treating cancer by customising each individual patient's care and treatment plan. Exactly what I wanted, Neon to be treated as an individual. Implementing "personalised medicine", employing the most current available technology to help identify *if* there is a problem, using a type of cancer treatment with a much safer, more precise and gentler approach, *should it be needed*. The American clinic's letter stated, "we customise our treatment for every patient based on identification of targets and implementation of targeted therapies, not blindly treating patients based on their type and stage of cancer."

Watching the testimonials and learning about antineoplastons, I thought it to be another preferred choice for Neon but when I contacted the clinic and explained Neon's circumstances the timing could not have been worse.

"Typically this would be the ideal case that Dr Burzynski has been successful with, but at this time the clinical trial that it is under has a hold placed on it by the FDA. We are currently unable to take paediatrics. We are hoping to have this hold removed early into the New Year, but do not know for certain."

With such restricted treatment options in the UK, a part of the problem was the draconian 1939 Cancer Act, which made it illegal to claim that any nonstandard approach could be used to combat cancer.

I had recently learnt about Lord Saatchi who had lost his beloved wife to cancer and wanted to pass a medical innovation bill through Parliament. His bill implied that the sort of experimentation that leads science forward is presently discouraged by the fear of legal suits.

"Innovation is deviation", Lord Saatchi states his claim. "So non-deviation is non-innovation, and here you have the explanation for why there is no cure for cancer. It's as simple as that."

It is hard for anyone to imagine how damaging the treatment is unless you have experienced it yourself or witnessed a loved one go through the pain, the torment and the humiliation.

Saatchi articulates:

> You have drugs that are over forty years old. You have surgical procedures that are over forty years old. You have a survival rate that is the same as forty years ago and the damage done to the immune system by the treatment is so severe that it's hard to know if the patient dies from the cancer or the treatment. All cancer deaths are wasted lives. Scientific knowledge does not advance by one-centimetre as a result of all these deaths, because the current law requires that the deceased receive only a standard procedure – the endless repetition of a failed experiment. In this way, the current law is a barrier to progress in curing cancer.

Nobody was in a more perfect position to fight the debate than Lord Saatchi. He nailed it. Yet even he was open to insults of "quackery", with an army of pro-treatment trolls running rampant ready to discredit anything he exposed, using deceptive ploys fostering mistrust, alleging the conventional "science-based, life-saving" medicine is the only means forward, despite Saatchi's continued efforts illustrating pertinent points.

> *I am not aware that the cancer dead or the victims of any other terrible disease are guilty of any crime. Death by hanging, by firing squad, by electric chair – no human being has ever devised a more brutal execution than death by cancer. Either way, those condemned by cancer suffer a worse fate than the worst mass murderer. While they await execution, they are tortured.*

———

I had always thought where there is a will there is a way, but the hurdles were getting higher. Every way I turned, I was blocked. I had been turned down for legal aid even though Imran confirmed I had a strong case and was eligible for public funding.

"It is our considered view that the Legal Services Commission (LSC) has incorrectly assessed our client's means."

The LSC disagreed without any justifiable grounds.

Imran and his partners of the firm who had reviewed the funding provision were of the view that the legal services commission had made a mistake.

"It would seem that you are now changing the goal posts in applying the criteria for my client's application."

Despite the ongoing correspondence and my situation meeting all of the criteria, the LSC was unable to confirm reasoning for the hitherto long delay or why my legal aid had been denied.

Imran proposed to make representations and get the LSC to get my public funding reinstated and lodge an appeal on that basis. However, all the procrastinating meant the treatment was about to begin, and there was nothing I could do about it.

Imran warned me that for now all we could do was wait. The cost of an appeal would be at least £80,000, and without legal aid, he would "need money in the kitty" before he could act as my lawyer and lodge my appeal.

CHAPTER TWENTY

Protons v Photons

On the 9th of January 2013, I arrived early in the morning at the hospital to meet with Dr Gadd, who was in charge of the radiology department. Dr Gadd said he was familiar with Dr Chang, the Proton Professor in America, yet claimed "there were no benefits to proton beam" and remained adamant there was to be "no more delay and treatment would start today".

Having provided Dr Gadd with the extensive email trail, including hard evidence proving PBT to be a more advanced and beneficial therapy, I thought he would agree it was in Neon's best interests to allow me to take him to America. However, Dr Gadd brushed me off and insisted: "Protons are no better than photons".

For over an hour I sat in his office trying to reason with him and two other nurses who were busy taking notes. Unable to accept the X-ray radiation treatment, I showed him the peer-reviewed reports and information I had printed out in the proton beams' favour, but Dr Gadd smugly reminded me of the

High Court ruling emphasising that there was nothing I could do without the authority of the court.

'Perhaps it is because it is unavailable in the UK and you have not received any training in proton beam therapy that you do not understand its advantages?' I suggested.

'I doubt that,' he replied callously.

When Neon and Ben arrived at the hospital, I was sitting in the radiology basement waiting room and stood up and held my arms out for Neon.

'What are you doing here?' Ben snapped.

'I've come to be with Neon,' I replied.

'We don't need you here, Sally. Go home.' Ben was furious. His eyes bulged from anger.

Neon looked at me with sadness in his eyes, holding Tallulah his treasured Jellycat tiger tightly up to his chest.

'Do us all a favour and leave,' Ben fumed, pulling Neon towards the looming ominous double doors.

Neon looked back misty-eyed almost losing his balance, still unsteady on his feet from the operation. Not wanting to make a scene I stood glued to the spot unable to hide the look of horror on my face as Ben lead Neon towards the radiation unit.

My seven-year-old boy had to trust the grown-ups who made his choices for him. He had no idea he was about to endure a treatment that as well as leaving him bald, sick and unable to eat, could potentially scar him both physically and mentally and make him drug dependent for life.

With my son's physiological and neurological health at stake, I feared what lay in wait on the other side of the doors. He would be asked to strip down to his underpants, lie on a hard table top and be fitted with a heavy-duty made-to-measure face and chest mask and then be bolted and screwed down to the table. How would he cope when the offensively loud beeper would go off alerting everyone to evacuate the room and then left alone, unable to move a muscle in the pre-moulded sci-fi plastic mesh shell, paralysed and facing an imposing radiation device resembling a vast robotic iron hand which would come at him and twist around his body? How would he feel being abandoned and left helpless in complete isolation for twenty minutes while the intimidating irradiating instrument spiralled around him and performed its duty?

Proton beam therapy was going to be available in the UK from 2018. The NHS acknowledged the benefits on their website. They had a list of different cancers for which they flew some patients abroad for treatment, but not medulloblastoma.

The representative for PBT in America said, "Neon is a perfect candidate for proton beam."

He also suggested Neon begin treatment in the USA and I could raise the necessary funds later. I was in full agreement, but unable to appeal and override the judge's decision, my rights were taken away. In a desperate attempt to make an application to the High Court, Linda had found me another solicitor.

At first the new hired gun was all fired up and set upon finding me a heavyweight expert who would be able to convince the judge that proton beam therapy and Dr Herzog's treatments were acceptable and better for Neon. My new lawyer's professional manner and optimistic disposition had me believe he would have me back in court in no time. However, after I received his invoice at the end of the month and paid him the £5,000, which was all of the raised funds through the NeonAppeal at GoFundMe, without moving forward at all I had to let him go.

'Well that was a lot of money for getting nowhere,' I said to him before transferring the funds.

'Mmmm,' he replied, 'I'm sorry you did not regard us as more helpful.'

I wrote an open letter to David Cameron. It was an appeal to the Prime Minister, not just as the leader of the country but also as a parent who loved his family above all else.

Mr Cameron on 24 October 2012, my heart was 'torn apart' when I was first told that Neon had a brain tumour, but now it's being 'ripped to shreds'; helplessly watching him suffer, knowing that the power to help him has been forced out of my hands. As our Prime Minister, you have the power and authority to overturn the NHS' decision and arrange for Neon's safe passage to America to start the proton beam therapy and other therapies immediately.

Time is of the essence and I am doing all in my 'limited' power to raise £250,000 to mount a court appeal for Neon to receive the necessary treatments abroad. Mr Cameron, the power is in your hands to end this blatant miscarriage of justice and save my son today.

The Prime Minister did not respond. However, my local MP in Brighton, Caroline Lucas, did get in touch but only to explain there was nothing she could do.

On a national policy level, I do have concerns about the Government's cuts to legal aid and I have done all I can to oppose them as they have passed through Parliament. The questions of whether you receive legal aid for your case is a decision for the Legal Services Commission and one which I, as your MP, am not in the position to intervene over.

————

'One of the side effects of radiotherapy which will happen almost definitely in the third week is hair falling out. Could you please get Neon's hair cut to lessen the ordeal?' I said to Ben over the phone.

'You want me to get his hair cut?' Ben questioned.

'Yes, Ben, you need to… very soon it's going to fall out in big clumps. Imagine how traumatised Neon will be, not if, but when that starts to happen. It will not be nearly so bad if you get his hair cut short.'

When I next saw Neon, Ben had respected my wishes and even gone military style himself. As the treatment went on, it was hard to know what I could do or say to make it any easier. Neon needed reassurance that he was going to be okay.

'Mummy, why are they doing this to me? Why are they making me so sick?'

'The people who work at the hospital are doing what they think is best. You know how you had surgery because you had a brain tumour, well the radiation treatment is what they believe they should do to make sure it does not come back.'

'But hasn't it gone already?' Neon asked. 'They took it out. I had the operations, and they took it all out?'

'Yes, it has all gone,' I answered.

'But the hospital is making me sick, not better. I don't want any more.'

Neon may have only been seven, but it did not take much to figure out they had a strange way of making him *better*.

Once bolted down to the table in his custom-made blue mask all that was exposed were his lips and eyes. Imprisoned in the mesh mask, the highly adept team would give Neon his hand-picked blanket, and he was allowed his trusty Tallulah. Hamstrung and immobilised, terror-stricken, he found it petrifying and would not let go of my hand. His eyes welled up with tears; he would plead with me not to leave the room. With the warning alarm ringing loudly and the nurse hurrying me out of the room, it was impossibly heart-wrenching.

'Mummy, I don't want to go there anymore. Every time I go to the hospital I feel okay, but they make me feel bad.'

'I know you don't want to go, Neon. I'm so sorry, but they say we don't have a choice.'

Elektra too was having a hard time understanding what was going on. 'Make them stop, Mummy. They are making him worse. Neon was okay before he started having the treatment.'

Before radiotherapy, he looked like a normal little boy. Several sessions of radiation later he looked grey and gaunt and sick and tired. Thinking back to what the Bristol consultant referred to as "frying his brain", these words rang true but it wasn't just his brain being fried, it was all down his spine too. Neon was bringing up bright yellow bile. He was off his food and rapidly losing weight, his skin looked burnt, the skin pigmentation was dramatically affected on the areas where he was being treated (neck and spine). Whatever little food Neon did manage to eat he had trouble holding down. The anti-sickness medication would stop him from constantly being sick, but they kept having to up the dose. He was fed up of being poked and prodded and wanted to be left alone.

The protocol stated that the course of radiation was due to run for six weeks; five days a week with the weekends off. Although Neon was going to the hospital every weekday, he was an outpatient and travelling to and fro by taxi from Knightsbridge. Elektra and I were living close by in an apartment I had spontaneously rented in Chelsea Harbour for the next six months. Needing to be close to Elektra's school and a short distance away from Neon, I used the money I had received from my "one-month deal" with the newspaper. Despite my continued efforts, over the coming weeks the only times I got to see Neon were at the hospital or on the doorstep of Ben's parents' flat. Even Elektra's time had been restricted as Neon was not keen to do much apart from build dens around himself. Elektra wanted nothing more than to be with her brother and strongly disliked her new school, which made the drive up the King's Road to take her there more and more difficult.

I attempted to take Neon for HBO several times and to have him over to my apartment, but it proved too difficult. After daily radiation and the weekly vincristine chemotherapy drug, all he wanted was to be in the comfort of his own familiar surroundings at his grandparents' place, where he had been spending time since he was born.

When Lucy told me "you are just not fun. He wants to go to SeaWorld, not the hyperbaric chamber." I took on board what she said and tried to lighten up. Although going through the worst time of my life and watching my son going through the unimaginable, it was near impossible to depict happiness, least of all fun.

As well as Ben not wanting me or Elektra around, the hospital had appointed a social worker to report on my every move. I was told Neon did not want any further oxygen therapy, and I was threatened with supervised access as well as recommending that I speak with one of the hospital councillors. I was told by Ben's legal team that "so far, you have not proved yourself trustworthy when it comes to being responsible for Neon's care."

Even accusations of madness or instability would not keep me away. In the coming weeks, while Neon was having radiation, because of a low red blood count (borderline), he had to have two blood transfusions (protocol). With the hospital in full control, I was not in a position to question their medical ethics. I continued to provide Ben with information about the advanced treatments in America and Germany, but since the treatment had commenced, he had become disinterested.

'Sally, Neon is not going anywhere. Just let the hospital get on with it.'

After the first week of treatment, I had become a shaky wreck. It only got worse. I could feel my whole head vibrating. I was petrified for Neon, who was also shaking and I could not see how the radiation could continue with how ill it was making him. I had been publicly grilled over how I could not want this treatment for my son. Witnessing it first-hand I questioned how anyone could think to inflict suffering in the name of healing was at all acceptable. After successful surgery, he should have been out of the danger zone, not thrown face-first into it.

Thinking the appeal would happen any day I still had hope, but the lead radiologist, Dr Gadd, was not providing what the team in America required – Neon's individual treatment plan. It became evident there was no personal individual treatment plan. Dr Gadd provided me with the phase one, craniospinal radiotherapy plan and the phase two, posterior fossa plan which was to be given with RapidArc, a form of intensity modulated arc therapy (IMAT). I had gone through the whole procedure to get *the plan*: it took perseverance and time. Due to the NHS' policy, all requests for information had to be made in writing with a signature, and after weeks of being at a standstill my lawyer had got involved.

All that effort to obtain an individual plan, only to be provided with the umbrella standard CCLG treatment plan. The guidelines were not specific to Neon yet formed the basis of his treatment. The proton beam specialist, Dr Chang, found it hard to believe there was no individual plan. It emphasised how the "gold standard" treatment was a "one-size-fits-all" protocol.

Without fail, my mother came to the hospital every day, and although Ben did not make us feel welcome we persevered. We all gathered in the waiting area outside Dr Gadd's room for the scheduled appointment on 23 January 2013, but well and truly on the conveyor belt, it was difficult to get off. Neon had been having treatment for two weeks; having had eleven sessions he had four weeks of radiotherapy left to go. The hospital's tight grip on Neon was suffocating but seeing the frightful effects taking hold I refused to stop pursuing. The PBT specialist had reassured me we could continue the second half of the treatment with them. Having had several conference calls with Dr Chang and the directors of SAH Global and being in constant contact with the UK representative, I was raring to go. I went to the hospital to meet with Dr Gadd, who was sporadically replying to my emails, above all, ignoring my requests to transfer his treatment.

'Oh my, there are so many of you. I don't think you can all fit into my office, would you mind waiting outside?' Dr Gadd asked Lucy who had her friend Sarah with her; the Smoking Pony producer. An unimpressed Lucy suggested, 'Shouldn't Sally's mother be the one to wait outside?'

'And who is this?' Dr Gadd asked looking at Sarah.

'Come on, Lucy, we will sit in the waiting area,' Sarah said backing away.

There were three clinicians including Dr Gadd, a member of the multidisciplinary team and a nurse taking notes, Ben, Neon, myself and my mum.

'Hello, Neon, how are you?' Dr Gadd glared at Neon.

'Good,' Neon replied looking at the floor and clasping Tallulah for comfort.

'How do you like your treatment so far?' Dr Gadd asked, leaning back in his chair and supporting his head with both hands.

'G… g… good,' Neon stuttered, his eyes not leaving the floor.

My eyes caught my mother's, whose facial expression told me she found the question equally as patronising. I knew I was skating on thin ice and had to stop myself asking Dr Gadd how he would like the treatment if it were him.

'Well, you are doing well, Neon.' Dr Gadd grinned, his intense gaze never leaving Neon. 'We are all very pleased.'

'Yes,' Ben added. 'He is responding very well.'

My mouth fell open in utter disbelief. We couldn't possibly be talking about the same boy. I was almost as repulsed by Ben's comment as Dr Gadd's. I had to stop myself muttering what I was thinking, *what an idiot*.

Words cannot describe how awful Neon looked and felt from the radiotherapy. He resembled *a limp rag doll with the stuffing knocked out of him*. Responding well to treatment? It was crippling him. I dared not think of the poor little mites who did not respond well if Neon represented a child who did. Although I found Dr Gadd to speak in a condescending manner, he was the man in charge, and I needed to talk to him. Sensing Neon's discomfort, I was relieved when he asked him to go to the art room with Ben. With his obnoxious undertone and fierce disposition, Neon undoubtedly found Dr Gadd to be intimidating, as did I.

'I can only presume you have not received my most recent emails as you have not replied?' I persevered. 'To avoid further harm, I would like Neon to be released so I can take him to America for proton beam therapy.'

'I am dreadfully sorry, Sally. I have seen your emails; however, it is a Trust policy to withhold certain information. I do hope you appreciate we get all sorts of requests... besides, I have already informed you that proton beam is of no use for medulloblastoma.'

'That is not what I have been told,' I replied. 'Specialists trained in protons have suggested the complete opposite. It would not be causing as much damage as your photon radiation. Dr Gadd, I have been asking for an individual plan, but it seems Neon does not have one. I am worried about how your treatment is affecting Neon. This cannot be a child doing well. Neon cannot physically or mentally cope with any more. He looks and feels awful. Proton therapy would not have this devastating effect on him, and we would avoid the X-ray radiation's "expected" long-term side effects. Please allow me to take Neon to America for the remainder of his treatment.'

'Mrs Roberts, with regards to protons, I am not supportive of your plan to take him abroad for proton treatment for phase two. I do not believe there is any significant clinical benefit for protons over photons delivered with an IMAT technique. I do not believe that a seamless transition from completion of phase one to the start of phase two is at all practicable. Finally, you do not need to be reminded that we are treating Neon here under the instruction of the High Court. For you to take Neon away from here, against my advice, to another country for treatment would, I believe, be in contempt of their order, unless you sought and were granted the prior authorisation of the court.'

———

Shortly after the appointment with Dr Gadd, I lost hope of Neon receiving the proton beam therapy when I received an email from the SAH Global correspondent:

> Dr Chang has still not received Neon's specific treatment plan and given that Neon will complete the first phase of his treatment on Monday, there is not enough time now to plan for the second phase using protons in the USA. We are sorry that there is not much more we can do at this stage. We are hoping and praying that Neon's chances in life are not prejudiced in any way by his treatment.

The Alliance for Natural Health put what I faced into words perfectly:

> To put it mildly, the NHS has shown itself in this instance to be so mired in dogma that it cannot deviate from a predetermined 'treatment pathway' – even when doing so could enormously improve the quality of Neon's later life.

The existence of a precedent in similar cases also raises worrying questions over the motivations of Neon's medical team: are they more concerned with saving face than with saving a young boy's future, more worried about preserving the integrity of their precious 'standard treatment pathways' than with preserving a decent function level for Neon?

Several times throughout the radiotherapy, Neon commented when he was left alone in the treatment room he could smell onions. I can only presume that it was the stench of the radioactive particles. I had pre-warning about the eradicating side effects of the radiation, but nothing could have prepared me to see Neon's health declining so rapidly.

To bear witness to your son not remembering what he ate for breakfast that morning and forgetting what he was saying mid-sentence as a result of cancer-prevention therapy was heartbreaking. My mother too was panic-stricken. It was painful to see Neon suffer and have difficulty with simple activities of everyday living because of the treatment. We discussed our concerns.

'I know it's all relative in terms of common reactions but how can Ben and that cruel doctor's assumption be that this is a little boy who is responding well?' I frowned. 'Neon looked good before treatment. It's only been two weeks, what are another four weeks going to do? What do they mean by that he is doing well? That he's still standing?'

'It is sickening.' Mum expressed bitterly. 'I feel awful for Neon. That doctor's manner was so patronising. How could he have asked Neon how did he "like" his treatment?'

'I have never encountered such arrogance,' I replied.

'It's all about making himself superior at our expense,' Mum continued. 'Neon could have had proton treatment and not been harmed in the way that he is now. I do not understand why they have not allowed you to take him to America.'

'The trouble is Dr Gadd is a photon radiation professor. His area of expertise is the management of cancer in children with *X-ray* radiation. It's the only way he knows how. It is the focus of his career. How can we expect a man who is only trained in photons to know anything about protons?' I remarked. 'His ignorance is causing Neon to deteriorate. It is medical negligence. It is a crime they are preventing Neon from receiving a safer, less aggressive treatment. They are making an example of him and forcefully administering an incorrect treatment. How are we going to reverse the catastrophic after-effects that are already taking hold?'

———

The end of treatment summary written by Dr Matthew Gadd, read as follows:

Craniospinal radiotherapy completed 20.02.13. In the first phase of treatment, the whole brain and spine were treated to a dose of 23.4Gy in 13 fractions at 1.8Gy/fraction using 6MV photons. In the second phase of treatment, an additional 30.6Gy was delivered in 17 fractions at 1.8/fractions again using 6MV photons with a dual RapidArc technique. During treatment Neon also had weekly concomitant Vincristine. The final administration of this is due on 1 March 2013. I saw Neon on the last day of his treatment together with his mother, maternal grandmother, father and sister. I am pleased to say that he seems to have tolerated this treatment remarkably well and has developed no side effects or complications other than those which would be expected. I have made no arrangements to see him again he will be seen by Dr Damien Harper on 25 February who will be responsible for his continuing chemotherapy over the next twelve months.

It was a matter of uncertainty why a cocktail of radiotherapy and chemotherapy were given together. Therefore, I questioned it. 'How long has this been in place for standard risk medulloblastoma? Isn't it unusual to give radiotherapy and chemotherapy together?'

'As I have explained to you before, Neon has been treated in this way as the CCLG guidance incorporates the international evidence base. Chemotherapy is more Damien's area than mine, so I hope he can explain more to you. As my part in Neon's treatment is now complete, I shall not enter into any further correspondence. Damien has taken over responsibility now.'

———

Neon's body broken by toxicity, the man in charge overseeing this excruciating process simply wiping his hands clean of us, his job was done. Neon's spirit was crushed. What hair remained was white and brittle. He looked deeply troubled and as a result of the radiation treatment was left with a ghost-like image of his former child self.

So how did our hospitals come to use a treatment that produces free radicals in the hope of healing by damaging the DNA of tumour cells (and all others), or in Neon's case (as a preventive) a phantom floating cell (if there was one)?

A free radical by definition is a molecule with an unpaired electron. You do not have to be a scientist to appreciate that bombarding the body with free radicals is a risky business. The X-ray radiation damages molecular structures, affecting non-cancerous cells. Cells that were healthy and as a result of radiotherapy, many would be damaged beyond repair. The potential risks of using such toxic treatment on my tumourless son far outweighed any benefits and could cause what they are said to be treating, yet it is all that is on offer in our hospitals as our mainstream cancer treatment.

Creating free radicals is dangerous and can have a counterproductive effect in more ways than one. Free radicals through the process of oxidation have the capacity to damage and destroy DNA, enzymes, fats and proteins. Causing damage to cells and DNA boosts the possibility of disease; it doesn't cure it.

The other "hit or miss" part of the much-feared trio-package-deal is chemical therapy. Chemotherapeutic drugs are also known to be mutagenic and cytotoxic. In a Q&A on CNN's website, a viewer asked if one of the chemotherapy drugs given to her husband may have caused his secondary cancer. Dr Otis Brawley, the chief medical officer of the American Cancer Society responded, "It is ironic but true that many cancer chemotherapies are known to cause cancers."

Is this not insanely tragic? Harming us in the name of medicine, praying (fingers crossed) it will work (but we may make you worse or kill you). The only hope we have to find a real cure is by re-evaluating the way our healthcare system attempts to overcome cancer.

It is crucial to understand why "many oncologists take the position that antioxidants by their nature undermine the free radical mechanism of chemotherapy and radiotherapy and should, therefore, be avoided during treatment," explained by Ralph Moss in a PubMed Abstract: Do antioxidants interfere with radiation therapy for cancer?

How many of us know that protection against oxidation (free radicals) can be obtained from antioxidants such as vitamins A, C and E?

If you and I know about this and we are not medical professionals, why do our experts on health ignore how valuable antioxidants are at a time when health-related quality of life (or even life itself) depends on it?

There is strong evidence according to Ralph Moss that "dietary antioxidants do not conflict with the use of radiotherapy and may significantly mitigate the adverse effects of that treatment." Because of research showing that high doses of intravenous vitamin C can benefit cancer patients, it is included in many integrated anticancer regimes.

Dr Ronald Hoffman tells us "research has shown that high concentrations of vitamin C can stop growth, or even kill a wide range of cancer cells. Only intravenous administration of vitamin C can deliver the high doses found to be effective against cancer."

At the London hospital, I was told by the medics not to give antioxidants while Neon was receiving radiation and chemotherapy. As Ben… and Lucy (who had taken a remarkable interest) accepted everything the hospital recommended as gospel, I sent them several peer-reviewed studies indicating that nutrients such as antioxidants had the potential to neutralise free radicals during radiation therapy and could reduce the treatment-related side effects.

Antioxidant supplementation while receiving the conventional treatment poses a conundrum for oncologists because antioxidants administered to protect normal healthy cells may provide the same benefits to cancerous cells, therefore reducing the effectiveness of the radiation and/or chemotherapy.

Whereas, the German integrated clinics encourage antioxidant booster infusions. It is dependent on the clinic and protocol at what stage they are administered. Ralph Moss reports "many integrative practitioners believe that antioxidants taken during cancer treatment not only alleviate some of the adverse effects of that treatment but also enhance the efficacy of cancer therapy."

Again we have the other side of the coin commonly ignored by our dominant health service providers. The Journal of Nutrition reveals "new findings that antioxidants induce apoptosis in cancer cells and protect patients from painful side effects of radiation treatment may prove these compounds useful in future adjuvant therapy."

Without everyone singing from the same hymn sheet, it was unrealistic to pursue a structured supplemental plan of any complexity without Neon in my care. However, with so much damage done and the hospital not taking charge of a detox/clean-up programme, someone had to deal with the mess. Like a nuclear bomb dropped on an innocent village. Who cleans up the hazard zone? The medics were experts in creating treatment-induced toxicity with little in place to deal with the destructive aftermath.

My aim was to lean towards a diet rich in antioxidants to target the rampant free radicals and to supplement essential nutrients. I devised a plan catered towards boosting Neon's immune system. This included increasing the protein content of his diet.

Proteins are composed of amino acids, which are the building blocks of our bodies. Their essential role includes repairing cells, tissues and organs and building DNA. Neon was happy to take supplements like spirulina when he was with me. Having provided Ben with various oils, powders and capsules, I could only trust he was giving them to him.

Another supplement that Neon needed was essential fatty acids (EFAs), ideally, through foods he ate and supplementing oils like flaxseed oil and hempseed oil. Our bodies do not make essential fats (omegas 3,6 and 9). They need to be provided through diet.

Considering the stance of the hospital proclaiming to be *anti*-antioxidants, I was advised not to give high-grade fish oils or chlorella alongside chemotherapy in case it prevented drugs such as cisplatin from "doing their job". However, research and reviews tell us they improve the well-being of cancer patients and superfoods such as chlorella can help to negate the effects of chemotherapy and radiation.

It is all very well to fixate on killing cancer (if it's in the body) but what about the patient?

Chlorella is one of the best sources of radiation mop-up as well as promoting cell/DNA repair. Well-sourced freshwater micro-algae such as chlorella and spirulina are bursting with nutrients and phytochemicals that can boost health and fight disease. Together with its detoxifying potential and nutrient-dense profile, chlorophyl-rich chlorella supports the body and has been shown to help minimise the toxic effects of conventional therapies. It would be beneficial for superfoods with immune-enhancing and anticancer properties to be offered in protocols to combat cancer. They can only improve the results, not hinder them.

One of the many issues, while Neon endured treatment, was the lack of support to the function of his liver. The liver is our main detoxification organ, and throughout treatment, it was going to be working hard to break down the liver-toxic medications and foreign substances.

Why was detoxification not part of the protocol? To be loading the body with lethal doses of radiation and chemically drenched drugs and only a saline solution to help "flush" it through? Surely the medical profession can offer more than that?

Neon's little liver would need all the help it could get to repair. It was heavily burdened detoxifying all the chemicals. There are ways to detox on a cellular level (apart from chlorella); dandelion and zeolite are two good examples. However, there were strictly pharmaceutically supplied drugs in the hospital. Turning a blind eye to proven natural solutions demonstrates the imbalance within our healthcare system.

Having seen the benefits from using it myself, I supplied Neon with milk thistle and asked Ben to give Neon at least ten drops of tincture in the morning (before food) alternating with silymarin capsules.

Milk thistle is a medicinal therapeutic compound shown to be beneficial in preventing and repairing damage to our liver. It should not be overlooked while receiving harsh liver-toxic therapies. There was a long list of what needed to be done, but with Neon living with his father, I needed Ben on board to implement it.

CHAPTER TWENTY-ONE

Taken its Toll

Neon, Elektra and I decided to have a party inviting friends from Devon and London to come and join us in Chelsea Harbour. It was to celebrate their eighth birthday, which fell in April 2013. I hid Neon and Elektra's presents all around the flat, including the biggest soft toys I could find. I bought Elektra a pink unicorn so big you could sit on it, and for Neon a huge cuddly tiger. Elektra was her usual cheerful self, but Neon looked and felt burnt and had difficulty eating breakfast before anyone arrived. He sat propping himself up with his arm on the table, his forehead in his hand with his head hanging almost touching the bowl.

Chemotherapy was scheduled to begin the following week. We had not discussed that he had to go back to the hospital after his birthday to begin the next stage of his treatment. All Neon wanted to do was build a world-within-a-world fort around himself and hide away.

Before the diagnosis, Neon had loved playing games and, like most children, just wanted to have fun. When everyone arrived at our apartment, being surrounded by his friends was hard. He felt "different" and withdrawn. It was also difficult for people to see him like that. His friends hardly recognised him, and could not hide the look of complete shock when they saw him, and to top it off Neon was feeling anything but playful. He had the *look of cancer*. Translation: the *look of the treatment for cancer*. He was frazzled. The few hairs remaining on his head stuck up like he had been electrocuted. His skin was rough and patchy, and he was severely underweight: having lost 4kg since radiation he was now 18kg. Already slender, it was weight he could not afford to lose. He could not walk in a straight line and found it hard to balance. He was like a feather blowing around in the wind. The expressions on friends' faces said it all, but none were as traumatised as Neon who refused to have his picture taken.

It was a beautiful early spring day. All the children except Neon were running around playing and hiding behind trees. We lay down a blanket on the grass overlooking the boats in Chelsea harbour but Neon was an emotional wreck, I have never seen him so frustrated and unhappy. He stood up, unsteadily veering from side to side and stumbled back towards the flat. 'I want to go back inside,' he cried.

'It's okay, Neon, let's go back we can sit inside together. Sometimes I prefer to be alone too.'

He went straight into my bedroom and shut himself in my cupboard and cried his eyes out. Six weeks of radiation had reduced him to a shaky shadow of the boy he once was. He had lost all of his energy, his confidence, his playfulness, his sense of humour and his self-worth. The look of cancer is not the look of cancer at all. The look of cancer we have come to know and fear is the look of the treatment.

A friend had recently given me a CD called *Folk Playground*. When we were listening to music, there was one song Neon wanted to listen to over and over again. It was called "Just Kidding" by Jon Gailmor. The lyrics hit a chord every time.

Originally, I had not been totally against chemotherapy. Kevin had made me see the positive side (that he could recover). Although I still considered it unnecessary, I had come to understand the inflexible protocol rather well and saw that we did not have a choice. Because everything I had read claimed that his body could recover from it, I did not fear it as much as the radiation, but I was starting to.

Seeing my once fun-loving son so frail and pale, I grew anxious and extremely apprehensive about what might happen if he had any more risk-filled treatment. The chemotherapy would further decimate his immune system and trigger side effects such as brain fog, hair loss, nausea, hearing and vision problems, stomach ulcers, candidiasis, diarrhoea, oesophageal erosions, cardiac problems, lung problems, liver toxicity, pancreatic problems, muscle wastage and possibly death.

There was an extensive study performed in Germany by Ulrich Abel (biostatistician and epidemiologist), who contacted over 350 medical centres worldwide requesting them to furnish anything they had published on the subject of cancer. By the time he finished his report, he was said to know more about chemotherapy than anyone. His report describes chemotherapy as "a scientific wasteland" and that "there was no scientific evidence that it worked".

———

Early Monday morning I called Ben to discuss if we could postpone the one-year's chemotherapy treatment until Neon was physically and mentally strong enough. My attempt to get the appeal back to court had failed miserably, having been turned down for legal aid and prevented from disputing the judge's decision at the Court of Appeal. The conversation with Ben went just as badly.

'Sally, when are you going to get it into your thick skull that he will die without the treatment,' he yelled down the phone. 'Just let them get on with it for fuck's sake.'

As per protocol, Neon had to have a Port-a-cath. A device fitted under the skin to the right of his chest used to administer intravenous drugs and blood transfusions. With direct access to a central vein, the *health* workers were ready to go. Preparations were in place to suppress his immune system with drugs so toxic, if accidentally spilt on the skin, it would burn more than bleach. If spilt, we would be asked to evacuate the room, and a trained team with protective masks and clothing would deal with the "toxic waste".

Pouring in poison when there was no tumour and no cancer left to fight. The explanation given to me was, "we need to stop cancer from coming back"; an illogical approach if you have any common sense.

Not everyone agrees with the view that it is a choice between "treatment or death". Chemotherapy is controversial. One doctor's statement: "There's a two per cent chance it will cure you and a twenty per cent chance it will kill you." Studies confirm chemotherapy is a variety of carcinogenic chemicals that destroys the immune system and can cause extensive long-term damage.

The founder of Natural News, Mike Adams, makes a good point. "Is it not a crime to inject a child with deadly chemicals against his will and his parents' will? If I loaded a syringe with the exact same chemicals used and injected them into your arm without your permission, I would be charged with attempted murder."

Using heavy immunosuppressive drugs in the hope of killing a phantom cancer cell is madness, yet the majority of people have been led to believe if you do not sign up for it no questions asked then you must be delusional. There is no denying handing yourself (or your child) over to modern-day cancer treatment is a perilous path considering the dangerous toxic levels resulting from these treatments which are capable of producing side effects like full-blown dementia, consequential diseases and death. How can a carcinogenic cause of cancer be remotely close to being considered a cure? Polluting our bodies and contaminating our way back to health does not make well-reasoned sense.

Chemotherapy drugs are designed to kill all fast-dividing, fast-growing cells, whether cancerous cells or normal healthy cells. Chemotherapy and radiation are used because cancer cells are weaker than normal cells, and therefore *may* die first. It is a gamble (a game of chance) what dies first – cancer or the person. The majority of people accept the prescribed nightmare as it is all we have on offer. It is drummed into us that it's life-saving. We are lead to believe it is our best chance. What if we have been misled?

The NHS were jeopardising my son's life in the *hope* they would destroy their (imaginary) target. It was a shot in the dark. They were using his beautiful body as a battlefield they would trash in the process... while *all* cells would be systematically nuked. *Any* cell caught in the act of division would be poisoned with cytotoxic drugs. Neon was tumour-free. How can it be acceptable to use a high-risk treatment as a preventive?

In addition to the dangers and side effects, research shows that chemotherapy can cause healthy cells to release WNT16B, a protein that helps promote cancer cell survival and growth. The result is that chemotherapy can potentially fuel the spread of cancer. Research says not only does this protein protect cancer cells, but it also causes cancer to be resistant to further chemotherapy treatment.

Neon was having routine MRI scans and numerous other tests. Each examination confirmed he remained in the all-clear with no macroscopic cancer cells detected. Howbeit, the NHS had a strict protocol to follow, and because of that, chemotherapy did proceed.

Elektra was sick in the middle of the night when the chemotherapy was pumped into Neon's body the first time. Although at home, his twin sister would throw up simultaneously with Neon when he was in the hospital and rigged up to the chemotherapy drugs.

The treatment was relentless and cruel. On one occasion, Neon was being violently sick, hooked up to the chemical substances and saline solution, projectile vomiting. Following the nurse out of the room, I begged her to stop. She refused and instead increased the dosage of the anti-sickness medicine, which he had been given so many times in different forms and variations it wasn't working. I was amazed at the amount of saline solution used to flush the chemicals through. The process was barbaric. The visible side effects were grim. Not only the way he looked and felt; if he wasn't constipated, it was diarrhoea, extreme pain, cramps, fatigue and on top of it all – total immune system destruction.

––––––

Having come to terms with the fact that the NHS was in complete control, and I was unable to take Neon to America, or Germany, confirmed by Ben that at this stage he would not allow it, I pushed for Neon to be seen at the London Hospital for Integrated Medicine.

However limited, I was keen to explore the use of complementary medicine to address the side effects that Neon was suffering due to the radiation and chemical combination, supporting him physically and emotionally. Even though the integrated hospital was next door to the hospital where Neon was being administered the chemotherapy, we had to wait several months for the appointment. After pushing for a referral, it eventually came through on my birthday in May 2013. I expressed an interest in vitamin B and C infusions, but the doctor looked at me blankly and shook her head. Neon was dreadfully sick as a result of the treatment. However, the integrated doctor commented he was "seen to be generally coping admirably well with this".

We talked about how Neon was suffering from the side effects of the treatment. The expected hair loss and generalised fatigue. Nausea and sickness. We discussed the leg and joint pain in his lower legs and how he was getting auditory issues, including ringing in his ears. After an examination and in-depth conversation with the practitioner analysing his symptoms, I hoped for some relief using any facilities, supplements or recommendations the integrated hospital had.

The "integrated" doctor prescribed some homeopathic remedies and nothing more, telling me that was all she could offer. *Helios* online takes five minutes to order. This appointment, including travel, had taken up most of our day. Given the lack of immune-boosting therapies, it was disappointing. We did not return to the Hospital for Integrated Medicine.

The repetitive cycle of Neon starting to look and feel better but being knocked back by the treatment was dragging on. It was a vicious circle. I wanted to focus on Neon being well again, yet all the hospital was focused on was a tumour that had been removed and consequently, treatment for it. Every six weeks just as he would start to feel a bit better, it was back to the hospital for another round. The proclaimed cancer-prevention poison would slowly drip into his body overnight, and chemotherapy-related nausea and sickness would escalate.

After six cycles of chemotherapy (approximately nine months later), the treatment was stopped due to toxicity, poor weight gain and delayed counts. Dr Harper, who had been in charge since chemotherapy had commenced, agreed with me that Neon could visibly not tolerate any more; his body had had enough. He barely had the energy to walk, and could not stand up straight, he stumbled everywhere and needed support. The fight to survive the treatment had Neon begging for mercy. He was mentally and physically broken.

It was common to stop the treatment since rarely could a child or adult complete the full course. As Neon was already tumour-free before he started treatment, his immune system could handle the toxicity of the radioactive particles and the cytotoxic drugs better than a child with cancer metastasised throughout their body. His body did not have to fight cancer. His body had to survive the treatment.

When the body is fighting cancer, it finds it difficult to deal with the treatment too. I had seen a statistic that sixty per cent of drug treatments prescribed in the UK are not completed, often due to the side effects. Having witnessed first-hand the brutality of the treatment used in our hospitals, it is hardly surprising that eighteen per cent of illnesses are caused by medical treatments. Iatrogenic illnesses are included/expected as part of the package when subjected to such harsh therapies. The anti-sickness medication plays a big part in both radiation and chemotherapy and would be verging on impossible to administer without it.

———

Throughout the summer, Neon attended many follow-up clinical appointments, including routine surveillance imaging and assessments. Every image and examination test, I would cry with relief on hearing NED, "no evidence of disease". Neon's hair was beginning to grow, and he was slowly getting his sparkle back. Finally, with no more treatment scheduled, he could recover.

I too was recuperating, although all my unreleased pent-up energy was causing me to shake. It was impossible for me to hold a pen still, and if anyone came close enough, they could sense my stress-induced vibration. After my short-term rental expired in London, Elektra and I moved to our home in Brighton.

'When can we get Candy back?' Elektra asked.

'I'm not sure we can. Sasha, Julian and the girls have fallen in love with her and have taken her in as one of their family,' I replied.

Tony was unimpressed on hearing the news. 'What do you mean? Candy can't stay in Devon. Neon needs her... he loves that dog.'

'We all do, Tony, but when I said to Sasha about getting Candy back, she flipped out.'

'You gave those friends of yours hundreds if not thousands of pounds' worth of stuff before you left. They took two truckloads, and now she wants to keep your dog? Does she not realise you bred Candy? She probably doesn't know you continued Jasmine's line. They can't keep her. Besides, Neon and Elektra and you need her. She's part of your family, not theirs. Does she not think about what Neon has been through this past year and that he needs his dog back?'

'Sasha wrote me a pretty unsympathetic email saying "I know you have had a tough time I feel for you... we all have tough times, not just you".'

'Well, there's tough, and then there is really tough. You call Sasha and tell her I am coming tomorrow. I'm going to pick up Candy,' Tony declared.

After driving over 200 miles from London to Devon and speaking to Julian, Tony wondered if he was making the right decision. He called me on his way back to Brighton.

'I'm not going to lie, that was one of the hardest things I have ever had to do, but I know I've done what is best for you and the dog. When I opened the door, Candy girl jumped straight into my car as if to say "let's go" and has been looking up at the moon ever since. I've never seen a dog look at the moon before, Sis. I kept thinking have I done the right thing and then I saw a sign,' Tony explained. 'On the side of the road there was a big sign, and it said "Sally's dog".'

'I don't believe you,' I laughed. 'An actual sign? Did you take a picture?'

'Yes, of course. I'll show you when I get there,' he answered.

———

All we needed now was Neon to be home with us, but he was still residing with his father, who lived two hours away. Moreover, stability and security had been stolen from me, on receiving orders to attend the High Court in London for a custody battle as well as being put in a position where I had to fight for the children's and my home. Talk about the straw that *almost* broke the camel's back.

Until now, I had been our children's primary caregiver. I had to fight my ex-husband's team of legal representatives in the High Court; filing statements proving my legitimate expectations based on letters and promises acted upon by me, to my detriment.

The court involved Cafcass, who represented our children. It was a lengthy, intimate process interviewing us all and observing the twins in our homes and the Brighton Cafcass office. Meanwhile, our children were living in limbo. Speaking on behalf of the children in court, the Cafcass representative came to the conclusion that it was in Neon and Elektra's best interests to reside with me. Taking no risks, hiring a barrister for the final hearing, I won custody. However, having not agreed to Ben's terms (custody of the children for him, in exchange for the house for me), I now had to fight for our home. Again, it was an unusual landscape where I was asked to sign paperwork that when the children reached adulthood, they could force the sale of our family home in exchange for an early inheritance.

Throughout the proceedings, it was never my intention to focus on Ben's unconscionable conduct. However, forced back into court by him, it was impossible to ignore it. Once again, a "litigant in person", I told the court how Ben had moved a mistress onto our property against my wishes and lived as a couple, causing distress to myself and our children.

Moving on from the unreasonable behaviour, committed to our children's welfare, I put forward what I considered to be the most favourable outcome, where our children would not realise their interest on our home until my death.

Ben fronted by his legal team had other ideas, pursuing a share of the equity where our children would gain monetary interest in the property when they reached the age of twenty-eight, placing Neon and Elektra in a position enabling them to sell our home to release their fifty per cent share. I crumbled at the end and, under duress, I agreed to his terms.

———

It was August 2013 when I received a voicemail message from Sarah. I listened to her triumphantly gloat about her achievement with malignant pleasure. Hearing Sarah's voice sent shivers down my spine. Her words were a force to be reckoned with and came at me like a verbal spear.

'The film is finished and is going to be out very soon.'

I had withdrawn when it became clear Sarah was linked to the mainstream media with an agenda to entirely in thrall orthodox cancer philosophy. That she was a family friend of Ben and Lucy had also (eventually) rung alarm bells. Having met up with her several times, I thought she had nothing to work with, and that would have been the end of it. Without my permission and any decent footage, how could Sarah use Neon or me in her film?

I soon discovered the programme had continued and was hijacked due to connections and influence from Ben and Lucy, who had invited the cameras into their home.

'In the absence of your fuller contribution other people have had to tell the story, and they have a different perspective to you,' Sarah explained.

In hindsight, it was naïve of me. Much like a scene from Spike Milligan's *Bad Jelly the Witch*. "Just step into this nice warm sack."

Back in January, even with my clouded judgement, it had not taken me long to realise Sarah's promises of the film to be a platform to raise the debate about cancer treatments were untrue. I had not been given a team of researchers as promised, and above all else, I questioned Sarah's intentions.

I had a good reason for concern: Ben's solicitors throughout treatment had contacted me with the ultimate blow of Ben going for full custody. The lawyer's letter stated Ben was going for custody because of my involvement with the media and commented that I had a "film crew", failing to mention it was Ben's sister who had organised it all in the first place. It was a case of the pot calling the kettle black, considering most filming done for Sarah's documentary took place at Ben's parents' flat and his comments had appeared in many a newspaper.

No matter how hard Sarah tried to coax me to film, after that final nail, I did not trust her and refused. I could not be part of a documentary with the producer having demonstrated such a biased view, and I had become wary of her split personality once the cameras were turned on. Discovering her plans to exploit us I turned down any offers to film, having also learnt that I would have no editorial control over the material.

I took comfort that I had never signed the waiver and called Linda.

'Sarah left a smug message telling me the film has finished. How can it air on Channel Four without my participation or consent? It's an infringement of the law. They are breaking regulations, and I told her she was not allowed to film Neon.'

'It can't be aired, Sally. You never signed anything. She needs your permission.'

'Isn't it a violation of mine and my children's rights?' I asked.

'Yes, it is,' Linda replied. 'She promised us editorial control. She fooled us both. It could have been a wonderful opportunity to discuss safer ways to treat a child who had a full resection of a medulloblastoma. She had a rare opportunity to raise awareness of the limited cancer treatments and the life-threatening dangers of what is currently being offered. Without your input, I can't imagine she's even touched on discussing anything of value about supportive anticancer therapies that would give people a better chance of survival. It is just so unfortunate and sad that the general public is being kept in the dark.'

'I guess it's going to be another case of having to rise above it. The only footage she has of me is at the beginning in your centre, and in the car on the way there. Also around the last court hearing, she picked me up from my flat and turned the camera on in the taxi. Oh, and there was that time when Lucy invited me over to her house to put the Christmas decorations on the tree with the children, a set-up as Sarah was there to film it. I'm not sure how she has managed to make a documentary out of that. It will make a terrible viewing. Fly on the wall rubbish.

'I wonder how bad she has made me look? She has probably steamrollered with the media's concept that my main goal is to subject my son to unproven treatment with dubious effectiveness. Documentaries can skew people's perspective by what they show and how they show it.'

In the hope of shedding some light on the truth of matters, I accepted another invitation back onto *Daybreak*. My one request: Please, not Lorraine!"

Although the presenter Kate Garraway was wide-eyed, her ingenuous sincerity was soft and gentle. She expressed innocence rather than a merciless and unsophisticated attitude. Not being put under attack-mode meant I could raise my legitimate concerns:

'The proton therapy is a far less invasive treatment that does not do nearly as much damage to the surrounding tissue. It is more targeted, more localised. I was contacted by a proton expert from the States who was willing to take him on.'

'This therapy has the same sort of statistical results of success, does it, as the one that's used by the NHS to treat this kind of problem?' Kate Garraway asked.

'Yes, that's right,' I replied. 'It will be used here in the United Kingdom from 2017. We have to consider our population here is less than somewhere like America, where they are using it with great success already.'

—

Going against my better judgement, I watched Sarah's film with my mother. I sat with my hands over my face as if witnessing a train-wreck. I did not recognise this woman on screen, yet it was me. The narrator told one lie after another. Sarah had profited off my hardship. I should have guessed any publication driven by my ex-husband's side of the family meant I was going to be edited to look like the baddie and Ben pure as the driven snow, portrayed as the superhero.

Neon was made out to be doing well (happily ever after), when in reality he was suffering terribly. It's a fair bet that anyone who watched the documentary would have believed I (in Ben's words) "abducted" Neon to prevent him receiving "life-saving" radiotherapy – at a time when according to Ben he needed "critical treatment".

The documentary opens with "a domestic scene" of us putting up Christmas decorations. The narrator speaks her first lie (as all tests indicate Neon is tumour-free). "Seven-year-old Neon has a brain tumour growing so quickly his life is in imminent danger. His mum, Sally, has just been found by the police after going on the run with Neon to prevent him from having the treatment he needs."

The narrator continues after showing some scandalous news reports. "We watched a mother risk her child's life on her faith in alternative medicine." Telling the audience that "the tumour had regrown" and that "Sally had grown hostile to conventional medicine altogether".

Sarah had managed to dig my hole even deeper into the ground; further convicted of crimes I did not commit. Sarah sensationalised an already distorted story and squashed my innocence to make her documentary. Through a script-reading narrator, untrue accusations were made. "Sally did not come over to see Neon, and so Ben took Neon to the hospital." Having not received an invite, Lucy staged a phone call for the purpose of the film.

My mother was furious and wanted me to take Sarah and Channel Four to court over the documentary crossing legal boundaries. Without my necessary permission or consent to partake in her film and the extent the viewers were misled by the narrator, they were breaching common laws such as defamation, libel and right to privacy.

'Sally, in court when the NHS QC interrogated you, do you feel like they were putting words into your mouth… that you were getting your information off the Internet?'

'It's frustrating it was falling on deaf ears. They did not want to hear I was getting my information from valued sources like published medical journals. Not once did I say in court I was getting my information off the Internet. I made a point of not saying it.'

In the documentary, Sarah, who knew how upset I was by these allegations, edited me saying 'thanks to the Internet these days some of us have educated ourselves.'

It got worse. 'Mum, the narrator just said I was not there after Neon's operation. Why would they say such a thing? They've already portrayed me as an irresponsible parent, and now I am a distant, unloving one?'

'You have to sue them. You can't let Sarah get away with this. You have proof you were there after the operation; your brother drove you to the hospital to be there. You signed a waiver form, and Tony received a parking ticket outside the hospital.'

'The medical notes say I was there. It's in writing. I have photos with Neon I took with him putting a cup on his head. However, as much as I am upset by the extent of the malicious lies, all I can think of are Imran's words, *"Sally, choose your fights wisely"*.'

'I never trusted her, Sally. Tony didn't either.'

'Well, I guess I fell into a trap. Pretty stupid as it was Lucy who opened the trap door.'

'You mean Lucifer? It's a disgrace that a dreadful documentary put together by an unknown producer has been allowed to air, especially without your permission or participation.' Mum spoke her mind. 'You have been edited so badly. You can see what she has done by cashing in on your misfortune. She never cared about you, Sally, and has exploited you and Neon for her own gain.'

I contacted Sarah to ask why she had continued with the film against my wishes and edited me in such an unfavourable way to which she replied that she "reflected the story both fairly and accurately".

Gasping in horror, I asked how was that possible when the narrator speaking over the film told a made-up story of misleading innuendos and untruths. The documentary from the moment it opened led the audience to believe this poor little boy still had a tumour/cancer. Full with critique and remarks of a derogatory nature, it was easy to see why people generally had a hard time understanding my viewpoint: radiation was one hell of a preventive. Sarah's documentary was filled with factual inaccuracies and left out vital information, that the tumour had gone and he was in remission.

Casting people as villains or heroes is childlike but is what Sarah had done to sell her film. It was a naïve telling by people who were unaware of the complexity of what they were presenting. Sarah put forward a one-sided, false view. In spite of that, what it did show the viewer is the effects of the radiotherapy. Sarah showed clips of Neon before radiation and three weeks in, and the "last day". Whatever you think about radiation treatment, I can tell you there is nothing worse than watching your child suffer from radiotherapy. To be strapped to a table and immobilised by a face and chest mask... and then what follows. If you have been led to believe it's all we have, then think again. As a modern-day treatment, it is not good enough. Our children deserve better. We deserve better.

Mum on The Run stirred up unwanted attention on an already crooked past.

On the flip side, some saw the bigger picture. "A recent UK Channel 4 documentary portrayed her in a very negative light and invited ridicule on her search for a gentler therapy for Neon."

It meant everything to have the support from people I respected at the Alliance for Natural Health (ANH).

ANH reported on matters in their news features and wrote me private messages.

Words can't really do justice to how horrified we all are at what has happened, and you're very much in our thoughts. Whilst we can never truly understand the extent of the trauma you must be experiencing, I just wanted to say that you came across on the recent Daybreak *interview as very balanced and composed, which did a lot to offset the damage attempted by such unscrupulous documentary editing; something that has*

*been reiterated by a number of people. How you are holding
it all together is a mystery to all of us, but if there is anything
else we can do, please do let us know.*

It was heartfelt to have ANH reporting accurately throughout,
something for which I shall always remain grateful. It was
incredibly refreshing having people I well and truly respected
fight my corner. They made me feel like there was a silver lining,
and my attempt to set the record straight had not entirely failed.
They wrote:

*Neon was cancer free prior to radiotherapy. This crucial fact,
that Neon was actually given the all-clear after his operation,
is entirely missing from the mainstream narrative.*

*UK Channel 4's recent documentary on Neon Roberts and
his mum, Sally,* You're Killing My Son… The Mum Who Went
On The Run *was a travesty of half-truths, misrepresentation
and subtle mainstream bias.*

As a result of the shameful fly-on-the-wall documentary, more
misinformation surrounded *our story*. At the end of 2013,
just after the documentary had aired, the producer Sarah was
diagnosed with sarcoma, a highly aggressive cancer. Sarah
raised money for *Race for Life* Cancer Research UK and did
everything the conventional offered her. She died three years
later, age thirty-four.

CHAPTER TWENTY-TWO

Vindication

In October 2014 the story of another young boy made the headlines. He was five years old and prescribed the "gold standard" treatment after the removal of a medulloblastoma brain tumour. In the beginning, the way the Kings' and myself were treated was a carbon copy of one another. Both grandparents were subjected to a lengthy invasion by police and treated like criminals, having their homes searched from top to bottom. Ashya King's mother and father challenged their son's treatment, requesting to discharge Ashya so they could take him abroad for proton beam therapy. The hospital in charge of Ashya prescribed radiotherapy and through the court issued an international arrest warrant for the Kings, who were captured and had to spend a few days in jail. To put a tight family unit through this ordeal at a time when a child needs his parents shows how the system does not always work in the child's best interests.

Have they not already been through enough by going through surgery to remove a brain tumour?

The media portrayed the Kings as irresponsible, bringing their religious beliefs into the equation to belittle them further, but full credit to them, they were good at presenting their case and immediately released a YouTube video to set the record straight. They were treated sympathetically and had the support of the public.

Soon after Ashya King's story became public, my father said he was proud of me for standing up for what I believed in. A huge contrast to how he originally felt. Sometimes new ideas take a while to sink in and for people to accept them, especially if it defies the scholars.

Putting to one side what it feels like to be the centre of controversy over torturous treatment and so shoddily treated by the media, the real dilemma we face is how are we ever going to overcome cancer in our society if we continue to be limited with our choices as to what treatments and conjunctive therapies we are offered. There have been many advances in medicine, but the treatment for cancer remains limited.

When the Kings' story broke, the media wanted to talk to me once more. I declined to do any interviews, but I did not ignore all the calls.

'It is interesting don't you think, Sal? How they are being treated and how you were treated?' A sharp-witted journalist (Carole Malone) asked me. 'There is not much difference between your cases. Both young boys diagnosed with a medulloblastoma whose parents don't agree with the conventional radiotherapy and want PBT. Do you think you did not get anywhere because you were seen as a single mother and possibly, dare I say... a blonde bimbo?' she cackled.

'I'd not thought of that,' I chuckled back. 'You are blonder than me though, Carole, is that how us blondes are perceived? Or, maybe, in all seriousness, is it because the Kings have the support of each other and form a tight family unit? I think the most significant difference between our two cases is the mother and father of Ashya are united in their stand against the hospital. Also, they knew what they wanted from the beginning, whereas it took me a while to learn about proton beam. Two years on from what my family went through, protons are now being recognised and accepted as a mainstream treatment. I could certainly argue there is more to be said on the issue of the *alternative treatment* it was made out to be in mine and Neon's case.'

Again, it was nice to have ANH-Intl News reporting accurately.

A media frenzy has erupted this week after a five-year-old brain tumour sufferer, was taken out of the UK's Southampton hospital by his parents and flown to Spain seeking a different, but still conventional, cancer treatment. Brett and Naghemeh King fled to Spain in the hope of getting their son proton beam therapy, but instead, a manhunt ensued, and they have been arrested, detained and denied bail. All the while their young son languishes alone in the Spanish hospital, bearing an uncanny resemblance to the terror and heartbreak of Sally Roberts and her young son Neon in a similar situation back in 2012.

Robert Verkerk, founder of ANH, wrote;

The Ashya King case, like that of Neon Roberts, shows just how far the NHS will go to use state power to manage the health of British minors. Surely British parents should have the right to seek medical opinions and treatment options outside of the UK? A mature discussion of the relative merits and risks of proton beam therapy versus the proposed NHS treatment among experts in Spain, the UK or elsewhere would also surely afford Ashya the best possible care, while also informing Ashya's family of the various options. The arrest of his parents, especially given that their actions appear

to have been entirely motivated by their love for their child,
looks to be an over-reaction – one which seemingly challenges
fundamental human rights relating to private and family life.

More from the Alliance of Health in the wake of the news reports:

Proton beam therapy – a new pioneering cancer treatment?
Proton beam therapy has hit the headlines again in the UK.
But instead of being associated with desperate parents
running from the NHS to save their offspring from the fate of
whole brain radiation, it's being heralded as a revolutionary,
new "pioneering cancer treatment". One can only imagine
how Sally Roberts, Neon Roberts' mother, is feeling reading
these new headlines. Sally was portrayed in 2013 as 'an
ignorant, perhaps self-obsessed woman determined to press
unscientific "quackery" on her suffering child' while fighting
for Neon to receive this much less invasive therapy than the
whole brain radiation that he was since forced to undergo.

As construction begins on the UK's first proton beam
therapy centre in Northumberland, slated to open by the end
of 2017, the therapy is now completely de rigueur, no longer
the territory of quackery. Proton beam therapy involves the
use of protons instead of X-rays which causes much less
damage to surrounding tissues and has fewer side effects, like
permanent brain damage.

Proton beam therapy, used on young Ashya King after
his parents absconded to Europe, is now being publicly
praised after he was given the all-clear. However, reports fail
to mention the previous proclamations made by the media
claiming Brett and Naghemeh King put Ashya's life in danger
when they 'kidnapped' him. Not to mention the authorities
throwing them in jail, all because they were desperate to win
their fight to seek the treatment in the Czech Republic and

avoid the fate of Neon Roberts. This complete about-face leaves a particularly foul taste in one's mouth. The needless suffering and permanent adverse effects of whole brain radiation that have been forced on British children denied the opportunity to have proton beam therapy in another EU country is downright criminal. If doctors have that power, we are in extremely dubious ethical waters.

An Australian health journalist, Anna Rogers, wrote:

Sally was a target for abuse because she went against the system. I met Neon when he was in the middle of his treatment and I will never ever forget what he looked like. I was speechless. This poor child resembled a ghost, so pale and thin, and bent over from the damaging effects of the treatment. I also will not ever forget the haunted look in his eyes – an innocent soul being destroyed by this treatment where he would often beg his mother 'to please stop this Mummy'. Kids are very intuitive and Neon knew that the treatment wasn't good. Sally too, wanted what was best for her son, and that was another type of treatment which is exactly what the King family wanted for Ashya.

Another reporter wrote:

When Proton therapy was sought by Sally Roberts she was written off by the press – and the courts – as an alternative nutcase who flouted medical advice to put her son at risk with experimental treatments. Roberts lost her fight, and custody of her son in her bid to avoid treating him with pre-emptive radiotherapy, which can have lifelong, life-limiting side effects – to avoid his cancer returning, although he was in remission at the time.

Carole Malone, for the *Daily Mirror*, wrote:

> *The father was told that if he dared to question their son's treatment the hospital would get a court order and take him away from them – then questions must be asked about the kind of doctor that does that. Probably the same kind of doctor who told Sally Roberts that they were going to fry her son's brain to cure him. When she objected to that because she knew radiation can cause blindness, deafness, infertility, she too was told if she questioned his treatment, if she tried to take him elsewhere, he would be taken from her. She did, and he was.*

————

What served me well throughout my ordeal was the ability to have a bird's eye view. Although it was impossible to have an entirely detached perspective while baring my soul directly in the line of fire, I have come to accept and understand my part to play. New ideas/concepts often get trampled. Challenging the thoughts of others invites critique and judgement as it can create confusion and be controversial. Walking one way when everybody is running the other way, it's going to be bumpy.

The current medical paradigm: giving doctors a demigod status, outlawing all other means to heal cancer aside from radiation, chemotherapy and surgery has its many flaws and deeply embedded cracks, which are showing. There is room for improvement, to say the very least. The well-protected cancer paradigm, although fiercely defended by a solid infrastructure and those who work within it, it is not made from steel and will eventually crumble.

Such arrogance has consistently continued to overshadow medicine throughout history from witch-hunts to vaccinations as it seems it is the way of the world and sometimes, like children, we have to learn from our mistakes. It can take many years for false paradigms to give way to make room for the new. We only have to look back to how cigarettes were once physician-tested and approved.

Even back in the 1930s, doctors were the authority on health and patients mostly trusted their expertise. Tobacco companies capitalised on this trust to quell all concerns in the years to come, using doctors smoking in pictures in advertisements to suppress any fears the public may have had about any unknown dangers in the cigarettes that were being so actively promoted as "healthy".

Then there was the (absence of) hygiene paradigm, something we all appreciate in this day and age – washing your hands.

The first doctor in the 1840s to recognise the importance of hygiene, Ignaz Semmelweis, was ridiculed and publicly humiliated after sharing his observations with his fellow physicians, who reported his "ridiculous" theory to newspapers, some going as far as to rebel and wipe their scalpels on their shoes before operating.

His message falling on deaf ears, he became the target of scandalous jokes, suffering years of abusive backlash at the very suggestion that washing hands would reduce death; he suffered a psychological breakdown and is said to have committed suicide.

Semmelweis was correct in his observations. Doctors now routinely wash their hands in-between patients and surgical devices are all sterilised. Hospitals advocate using anti-bacterial gel, stressing the importance of a *germ-free* zone.

The moral of the story is "don't shoot the messenger". Sometimes it takes many years for false paradigms to fall away, however obvious (or not) they may seem.

CHAPTER TWENTY-THREE

Best of Both Worlds

Nobody could ever be prepared for a brain tumour to enter into their lives, but if it does, following the diagnosis, everyday *problems* become so petty and meaningless. A life-threatening illness like childhood cancer shreds normalcy into microscopic pieces and throws them into the wind.

The intensely insane weeks that followed the initial surgery and nursing Neon back to health was nothing short of an emotional roller coaster. The surgery, having been deemed a success, had turned my tears of sadness into tears of joy. However, I had no warning about how difficult the recovery process would be. Unless you have witnessed something like this, it is difficult to comprehend the hardship that you, your family and suffering child are faced with. Having seen my sunshine suffer from the symptoms of a medulloblastoma (headaches, double vision, stiff neck, nausea and fatigue) leading up to the diagnosis, then the operation followed by steroid psychosis, paralysis and sickness, it felt endless.

Then for the real nightmare: the treatment.

The following two years included nonstop hospital appointments involving MRI scans, CAT scans, radiation, chemotherapy, blood tests, audiologists, ophthalmologists, physiotherapists, endocrinologists and psychologists. That is not including the complementary therapies I sought out to help with the side effects of the treatment such as cranial osteopathy, kinesiology, EFT, acupuncture, vision therapy and HBOT.

'It, of course, is important that he is reviewed by both oncology and endocrine with regards to monitoring of his long-term effects,' Dr Harper wrote in a letter dated May 2018, also referring to the strabismus that Neon had recently been diagnosed with as an aftereffect of having radiotherapy. 'I am pleased to say he is in remission; however, as a consequence of his treatment, he has squint associated with sixth nerve palsy. He has seen a number of ophthalmologists both in Brighton and London who discussed various options such as surgery, prism glasses and botulinum toxin [botox].'

The reality of surviving cancer comes down to surviving the treatment for cancer. After full brain radiation, Neon's ears don't work as they should, nor do his eyes, and the journey has been a testing one. However, I remain grateful. There are parents whose children did not have a positive outcome, who live a life sentence suffering from their loss. My heart goes out to them. So, despite the "bad hand", we count our blessings and are bumping along as best we know how with no hard and fast schooling schedule.

After missing two years of school, Neon started at the same primary school as Elektra. He made it there about fifty per cent of the time, if that, and often only for half days.

'Do the other children know why you have so many days off?' I asked him on one trip home. He was too tired to be there.

'I think so,' he replied thoughtfully.

'So, they understand why you are sometimes not there?'

'Yes, Mummy, they do understand, but it was only a brain tumour you know,' Neon replied in all seriousness, making out as though having brain surgery to remove a tumour was a minor case of the flu.

'Of course, Neon.' I could only laugh. 'It was *only* a brain tumour!'

That pretty much sums my Neon up; a true warrior. To think it quite normal to dance with death and with such skill and strength. The admiration I have for him is beyond words. That said, there is no denying he often struggles to find the energy, has difficulty walking in a straight line and riding a bike again is a milestone achievement not yet fulfilled. When it came to it, secondary school proved to be unsuitable.

The radiotherapy side effects are constant and ever-changing. It has been an ongoing battle to deal with the rigours of the treatment. Neon remains under the wing of the hospital in London. Their tight grasp has recently loosened but not enough to be transferred to Brighton. Long-term effects can occur months to many years after treatment, and the risks vary depending on the areas included in the field of radiation, which explains why the hospital needs to keep a watchful eye and monitor his progress.

Neon's body was bombarded with chemicals and radioactive particles to destroy one or two elusive cancer cells (maybe there, or maybe not). Billions of healthy cells were affected in the process, many damaged beyond repair. Cranial irradiation causes harm to the pituitary gland, which affects hormone levels in the body, and thyroid, and sex hormones. The late-occurring problems are a common occurrence because the endocrine system is damaged by the radiotherapy treatment. I was warned before the treatment started that it would lead to a lifelong need for endocrine care.

Radiotherapy inevitably affects growth. This was a side effect that I worried would unravel itself, although even in the first appointment with Dr Lucock, I was told there were drugs to help. After treatment, Dr Harper reiterated this point. "In my sixteen years as an oncologist only two children have not needed the growth hormone, but don't worry, Sally. It is natural."

'Natural? But isn't it synthetic?' I queried.

'Yes,' Dr Harper confirmed, his head tilted down peering at me over his rounded glasses. 'It is synthetic but naturally occurring.'

Only growing a few centimetres since treatment, before Neon reached puberty and his bones began to fuse, he was prescribed the growth hormone (GH), which he has been advised by the endocrinologist to inject every day until he stops growing and probably longer. "Once you begin a replacement hormone you are likely to need it for the rest of your life," says the fine print.

I read the package leaflet about the possible side effects of Saizen.

"The growth hormone (somatropin) contained in Saizen is almost the same as humans' natural GH except that it is made outside the body by a process called *recombinant DNA technology* (genetic engineering)."

Without growth hormone, the endocrinologist told me that that Neon would be lucky to reach five foot four. With myself six feet, and Ben about the same, Neon would have reached at least six feet. With GH, the specialist said Neon should reach five foot nine. Besides it hurting Neon from having to inject daily, the precautions on the enclosed information come with warnings. "If you had a tumour in your childhood and were treated with Saizen, there is an increased risk to develop a new tumour."

Our six-monthly ongoing endocrine appointments come around too quickly. We dread the trek to the London hospital.

The lead endocrinologist is not Neon's favourite person, informing us that Neon would likely have to take another drug as a preventive for developing thyroid cancer. The leaflet tells me: "Saizen may affect how your thyroid works. Your doctor will prescribe another hormone if you (or your child) are found to have developed a lack of thyroid hormone."

What else can one expect from a treatment that uses high-energy X-ray machines to treat a disease (or prevent it), which works by damaging the nucleus of any cells that it passes through? A treatment so harsh the clinical team administering it have to leave the room because of the risk of being exposed to it.

The difficulty we face is that our practitioners are only treating symptoms with what they have been trained in; prescription drugs and therapies. These "approved" lethal concentrations of drugs and therapies often lead to having to receive more drugs/treatments. This is acceptable if we were talking about a desirable result such as prolonging life, but realistically the hit-or-miss approach is far from curative and can have the opposite effect (sickness/death).

The clinical team did do their best to their ability. However, given the lack of state-of-the-art expertise, it is a fine example of "I can forgive, but I cannot forget". It will always remain with me that there were improved treatments available, but not in this country and I was blocked from accessing them.

The "usual" side effects would have been avoided had we been granted the right to use the advanced treatment. All systems were set in place, but the NHS would not let Neon go. The NHS, backed by the power of the High Court, prevented me from appealing. I then had to watch my son suffer while being publicly persecuted for daring to seek out safer solutions.

Worldwide, there is no treatment (mainstream or alternative) that can give any guarantee of being healed from cancer. Whatever treatment we choose should be our informed choice to make. It should not be something that is forced on us based on fear and biased extremes.

———

I will never forget my friend Clementine telling me, 'Sal, you've started a revolution.'

It was not my intention. As any loving mother would, I saw it as my duty to do right by my son.

Perhaps, I had thrown seeds into the air, and a few had fallen into the cracks, but we have a long way to go. It is one step in the right direction that public awareness is increasing and we are understanding more every day that a higher standard of treatment is not only needed in our healing centres, but it should be a parental right to make an informed decision on what is best for their child. If the healthcare system didn't involve rapidly descending into a downward spiral and without a doubt served the child's best interests, then all very well, though alas it does not.

It is a double-edged sword that the unorthodox treatment I sought out for Neon is now accepted as a mainstream therapy. This demonstrates perfectly how easily misled we can be; by the press who couldn't have got it more wrong, by the medics who are restricted in their duty of care and by the court system who served a miscarriage of justice by actively preventing Neon from receiving a safer treatment.

A blunder was made by the medical establishment. My son was subjected to radiotherapy when I provided substantial evidence that it would be more beneficial for him to receive proton therapy. An acknowledgement that a mishap occurred would be courteous. The body of clinicians treating Neon breached its duty of care by not allowing him access to PBT; a treatment I became an object of ridicule for seeking and without permission from the court, unable to pursue. Only to see, several years later, the same physicians who treated Neon to be receiving training in and recommending proton beam as the way forward for overcoming cancer.

If our physicians are uninformed, how can we expect them to inform us?

—————

With the risky radiation and lethal chemicals dominating our hospitals as a treatment to cancer, more needs to be done towards raising awareness on safer treatments and complementary therapies, and if treated with the conventional, with quality of life paramount, what can be done to mitigate the side effects of the treatment.

Ten years ago I had known one person to die from cancer. In the last decade, having had my child and my beloved brother among the many other millions diagnosed, I have seen the suffering that nobody should bear witness to. It now affects almost every family at some time in their lives.

With the cure around the elusive corner, why do we not focus more on prevention?

Scientific evidence says seventy per cent of degenerative conditions could be prevented, suggesting that the lifestyles we lead and the choices we make impact on our health.

Dare I mention that none of the vaccines injected into children is tested for their carcinogenic potential? It is a probability that children are developing cancer from vaccinations given to avoid illnesses far less concerning than cancer. Cancer is better understood than many of us believe. Many enlightened practitioners successfully overcome cancer by using approaches not yet embraced by the mainstream.

How much longer are we going to tolerate the massive insult on the environment from pesticides, fluoride, asbestos and nuclear radiation, to name a few? It is up to us in our homes to do our best to avoid excitotoxins such as aspartame, MSG, microwave exposure and to choose organic, whenever possible, and to lessen our consumption of pesticides and other hormonal disruptors. The less we expose ourselves to the liver-toxic onslaught, the better off we will be.

If you have done some research on cancer, you would have probably noticed there is an overwhelming amount of information at your fingertips.

You need to be savvy and look deep into the murky waters to understand that many effective cancer treatments are out there and despite what your doctor may tell you, to always have hope. It takes months if not years of dedicated research to get a truly comprehensive understanding of the widespread misconceptions on non-toxic cancer treatments. If you are relying entirely on the mainstream media to get your information, with all due respect, there are more reliable sources.

"Don't believe everything – or indeed, anything – you read, see or hear in the mainstream media if it relates to medicine and cancer, without looking into all sides of the issue first!" ANH reminds us. "The relationships between media and orthodox medicine are deep and complex and include shared ownership, overlapping board members and advertising revenue. With such relationships, bias is likely to be the norm, rather than the exception."

It is said relying on alternative treatments is unreliable, but the truth is, so is relying only on the conventional. There is a multitude of natural approaches proven to work by rigorous research performed by respected physicians, biochemists and Nobel Prize-winning scientists.

Why has this information been suppressed? If integrative treatments have been proven to work, why are our healthcare providers restricted and prevented from offering them to us?

Imagine how much better the outcome would be to be informed by our healthcare providers that we shouldn't rely entirely on toxic measures, and there are herbs, vitamins, minerals and enzymes with immune boosting and cancer-fighting properties, and it is possible to heal from cancer with non-toxic approaches.

The people (adults) who have chosen *not* to have radiation and/or chemotherapy and have survived are labelled "miracles" but it's more than that, they are courageous people who have declined procedures they felt were not in their best interests. They are brave people who took control of their own health rather than handing over their lives to an industry that may or may not save them.

———

Cancer is not a mysterious affliction that we know nothing about. Moreover, the toxic shotgun method is not as reliable as it should be given the aftermath. The standard procedures can cause more problems than they are solving, yet it continues.

The definition of the current cancer *cure* is misleading: *the conventional cancer cure is the lack of symptoms for five years.* If a patient dies after the five years, they remain in the *cured* statistic. Cured and dead? How can you be cured and dead?

Who can challenge a system that has become a wildly out-of-control industry when it has no true independent monitor?

People are being let down by the lack of state-of-the-art treatments available. We should not be denied *alternative* strategies just because they have not been embraced by our mainstream healthcare providers. It was "criminal" Neon was denied a safer treatment as well as denied immune-boosting therapies. Although not offered by our medical practitioners, herbal approaches alone have helped people overcome cancer.

Essiac is one of the best-known formulas. I gave it to Neon as part of our anticancer approach. Herbal remedies are biodynamic living organisms and powerhouses in their own right. In days gone by, the meaning of *simple* used to be a *remedy*. With complex prescriptions often causing severe reactions, it is no surprise people are searching for more natural and simple approaches to restoring health.

It is a travesty to ignore that nature has provided us with many answers to health problems, including an ingenious defence against cancer, a common dietary nutrient. Vitamin B17 is a cancer bomb that all we need to do is eat an abundance of fruits, vegetables, grains and nuts to get plenty of it. Laetrile is not a bogus treatment that fizzled out years ago. Why would President Reagan choose to have intravenous shots of B17 and oxygenating therapies as opposed to the conventional? Alongside nutritional therapy, diet changes and following a vigorous non-toxic anticancer regime, many cancer patients have overcome their cancer naturally and remain cancer free.

———

In 2016 I found myself sitting in the back of the car to a newly made friend's funeral, who had lost her battle with leukaemia; she had been diagnosed with blood cancer less than one year before. Two fellow mothers discussed what Becky had been through acknowledging how devastating the chemotherapy had been on her towards the end.

'But what chance have you got without it?' one mum asked, referring to the chemotherapy. 'You've got to throw everything at it. You'd be mad not to give it everything the doctors are offering.'

I sat in silence in the backseat and reflected on how I had once been the subject of attack simply because of naïveté and that our knowledge base in this country was limited or perhaps just restricted. I did not want to be the one to tell this kind, trusting lady about the extensive corruption within our healthcare system, with some analysts reporting the cancer industry was sustained by a policy of deliberately facing in the wrong direction.

The majority of the population have been kept in the dark, not giving much thought to the depth of deceptive conduct by the powers that be, including laws that were passed by our government back in 2011 which legalised the removal of hundreds and thousands of (proven) safe natural health products.

Contrary to mainstream reports, I would like to echo how I was not completely against orthodox treatments. I simply wanted the opportunity to exercise my right to choose safer and more effective options. The objective of cancer treatment should be to avoid recurrence, not create it. Especially in Neon's case when he had already been confirmed in the clear. Put irony to one side; is it not insanely tragic that cancer is treated with something that could make you worse than you already are?

Disagreeing with the norm, I found myself caught in a web of procedures rather than an unimpeded scientific assessment of less harmful approaches. I fought bureaucrats instead of working alongside clinicians to evaluate the best choice of treatments that would have produced the most favourable outcome for Neon. However, in my quest, I uncovered a huge range of successful cancer treatments which should be on offer to anyone who ever faces the dilemma I found myself in.

It is vital we have a full understanding of the crucial role the 1939 Cancer Act plays in preventing promising information reaching the light of day. This Act was passed solely for the purpose of supporting *scientific methodologies for experimental cancer drug-treatments* and *not for research into the prevention of the disease.* Therefore, the 1939 Cancer Act prohibits and makes it illegal to promote or advertise any effective natural product or therapy proven to heal, prevent or control cancer. Consequently, only radiotherapy, chemotherapy, new trial drugs, and surgery are prescribed.

The present state of cancer treatments is unsatisfactory. We have the cancer investigators and their funding agencies ignoring complementary therapies due to restrictive legislation and the lack of financial reward. To the average person, it makes sense to improve the healthcare system by incorporating well-known, inexpensive therapies that work. It is the integrative cancer foundations that have funded the much-needed research, proving the value of safer therapies, while the conventional turn the other way. How are we going to move forward and overcome this dreadful disease in our society when the mainstream academic environment remains uninterested in a balanced, integrated healthcare system?

Despite the seventy-year war declared on cancer, drug-based advances are not making a dent in the rise of cancer prevalence. With an industry so focused on disease yet failing to address lifestyle-related issues, such as lack of sun (vitamin D) exposure, DNA disrupting wireless/microwave technologies, chemical exposure, diet and stress levels, we may remain stuck in a downward spiral much like a dog chasing its tail.

Prior to the 1939 Cancer Act, cancer affected one in fifty people. The latest statistic is one in two people. It used to be a rare disease; since we have been accepting radiation and chemotherapy to be the only methods to *beat* cancer, together with the forming of the NHS and its cousin Cancer Research UK, cancer has become wildly out of control. With our government in support of the extraordinary increase in the intensity of electromagnetic microwave transmissions, it's not going to get any better. Nobody knows what impact this hazard will have on humanity and life. Whatever advantages the latest hype, 5G, comes with, it is at the expense of our health.

———

Science tells us we are no closer to finding a real cure. Recently, the press carried the very latest pronouncement from Orthodox Medicine/Big Pharma – "we have discovered that cancer can not be cured but only managed – by the wonderful new cancer drugs we are developing with this aim. Therefore we are no longer seeking a cure for cancer."

The conventional treatment offered does not qualify as saving lives. Draining patients of their life essence and turning people into zombies is not healing them. Despite advances in technology, scientific know-how, medical breakthroughs and billions raised for cancer research, what has changed except for the escalation of the disease and increased deaths?

There is always hope. Reported in the *i* paper under Health on Wednesday 20 June 2018:

> *New 'beating heart' for cancer patients.*
> *A 90-tonne piece of cancer-fighting equipment that will improve the lives of hundreds of patients every year has been carefully lowered into place in its new home. The cyclotron is described as the beating heart of the new proton beam therapy centre at University College London Hospital.*

Although I am happy a more humane therapy is emerging as a mainstream treatment, it is upsetting Neon was blocked from having PBT. We could have avoided so much suffering.

January 2013; I was bound to a court order and prevented from taking Neon abroad for proton beam. The consultant's antiquated attitude was condescending and clearly a result of his medical schooling. He had not (yet) received any training in PBT. As a result of such injustice, Neon was forced into the treatment the professor was trained in and is left with the known side effects.

Despite my efforts, the lead radiologist brushed me off and claimed "photons had no benefits over protons", only to five years later be tweeting "off to Proton School".

What compensation will Neon ever receive as a result of being subjected to the outdated photon radiation? Have we even crossed the minds of the people who enforced the treatment I opposed? Have they reflected on their error?

Quality of life is a big price to pay. One can only imagine the heartache I feel considering how hard I fought for a better treatment plan, and to have been scoffed and scorned at throughout the process, to a few years later see the treatment I had in place for Neon to become available in the hospital he was treated in. Furthermore, to see the consultant who went to great lengths to prevent Neon receiving proton beam, publicly announce through social media that he is "looking forward" to the proton therapy he once so confidently condemned and prevented Neon from having. It is the ultimate insult, a slap in the face and we are left to carry the consequences.

The professor's tweet I saw sight of in January 2019: "Our mission is to ensure that children get the best radiotherapy. Radiotherapy for children is changing quite dramatically across the UK with the introduction of proton beam therapy services in Manchester and London."

If only he had this open mind in 2012, as it is an entirely different perspective considering he did everything in his power to ensure that Neon received his photon radiation and not protons.

Time has vindicated my actions. A treatment once shunned by the professor and medical profession is now an orthodox treatment within our grasp.

The 1939 Cancer Act ensures that we are led to think there is no choice in treatments.

A reform of the 1939 Cancer Act is long overdue. Until it is revoked, it prevents us from being able to move forward. Independent scientists, oncologists and doctors have confirmed that more people die from surgery, radiation and chemotherapy than cancer itself.

The whole ethos of the approach to cancer treatment needs to be reviewed, and become more open so we can have a comprehensive understanding of all treatments including immune-boosting therapies, which need to be made readily available to optimise the patients' outcomes.

What will we think in years to come when we look back at the horrific suffering inflicted on children with cancer? The modern era or the Dark Ages? How could it be that such a civilised society could not have prevented it?

Britain cherishes its right to freedom of speech, so why is it the Advertising Standards Agency close down educational open days on treating cancer advocating alternatives?

We should not be fear-filled thinking we have no choice but to accept and be degraded by humiliating treatments. We deserve humane treatment options that do not make us lose our dignity, appetites, energy, hair, hope, will and the biggest price of all – our precious lives. Pandora's box on cancer and its treatments is open. It is time to create a level playing field offering choice. Ultimately, bringing to light safer treatments and encouraging integration within the general healthcare system; combining the very best of conventional and complementary.

Isn't it Ironic?

First and foremost to anybody so quick to judge, it helps to know all the facts before jumping to conclusions and persecuting someone. It does nothing to promote justice or righteousness to ridicule a loving mother for seeking safer treatment options for her child.

Strabismus, injecting growth hormone every day, chronic fatigue, and the other debilitating side effects Neon has since faced could have been avoided should I have been granted permission to treat my son with the best treatment available.

When I learnt about proton beam therapy, mere moments after the ruling of the court case in 2012, and went onto the NHS website to discover they recognised the advantages of PBT confirming that it would be available in the UK from 2018, I could see it was already accepted as a mainstream treatment. I had everything set in place to transfer his treatment to America but was blocked by the professor/hospital treating Neon and the court system.

Doing everything in my power to save Neon from being blindly treated and needlessly suffer the consequences of the damaging effects of photon radiation, I had Neon booked in for proton beam but was told by the chief radiologist, Professor Gadd in January 2013: "There is no significant clinical benefit for protons over photons delivered with an IMAT technique." Yet this very same Professor Gadd in 2018 tweeted "looking forward to high energy proton beam in the UK."

The decision to prevent Neon receiving proton beam carries serious consequences. Where is the justification?

The hospital where Neon was treated promotes PBT on their website: "A new hospital with state-of-the-art facilities using cutting edge technology."

We cannot turn back the clock.

Will I ever get an apology? An apology from the hospital that denied Neon a less intrusive treatment and most of all an apology from Dr Gadd, the professor who forced Neon into a treatment against my better judgement which has caused my son much harm because of his ignorance. The doors open in 2020 to the treatment that I had slammed shut in my face.

Moreover, not only would I like an apology, I would appreciate an acknowledgement that a blunder was made by the medical profession; the more advanced treatment I sought out for my son and had set in place is now an accepted preferred treatment.

The whole experience has been an eye-opener. From the callous reporter saying that 'nobody will care in two weeks', to the bullying tactics used by the medical establishment which highlighted the limited procedures and antiquated mindset we are faced with in our treatment centres.

There is no doubt that the direct proton beam is better than the scattered photon particles. However, to reach state-of-the-art claims, a balanced and integrated approach to healthcare must be pursued and achieved. If you are going to bring the immune system to its knees, you need to give it a helping hand back up again.

Six years from my ordeal, in September 2018, I received a letter from the Legal Aid Commission, stating "Imran Khan's bill has been paid". It is an added insult to injury to be asked to pay a large sum of money for an appeal to the High Court that never happened. If it did, perhaps Neon would have been granted access to receive proton beam. If only I had found a solicitor who would have moved forward without "money in the kitty". It was "downright criminal" that I was prevented from an appeal and he was denied a safer treatment. Should a well-informed mother have to wait for medical advancements to be accepted by a reasonable body of clinicians to the detriment of her child?

Acknowledgements

In the height of my turmoil, I was asked, "You must have a wonderful support network around you?" Although I would have loved this to be true, at times, it was the complete opposite. Thinking outside the box and not agreeing with what is recommended by the health service is controversial and not only caused friction with the medics, it made friends question my ethics, and my own mother asked if I had lost the plot.

"Why don't you just do whatever the doctors want?" I heard it so many times I lost count.

To all of you who ever lost faith in me, I can only thank you. It helped me understand the true depth of the dilemma we are faced with and helped push me to write this book. Which leads to the second most asked question by my friends and even family...

"What are you writing a book about?"

By writing my book and sharing my story I have had to relive painful memories. Having a child diagnosed with medulloblastoma is deeply traumatic, but it became even more heinous by not being satisfied with what the medical establishment was offering to overcome a tumour that had been removed. It became even more complicated with the court, and then the media becoming involved, "my story" was told by people who knew nothing about the circumstances, and I had to come to terms with being exploited and scapegoated. By revisiting these ordeals and facing them head-on by describing them in intimate detail, I have "done myself justice", expressed my truth and healed old wounds. What else can be done when you find yourself the centre of a high-profile case and accused of misdoings, all while the NHS gets their wicked way and inflicts the harshest of therapy's on my son? It is impossible to escape the harsh reality of having been thrown face first into the centre of controversy over radiation treatment and to be so shoddily treated by the media, only to see a few years on, the proton beam therapy Neon was denied emerge as a mainstream treatment. It was inevitable my side of the story had to be told, and nobody else could tell it but me.

My memoir has been written from the heart. Neon and Elektra should know my version of events. Writing my book was a necessary part of the process for me to have a sense of closure. Although I always wanted what was best for Neon, I was put in a position where I have had to free myself of allegations and vindicate my actions while justifying why I fought for *the* best *treatment* plan for Neon.

I felt compelled to set the record straight from the distorted "soundbite" media perception. Although we know the media to not always be the most credible source of information, how many believed the news reports to be true and judged me for denying my son "life-saving" treatment? It demonstrates perfectly how easily fooled we are and even the "greatest of lies"; if an outlet like the media says the same thing over and over, people can believe it to be true. Saying that, as always in every area of life, the media has some absolute diamonds. A few of you held out your hands and did whatever you could to pull me out of the dirt.

Moreover, there were the people that sympathised and sided with me, understanding the multi-faceted enormity of what I faced. I would like to thank all the people that offered their help and expertise. The team at the Alliance of National Health (ANH), you truly are incredible. Your accurate reporting was refreshing. Thank you to the magazines like *What Doctors Don't Tell You* and *Juno* for your attempts to set the record straight. Thanks a million to Katherine Smith, editor of *NZ Journal of Natural Medicine*. Words cannot describe how much I appreciated your time, expertise and efforts to help me. Dounne and India, you absolute angels, thank you from the bottom of my heart, you were my rocks.

The two most amazing people who I need to thank the most are my parents. Thank you for your love and support, and although at one point you doubted my antics, throughout the journey once you understood my plight, nobody has supported me more.

I also thank my big brothers, Michael, Russell and Tony – you are all legends in your own right.

Linda and Kevin, thank you for both being you. You were lighthouses in the stormiest of seas. Thank you for your support and friendship when I needed it the most. I am forever grateful. I also would like to thank Tracey Hall-Roberts, my McKenzie friend. Anna Rogers, Sarah Best, Elaine Godley and Kate Magic, you are all very lovely ladies, thank you for your support and kindness when I needed it.

———

To my darling Neon and Elektra, thank you for all the love letters and reminding me that I am beautiful, even when I felt anything but. Thank you for being the most amazing twins in the whole wide world. I am so proud of you both and love you with all my heart. It is the biggest honour to be your mother.

My darling Mes, you are the man of my dreams. Not a day goes by that I don't feel gratitude for you coming into our lives. I treasure your warmth, love and companionship.

I would like to take this opportunity to thank all the people involved in Neon's recovery process. We met some real gems amongst the rough.

The names of any people working in the medical establishment I have changed to protect the privacy of those depicted.

Throughout my book, I have mentioned parts of the anticancer strategy I embraced. It is always a good idea to do your own research and make up your own mind. The list is long with ample integrated solutions, and I only touched the surface by sharing my experience. It would be unwise to not pay attention to all the information available on reversing cancer. Nobody cares more about your health than you.

To all the parents and people who have found themselves thrown into the cancer camp. Stay strong, stay positive, stay true, stay focused, look at all the facts and never lose hope.

Lastly, a big thank you to all the people who took the time to contact me offering me advice, support and kindness. It touched me how many of you reached out. It showed me that the greater the darkness, the brighter the light shines.

A final thank you to Gary at Bubblecow, the team at Matador and, Tamsin Banks, for kindly giving my manuscript the final eye. I am so pleased to have finally completed my memoir and am grateful to everyone who helped in the process.

About the Author

Sally Jane Roberts was born and raised in Auckland, New Zealand. British roots led her to the UK where she has lived since 1999. Sally resides in East Sussex with her boyfriend Mes, fourteen-year-old twins Neon and Elektra and their two Staffordshire Bull Terriers, Candy and Ziggy.

Glossary

Acidic – pH of lower than 7

Acupuncture – Traditional Chinese medicine used to restore, promote & maintain health

Adaptogen – A substance that can adapt to the needs of the body and support homeostasis

Alkaline – pH of 7 or higher

Antioxidants – Compounds that inhibit oxidation. Anti (against) oxidants (free radicals)

Apple cider vinegar (with the mother) – Web effect living enzymes

Apoptosis – Programmed cell death

Apricot kernels – Anticancer vitamin B17. Otherwise known as laetrile or amygdalin

Ambulatory – Outpatient medical care

Amygdalin – A cyanogenic glycoside (natural plant toxin) otherwise known as nitrilosides

Bee pollen – A high-profile complete food source made by honey bees

Beta-glucans – Naturally occurring polysaccharides

Beta-glucosidase – An enzyme only present in cancer cells

Bicarbonate of soda – A compound that can help neutralise acid and regulate pH

Bromelain – Anti-inflammatory, anticancer (pineapple)

Cannabis oil – Hemp strain cannabinoid used for medicinal purposes

Carcinogenic – Carcinogens are substances which can cause or promote cancer

Chaga – Adaptogen. Alkalising. King of the medicinal mushrooms

Chlorella – Freshwater micro-algae good for cell renewal and detoxing

Coconut oil – Multi-purpose EFA. Anti-fungal, anti-viral, anti-inflammatory

Complete resection – A desired surgical procedure where the 'growth' is removed in full

Complementary therapies – Supportive treatments used with or instead of the conventional

Cranial osteopathy – Gentle pressure to realign, rebalance and stimulate healing in the body

Curcumin – An anticancer bright yellow chemical. The principal curcuminoid of turmeric

Cyanide – A naturally occurring chemical found in many plants used as a lethal agent

Dandelion – A bitter medicinal herb good for stimulating the liver and digestive tract

Dr Herzog – Integrative cancer treatment clinic in Germany

DWI – Investigation of tissue functions

Dynamic living medicines – Organisms that can help bring the body back to equilibrium

E3 – A nutrient dense freshwater blue-green algae superfood

EFAs – Building blocks that are essential to human health but not made in the body

Electrophilic – Electrically unbalanced

EFT – Fingertip tapping on acupuncture points to overcome emotional distress

Flaxseed oil – One of nature's richest sources of omega 3 and omega 6 (EFAs)

Free radicals – An unpaired electron/unstable molecule

Gerson therapy – Nutritional immune-boosting non-toxic cancer treatment

Goji berries – Antioxidant adaptogen super berry that stimulates HGH

Healing powers of nature – Electron-rich connection with the Earth (grounding)

Hempseed oil – Nature's perfectly balanced ratio of omega 3,6 & 9 (EFAs) super oil

Hufeland – Holistic immunobiological therapy clinic in Germany

Hydrogen peroxide – H202 – Oxygen with an extra molecule – strong oxidiser

Hyperbaric oxygen therapy – Increases oxygen levels in the blood plasma

Hyperthermia – Infrared heat (fever) therapy stimulates cellular metabolism

Hypoxia – Lack of oxygen to the blood/tissue/cell

Iatrogenic illnesses – Illness caused by medical treatment

Immunotherapy – Immunology. Immunomodulation. Activating the body's own defences

Infrared heat therapy – Invisible band of light felt as heat, increasing regenerative abilities

Integrated – A holistic complementary approach alongside orthodox treatments

Johanna Brandt's grape cure – Resveratrol

Kinesiology – Muscle testing procedure identifying any areas of imbalance

Laetrile – Is the commercial semi-synthetic patented form of amygdalin (B17)

Life-saving – A broad term describing treatment advocated by a body of clinicians

Maca – Superfood adaptogen (hormone balancer)

Macroscopic – Visible and measurable to the naked eye

Magnetic field therapy – The use of magnets to increase oxygen transfer to the cells

Manuka – Antibacterial honey made from bees that pollinate the Manuka bush (tea tree)

Marine phytoplankton – A nutritious superfood micro algae sourced from the ocean

Medicinal mushrooms – Mushroom family w/ immune boosting + adaptogenic properties

Medulloblastoma – A brain tumour originating in the cerebellum

Metastasis – Cancer that has spread to other part/s of the body than where it started

Milk thistle – Liver detoxifying herb

Miracle – A mainstream term used to describe surviving without "life-saving" treatment

Multidisciplinary team – A group working together on complex medical conditions

Monosaccharides – Small sugar molecules bonded together (the most basic carbohydrate)

Nasogastric tube – A thin plastic tube through the nose, throat & into the stomach

Nettles – Super herb with medicinal properties

Neuroblastoma – A tumour that affects the nervous system including the adrenal glands

Neurological – Science of the nerves & the nervous system (& the diseases affecting them)

Orthomolecular therapy – Treating disease by substances already present in the body

Oxidation – The attack of unstable molecules (free radicals)

Oxygen therapy – Supplemental oxygen as a medical treatment (HBOT)

Ozone therapy – Supercharged oxygen with a molecular structure of O3 rather than O2

pH – The measure of acidity and alkalinity from 0–14

Physiological – Normal function of living organisms and their parts

Plasma – The largest component of blood, which carries platelets, red & white blood cells

Proton beam therapy – A direct radiation of high energy positively charged particle beams

Polysaccharides – A large molecule made of many smaller monosaccharides

Port-a-cath – A device used to administer intravenous drugs and blood transfusions

Posterior fossa syndrome – Symptoms occurring after operations to the cerebellum

Quality of life – Health and happiness

Radical scavenger – A substance that helps protect from damage caused by free radicals

Radiotherapy – High energy X-ray radiation

RapidArc – IMRT therapy – 3D dose distribution with a 360-degree rotation

Remission – Showing no symptoms. No evidence of disease

Resonant light machine – Sound frequency treatment

Resveratrol – An anticancer compound found in red and purple grape skin and seeds

Rhodanese – An enzyme found in our cells throughout our body (not cancer cells)

Selenium – A vital trace element (mineral)

Turmeric – A root spice containing an anticancer medicinal compound called curcumin

Zeolite – Volcanic minerals used for detoxification and boosting the immune system

Abbreviations

ACV – Apple cider vinegar

ANH – Alliance for National Health

B17 – Vitamin B17. Amygdalin. Laetrile

CAFCASS – Children and Family Court Advisory and Support Service

CBD – Cannabidiol (cannabis) oil

CBT – Childhood brain tumour

CCLG – Children's Cancer and Leukaemia Group

CSRT – Craniospinal radiotherapy

CT – Computed tomography

DWI – Diffusion weighted imaging

EFA – Essential fatty acid

EFS – Event free survival

EFT – Emotional freedom technique

EMF – Electromagnetic fields

EVD – External ventricle drain

FDA – Food and Drug Administration

GH – Growth hormone

GI – Glycemic index
GMC – General Medical Council
GMOs – Genetically modified organisms
HDU – High dependency unit
HBOT – Hyperbaric oxygen therapy
HGH – Human growth hormone
HRQOL – Health-related quality-of-life
IMRT – Intensity modulated radiation therapy
LSC – Legal Services Commission
MDT –Multidisciplinary team
MSG – Monosodium glutamate
MRI – Magnetic resonance imaging
NCI – National Cancer Institute
NED – No evidence of disease
NHS – National Health Service
pH – Power/potential of hydrogen
PBT – Proton beam therapy
PFS – Posterior fossa syndrome
RCT – Randomised controlled trials
WBRT – Whole brain radiotherapy

The Studies

Treatment of medulloblastoma by postoperative chemotherapy alone
https://www.ncbi.nlm.nih.gov/pubmed/15758008

SKK study (Treatment of medulloblastoma by postoperative chemo
& deferred radio)
https://www.ncbi.nlm.nih.gov/pmc/articles/PMC2718992/

Late effects: Survivor Study
https://www.ncbi.nlm.nih.gov/pubmed/12548609?dopt+Abstract

Adverse health outcomes
https://www.ncbi.nlm.nih.gov/pubmed/17595271

Proton Beam
https://www.ncbi.nlm.nih.gov/pmc/articles/PMC5772792/

Radiation-induced growth hormone deficiency
https://www.ncbi.nlm.nih.gov/pubmed/19640651

WBRT versus observation: HRQOL results
https://www.ncbi.nlm.nih.gov/pubmed/23213105

HBOT and cancer – a review
   https://www.ncbi.nlm.nih.gov/pubmed/23054400

WNT16B promotes tumour growth
   https://www.ncbi.nlm.nih.gov/pmc/articles/PMC3572004/

Antioxidants and radiation
   https://academic.oup.com/jn/article/134/11/3207S/4688649
   https://www.ncbi.nlm.nih.gov/pubmed/17283738
   https://journals.sagepub.com/doi/abs/10.1177/1534735407305655
   https://www.ncbi.nlm.nih.gov/pubmed/16484715

The effects of Vitamin C on cancer cells
   https://www.ncbi.nlm.nih.gov/pmc/articles/PMC3798917/

Beta-glucans (medicinal mushrooms)
   https://www.ncbi.nlm.nih.gov/pubmed/17895634

Milk thistle
   https://www.ncbi.nlm.nih.gov/pmc/articles/PMC3542639/

Bromelain
   https://www.ncbi.nlm.nih.gov/pmc/articles/PMC3633552/

Additional References

Dangers of radiation
> http://www.encognitive.com/node/1575

Chemotherapy makes cancer worse
> http://naturalsociety.com/chemotherapy-makes-cancer-far-worse/

Hyperthermia
> https://www.cancer.gov/about-cancer/treatment/types/surgery/hyperthermia-fact-sheet#r1
> https://www.canceractive.com/article/whole-body-hyperthermia-helps-kill-cancer-cells
> https://academic.oup.com/jnci/article/102/2/79/927263

Vitamin C
> https://drhoffman.com/article/intravenous-vitamin-c-for-cancer-2/

Long-term survivors: The late effects of therapy
> http://theoncologist.alphamedpress.org/content/4/1/45.full

Childhood cancer
> https://www.cancer.gov/types/childhood-cancers/child-adolescent-cancers-fact-sheet

All PDF references including the NHS's 1940s study by Bodian and Lason are available on the authors website sallyjroberts. com

Recommended Books

The Cancer Industry by Ralph W. Moss PhD
Anticancer: A New Way of Life by Dr David Servan-Schreiber
Killing Cancer, Not People by Robert G. Wright
The Only Answer to Cancer by Dr Coldwell
Natural Strategies for Cancer Patients by Dr Blaylock
Excitotoxins by Russell L. Blaylock
The Nutritional Medicine of Cancer by Dr Plaskett
Fats that Heal, Fats that Kill by Udo Erasmus
German Cancer Breakthrough by Andrew Scholberg
The Cancer Cure that Worked by Barry Lynes
Healing with Whole Foods by Paul Pitchford
Bad Pharma by Ben Goldacre
The Gerson Therapy by Charlotte Gerson and Morton Walker
The Powerwatch Handbook by Alasdair & Jean Philips
Mum's Not Having Chemo by Laura Bond
Cancer: Why We're Still Dying To Know The Truth by Philip Day
Beat Cancer by Robert Olifent
Cancer – Step Outside the Box by Ty Bollinger
Chris Beat Cancer by Chris Wark